Customer-Driven IT

Customer-Driven IT

How Users Are Shaping
Technology Industry Growth

David Moschella

Harvard Business School Press
Boston, Massachusetts

Library of Congress Cataloging-in-Publication Data
Moschella, David C.
   Customer-driven IT : how users are shaping technology industry growth
/ David Moschella.
      p. cm.
Includes bibliographical references and index.
   ISBN 1-57851-865-2 (acid-free)
   1. Information technology. 2. Business enterprises—Technological innovations. I. Title.
   HC79.I55 M673 2003
   338.4'7004—dc21
                                    2002012680

In memory of my parents

Contents

Introduction: The Evolution of an Idea

IN MANY WAYS, this is a book that stems from a single idea, one that I hope will give you a fresh perspective on the evolution of our increasingly technology-driven economy. So as a way of introducing both this idea and myself, allow me to briefly explain the roundabout way in which this work actually began.

The story starts back in 1997, a few years into the dot-com boom. At that time, it seemed that just about everyone in the technology, media, consulting, and punditry businesses was full of ideas about what the Internet would or could be and why the Net was so fundamentally different from previous generations of technology and media. There was, if anything, a surfeit of potentially powerful theories. Bits and atoms, dis-intermediation, increasing returns, critical mass, first-mover advantage, and clicks and mortar were just a few of the more prominent concepts, each with its own vocal proponents.

Back then, I was very much one of these voices, working as both a consultant and as a weekly columnist for *Computerworld,* the IT industry newspaper. Having analyzed and forecasted the information technology (IT) business for more than twenty years, my approach was to focus on the sector's ever-shifting value-chain dynamics, those series of relationships and activities that define how an industry actually operates. This technique had proved quite effective in assessing the evolution of the IT industry through the mainframe, minicomputer, and PC eras. Indeed, it had become the basis for my first and only other book, *Waves of Power,* written in 1996.

As the potential of the Internet became increasingly visible, there seemed to be little doubt that the IT industry's value chain was once again being greatly transformed. After all, there was now a whole new set of important market participants. In addition to the rapidly increasing number of dot-com companies, all manner of established publishing, education, media, retail, financial services, and other firms that had never been part of the IT business were suddenly becoming key Internet industry forces. The inclusion of so many new types of companies meant that, almost by definition, a very different IT industry value chain was emerging. To me, the big question was what this would mean for new and existing industry participants alike.

One day in the spring of 1997, I was sitting around with some of my colleagues at *Computerworld*'s parent company, International Data Group (IDG), the large IT media and research conglomerate with which I had spent many years as a researcher, consultant, and executive. We were trying to come up with some new themes for an important upcoming IDG client seminar. During our discussions, I mentioned that I had been developing a new idea, but thus far I was struggling with an apparent lack of compelling implications.

What had struck me was that with the arrival of the Internet, for the first time in this business's history, IT customers were intentionally and systematically creating value for other IT customers. More important, the value that these customers were creating was much more meaningful to most IT customers than the value that major IT suppliers were creating. Consequently, for the first time, the IT industry seemed to be moving from a supply-driven to a demand-driven value chain.

While the previous paragraph contains a lot of abstract language, the real-world examples couldn't be much more obvious. Consider that from their very beginnings, firms such as Amazon.com, E*TRADE, and eBay were not IT suppliers in any traditional sense. They were selling books, financial services, or Cabbage Patch dolls. Yet, since at least 1995, it had been clear that for many consumers, the ability to access these new types of services was a much stronger incentive to get on the Internet than anything that Microsoft, Dell, Cisco, or even America Online (AOL) were offering. Better browsers, more powerful PCs, and faster, simpler networks were all important, but they were far from the driving force behind market demand.

The fact that technology customer organizations such as Amazon had suddenly become the main creators of IT demand meant that these firms were now, by definition, formally part of the IT industry value chain. Customers, of course, have always been the ultimate source of IT demand, but before the Internet they were largely absent from the demand-creation side of the business. Historically, what one company did with its mainframes, minis, PCs, or networks typically had little or no impact upon the total demand for computers by other companies, except perhaps in the relatively modest sense of a best practice indicator of what could or couldn't be done.

But with the emergence of the Internet, IT customers were now systematically creating IT demand for other IT customers, and this was now the driving force in the marketplace. All of my previous experience suggested that this type of major change in value-chain dynamics would almost certainly have enormous effects on the rest of the IT business. Yet, at the time, when my colleagues and I looked at this theory, we all had the same basic reaction. Although the idea seemed both theoretically sound and inherently interesting, we really couldn't get past the "So what?" test. Why exactly did this change matter?

After all, the IT industry was booming on all fronts, and there didn't seem to be any fundamental changes in competitive or behavioral dynamics. If, in 1997, you had asked executives at Microsoft, Dell, or Amazon how the fact that customers were becoming part of the IT industry value chain had affected their business, they would have simply and correctly said "not at all." Consequently, this seemed to be a theory without much of a purpose, and thus it was largely relegated to a folder on my PC where I keep ideas that might someday be useful.

New Thinking for the Post-Bubble Era

However, beginning in the spring of 2000, after the dot-com bubble began to burst, there was clearly a need for new ideas to help think through what would follow this dramatic, although certainly not surprising, shift in the IT industry's fortune. Having a background in economic history, I had long been fascinated by society's periodic bubbles of business activity. Over the years, I have regularly revisited the indispensable *Extraordinary Popular Delusions and the Madness of Crowds* written in 1841 by British journalist, Charles Mackay. This still-underappreciated work recounts the Dutch tulip bulb craze, the hyper land speculation in the New World, and many other examples of irrational and often disastrous mass-market behavior.

Yet while it is easy to dismiss the dot-com boom as merely the latest example of money's ability to make otherwise sane people abandon just about all sense of judgment, history suggests that this is only part of the story. The evidence shows that not all bubbles are alike, and that the distinctions between them are often instructive and even predictive. In other words, to forecast what will happen next, it's often worth understanding the underlying nature of each particular bubble.

Looking back, it seems clear that the heart of the Internet bubble was the mistaken expectations regarding the overall rate of business and societal change. Many participants and investors expected the economy to be rapidly transformed, and when it became clear that it would not, the bubble burst. Consequently, correctly forecasting the rate of business and social change is still the key to assessing the overall prospects for the IT industry. And it is here that the concept of a customer-driven value chain resurfaces as an important, and I think necessary analytical tool. Certain IT industry segments have always borne the burden of IT industry leadership, but for the first time, this leadership has shifted from IT suppliers to IT customers, who are now taking on the historically difficult task of making computers more useful and appealing.

Customers Must Take the Lead

Consider this list of current IT industry challenges. Creating compelling new online content has proven to be more difficult than for previous technologies such as television and radio. The content that has been created isn't something most consumers are willing to pay for, and online advertising techniques are still immature. E-commerce has proven surprisingly complex and often requires large up-front investments. Established industry leaders often have mixed feelings regarding market exchanges and other forms of cooperative commerce, and thus industries such as banking, insurance, retail, and health care aren't about to be transformed overnight. Using the Internet for online learning has often been no more effective than previous generations of computer-based education. The music industry would rather shut down Napster than lose control over its copyrighted content. These realities have been remarkably consistent all around the world.

In fact, it is this very list of problems and barriers that reveals how the IT industry really has changed. The common thread of all of these obstacles is that they are primarily IT customer issues. Over the course of this work, we will see that the IT industry faces a long list of opportunities and challenges that traditional IT suppliers can't really address, but customers can. Indeed, the degree to which customers respond to these challenges will determine where the IT industry goes from here.

The Evolution of an Idea

As we will see throughout part 1 of this book, computer industry progress has often been difficult. However, for the first time, this is more a customer challenge than a supplier one.

From a longer-term perspective, today's customer-centric IT industry should be seen as just the latest example of the refocusing of the IT industry's energies, much as innovation was once centered around mainframes, minis, and PCs. A summary of these shifts is provided in figure I-1, which is an updated version of the chart that was central to *Waves of Power*. But whereas previous shifts have tended to be led by one group of suppliers or another, in this case the position of IT vendors is becoming subordinate to that of their customers. For the first time, even the IT industry's strongest players such as Microsoft, IBM, Sun Microsystems, Oracle, and Cisco can't by themselves address many of the problems the industry needs to resolve to aggressively move ahead. This represents a huge cultural and business change.

Of course, one can't take this argument too far. Clearly, IT suppliers will continue to innovate furiously in just about every sector, new and

FIGURE I - 1

Major Stages of IT Industry Expansion

As the figure suggests, approximately every decade the IT industry's center of gravity tends to shift, with profound implications for new and existing IT industry participants. And while this book will focus on the customer-centric era, it should be noted that the effects of previous waves of computing are still very much with us.

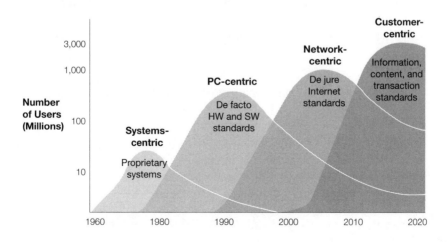

old alike. In established areas such as PCs, servers, networking equipment, and especially an endless array of software, competition will continue to require vendors to rapidly improve their products. As in the past, the cumulative effects of these improvements will be profound and will provide the ever-more-sophisticated enabling technologies that customers require. Additionally, in emerging markets such as handheld devices, wireless data services, speech and video recognition, biotechnology, nanotechnology, and other nascent areas, supplier innovation will continue to play the lead role in helping these markets become more viable and eventually reach critical mass.

However, at this particular time in the IT industry's history, neither incremental improvements to existing markets nor leadership in emerging areas is likely to be sufficient to drive a major industry expansion. For that, the leadership of customers will be required to establish a whole new range of industry and even societywide systems, applications, platforms, and standards. Should customers move aggressively in these areas, the business of IT suppliers will expand accordingly. However, should customers prove unable to make progress in many of the areas mentioned above, the overall IT business will almost certainly stagnate. It's a whole new level of dependency, and it should be the dominant IT industry dynamic for the rest of this decade.

More personally, I want to make it clear that I do not come at these issues from anything even resembling an anti-supplier or anti-technology perspective. For the majority of my career, I have worked as a consultant with IT vendors, helping them develop strategies, launch markets, and both compete and cooperate with their rivals. Although the IT industry has recently been hurt by a number of high-profile scandals, I have nothing but admiration for the faith, confidence, and commitment that so many companies have exhibited over so many years to keep the IT business moving forward. These firms and their employees have faced many difficult challenges that have required great perseverance and ingenuity. I have no doubt that their efforts and resilience will continue.

Indeed, one of the motivations for writing this book is my belief that it is now the turn of IT customers to show the same level of faith and commitment that IT suppliers have consistently provided in the past. In inherently difficult long-term tasks such as fully exploiting the potential of information technology, nothing is more important than a gut-level commitment to the possibilities of the future. Historically, and through this industry's many ups and downs, this driving energy has mostly been supplied by IT vendors, particularly entrepreneurs who were often the biggest supporters of change and who assumed the highest levels of risk. While customers have occasionally taken the lead, they have usually had the luxury of sitting back and seeing how the IT market evolved. This book will explain why this is increasingly no longer the case.

Consequently, one of the great questions of the next few years is the extent to which IT customers will succeed in showing supplier-like levels of IT commitment and leadership, effectively operating on the very frontier of IT industry change. Establishing a new generation of both industry-specific and societywide applications will require significant customer transformation, often including close industrywide cooperation. More broadly and fundamentally, it's during the next few years that the impact of the Internet on the very structure of the U.S. economy will be largely defined. All of the IT industry's history suggests that, once defined, these changes will prove long-lasting. Thus, I expect that this post-bubble period marks the beginning of the truly formative years of what will be an increasingly Internet-based economy.

About This Book

The primary goal of this book is to make sure that readers fully understand and appreciate that customers are now the driving force of IT industry progress. Thus, its initial mission is to provide the mental map with which readers can envision the IT industry of today. Using a consistent value-chain approach, the book assesses the IT industry's most important dynamics and challenges across a wide range of business, education, government, and consumer activity. This broad perspective will then be used to identify and forecast the many specific issues that will determine the health and structure of the IT business over the rest of this decade. The purpose is not so much to examine each issue in detail, but rather to show how so many of today's seemingly diverse challenges are actually part of a common customer-driven pattern.

Of course, the more important question for most readers is what these changes will mean to them. For IT suppliers, this work will identify the forces likely to drive the next major cycle of industry expansion. It will also explain why even the largest of vendors won't be able to control their own fate to the extent they have in the past. Increasingly, the most decisive events will take place in particular industries and applications as customers develop key new platforms and standards. This work predicts, among other things, that, for the first time, IT industry talent will begin to migrate away from the supplier to the customer side of the business and that the traditional venture-capital backed start-up company will become a smaller part of the overall IT industry picture. Indeed, we will see why many of the great companies of the future are likely to be the result of customer-driven change, not the cause. This will be a major reversal of the traditional industry pattern.

For IT customers, the changes are even greater. They are being asked to develop major new industry systems, platforms, and standards. Whether the issue is online music, more effective advertising formats, health care, business exchanges, payment systems, e-learning, or government services, customers must take the lead in moving IT usage forward. In the past, IT suppliers and various associations have dominated many standards areas. But increasingly, specific customer leadership is required. Going forward, the big questions are how aggressive customers will be in establishing these new information uses and how long this formative stage will last. Assuming that the world can avoid a major war, paralyzing terrorism, or a steep recession, the answers to these questions will determine when the next cycle of growth and expansion will begin.

The book itself is broken down into three largely chronological sections. Part 1 explores the changing patterns of IT industry leadership. By looking back at the evolution of key twentieth-century technologies, we'll see how difficult IT industry progress has often been and how this resulted in a supplier-dominated IT business. This history will also be used to show how an overreliance on supplier-centric business models led directly to the Internet bubble. This sets the stage for chapter 3, in which the concept of a customer-driven value chain is explained in detail. Part 1 concludes with a number of important historical examples of industries and applications where customers have taken the technology lead and established important industrywide and societywide systems.

Part 2 focuses on today's most important IT challenges and opportunities, with a particular emphasis on the impact of Web Services and metadata-driven Semantic Applications. While businesses, educational institutions, consumers, and governments each have their own IT priorities, there are now some remarkably consistent patterns. For example, in each of these areas the key is not so much deploying exotic new applications such as software agents or voice recognition, but rather much more fully exploiting ideas and technologies that are already available. Additionally, on the majority of new frontiers, successful IT industry expansion will require unprecedented levels of customer cooperation. Indeed, this ongoing need for close industrywide interaction will be one of the defining differences between the supplier- and customer-driven eras.

Finally, part 3 will bring together the implications of this formative period for both IT suppliers and customers alike, including a number of specific recommendations and predictions. The emphasis will be on defining the adjustments that many IT suppliers and customers will have to make in their strategies, tactics, and perspectives. By summarizing the book's key themes, the final chapter shows that a new value chain has truly taken hold, but suggests it could take time before the next phase of IT industry growth and expansion can emerge.

A Note on Terminology

Over the course of this book, the term *IT industry* will be used countless times, and since the term is used in a somewhat expansive way, its meaning should be carefully explained. Before the Internet, the world of information technology could be divided pretty cleanly between IT suppliers and IT customers (often called IT users). Within this framework, the term IT industry typically included only the IT supplier side of the business. However, now that the efforts of both IT suppliers and IT customers are part of the same industry value chain, it's important to see both groups as essential IT industry participants. While we still often need distinctive terminology such as, for example, the information systems department or specific product user groups, we also need a unified term to encompass an increasingly unified industry. As the saying goes, in many ways we are all technologists now, and therefore when viewed broadly just about every knowledge worker is now part of the IT industry story.

Similarly, the phrase *IT customer* is also used very extensively, and in today's business world, it too has several different meanings. In this work, IT customer is almost always used to refer to those organizations that buy and use IT products and services from some sort of IT supplier. Thus, when this book refers to customers creating value for other customers, one could say that it is IT buyers creating value for other IT buyers, or IT users creating for other IT users. Clearly, these IT buyers often have their own customers, both inside and outside of their organizations. When the word *customer* is used in this latter way, it will be clearly indicated as such; these latter types of customers are also sometimes referred to as "end users." In contrast, the word *consumer* is almost always used to talk about individuals acting largely outside of any business or other organizational context. In this sense, they are a subset of the universe of IT customers.

Additionally, throughout this work, the phrases *IT supplier* and *IT vendor* will be used almost interchangeably. Supplier is probably the more generally recognized business term, but many IT suppliers often refer to themselves as IT vendors. There is no real difference. Of more intellectual interest is the increasingly blurred line between customer and supplier organizations, as technology-oriented services companies (especially those providing Web Services) become important parts of many industry sectors. In this work, the phrase *traditional IT vendors* will be reserved for general-purpose hardware, software, telecommunications, and professional services suppliers. More borderline cases will be identified as such.

Finally, the words *value* and *value chain* are also used extensively. Value refers to the actual utility of an individual product or service, whether it can be reflected in a specific price or not. Value chain refers to those interrelated activities and players that come together to design, build, deliver, and support a particular product or service. (The particular type of value chain in place is often equated more or less synonymously with the phrase *industry structure.*)

This is a deliberately broad value chain definition in that it includes processes that are both within and between particular companies. (Some people now use the phrase "value network" to describe this broader internal and external perspective.) Much of this book will stress that IT industry participants often put too much emphasis on supply-chain efficiencies, as opposed to demand-side expansion. In the end, the IT industry has always grown by establishing important new frontiers of usage and demand. Much of this work will be aimed at explaining how these new frontiers are likely to come about.

The Evolution of an Idea

Acknowledgments

Much of the content of this book has accumulated over many years of consulting with IT suppliers and customers and writing about IT industry trends as part of my regular *Computerworld* columns, and thus many individuals have contributed to this book without ever realizing it. This is especially true for all of my readers, whose comments have often proven invaluable. Looking back, I am particularly indebted to my friends at IDG, particularly Kelly Conlin and Gary Beach who were the first people with whom the ideas behind this work were discussed, and who provided me with important conceptual feedback.

Once the work commenced, particular individuals have been very helpful with certain chapters. For example, in the world of online education, I am indebted to many of my former colleagues at MeansBusiness, especially Trish O'Hare, Nancy Adams, Matt Toolan, David Wilcox, and James Coleman. This is where many of my ideas regarding the e-learning business as well as the whole subject of Semantic Applications were first developed. The comments of Paul Pastrone were also very helpful in this area.

Similarly, the chapter on government was greatly informed by my experience working with the staff of the Progressive Policy Institute, especially Rob Atkinson. It is here that I first began to explore the full scope of interaction between public and private sector forces. In terms of the value of business computing, the comments and work of David Vellante, and his colleagues at ITCentrix, have also been much appreciated.

I would like to thank Steve Milunovich of Merrill Lynch for his insightful comments on the early draft of this work. The steady stream of research from Merrill's analysts has also greatly helped me keep up with the many topics covered. The same can be said for my editors at *Computerworld*, Richard Saia and Mary Fran Johnson. Many of the key ideas in this book were first experimented with in my *Computerworld* columns. *Computerworld* and *CIO* magazine are the two IT publications that most closely cover the types of customer leadership issues described in this book, and both have been an important ongoing source. Other important background sources are listed in the works consulted.

Finally, this work would not have been possible without the unwavering support of Jacqueline Murphy, my editor at Harvard Business

xix

School Press. Jacque's wisdom, advice, patience, and enthusiasm have been relied upon countless times, and she deserves great credit for whatever parts of this book are well organized and/or clear. Additionally, I would like to thank the entire team at HBSP, especially Jill Connor and Timothy Maher for their careful editing of this text, and Astrid Sandoval for all that she has done to help keep this project on track.

Most of all, I would like to thank Alev Danis, my dear wife, who created the environment from which this work's thinking and writing could eventually emerge. Her support has made everything possible.

I

IT Patterns and Tendencies

CHAPTER ONE

Computers Have Always Been Difficult

SINCE THIS IS a book about customers and computing, I thought I would start off with a perspective on how customers have historically viewed the idea of computing. A recurring theme of this book is that the effective use of computers has almost always been difficult, and therefore it has often taken a long time to bring a particular information technology idea or capability to fruition. This is why commitment and perseverance have always been essential parts of the IT industry story. Over the course of this book we will see why many of the key applications of the future could also take considerable time to emerge on a large-scale basis. This chapter explores how this pattern has been true since the IT industry's very beginnings.

Oddly enough, many of us in the IT industry often seem to overlook or forget this clear historical pattern. Consequently, our industry has had an unfortunate tendency to indulge in somewhat self-congratulatory attitudes and behavior, typically based on the mistaken view that computers are the fastest growing, most dynamic, and most revolutionary industry sector ever. Admittedly, these sentiments have cooled considerably since the Internet bubble burst, but the general sense of unprecedented change remains. Perhaps every age has felt this way about its own frontiers, especially ones that have created so much opportunity, wealth, and status.

A sense of being in a truly special time can be a comforting thought for just about any industry participant, and in the whir of day-to-day IT industry events, it does often feel as if our world must be changing faster than ever. But it is important to realize that this is really not the case. Computers are part of a long stream of significant nineteenth- and twentieth-century electrical innovations—lights, radios, telephones,

TVs—and compared to what these earlier technologies meant to society, computers and IT shine in some areas but come up lacking in many others. Someday, the IT industry will likely achieve its goals and become the most important of all electronic applications, but at least from a consumer's perspective, this day remains a long way off.

It is, of course, difficult to directly and fairly compare the usage, evolution, and impact of very different industries that emerged at very different times. However, the research in the fields of technology and economic history is quite extensive, and a review of this literature reveals that there are enough common challenges, issues, and data points that the growth of the computer industry can be accurately placed into a wider technological context. (Some of the key texts that I have relied on in these areas are listed in the bibliography.) In looking back at the last hundred years or so of technological innovation, the following four questions have been particularly relevant:

1. How excited was the general public by what this technology had to offer?

2. Why have some industries caught on considerably faster than others?

3. How were resources mobilized to develop this industry?

4. What role did the public sector play?

The answers to these questions will help us see why utilizing general-purpose computers based on software programs has generally been a more difficult and time-consuming task than taking advantage of previous twentieth-century innovations. Thus, the fact that the commercial success of the Internet is taking a few years longer than many of us had hoped or expected is neither surprising nor really of any great long-term consequence. Much of the Internet's potential will eventually be fulfilled.

Customer Enthusiasm

A comparative analysis of the initial levels of consumer enthusiasm reveals some of the sharpest differences between computers and other twentieth-century inventions. Although every period has had its skeptics, the overall excitement regarding earlier electrical inventions was often almost palpable. We've probably all heard stories about whole neighborhoods gathering around a single radio receiver to hear a war report, a prizefight, a presidential address, or simply some music. Looking back, the period from roughly 1922–1952 witnessed the greatest explosion in information and communication in human history. Five major new media—radios, telephones, film, recorded sound, and television—all became widely, often wildly, popular and forever changed U.S. culture.

Yet, as impressive as all of this was, the single strongest example of unbounded consumer excitement came from electricity itself. It is almost impossible to imagine what the arrival of electric light meant to the typical town or home, where for many, the ability to light up the night sky took on an almost spiritual dimension. Similarly, it is all too easy to forget how much now seemingly mundane appliances such as electric irons, vacuum cleaners, stoves, and refrigerators meant in terms of reducing some of the physical drudgery of everyday life. Consumers often stood in long lines to see special exhibitions of the latest ideas in home technology, and there was a great deal of utopian and futuristic literature promising the better world to come. Even today, there still isn't much higher praise than to be called "electrifying," and the most productive of our citizens are often deemed human "dynamos." More than any other innovation, past or present, electrical energy had the potential to create truly better lives.

But whether one is looking at electricity, radio, or television, the initial level of consumer enthusiasm significantly exceeded the initial consumer reaction to that of computers. Consider that the great majority of early computer usage was for business purposes, and businesspeople are typically much less utopian and excitable than consumers. But even in the consumer market, especially after the introduction of the IBM PC in 1981, the use of home computers often simply meant that people were able to work from home. Convenient perhaps, but hardly inspiring. Whereas being called electrifying was undeniably flattering, being seen as a human computer still connotes a considerably more mixed message.

Certainly, there was and still is a large group of hobbyists fascinated by the art of programming and the way computers work, much as amateur radio operators and automobile mechanics flourished in the early

TABLE 1 - 1

Relative Rates of Consumer Acceptance, Major Electronic Technologies

	Approximate Year Developed	Approximate Year Major Consumer Growth Began	Percent in U.S. Households Twenty Years after Growth Began	General- or Single-Purpose (GP or SP)	New Infrastructure Requirements
Telephone	1876	1899	35	SP	High
Electricity	1878	1907	63	GP	High
Radio	1907	1923	78	SP	Medium
Television	1927	1948	93	SP	Medium
Computers	1941	1976	35	GP	Low

All market data is from U.S. Statistical Abstracts, except 1976 PC data, which is from the U.S. Department of Commerce. It is noteworthy that the two general-purpose technologies are the ones where customer and application leadership have proven most important.

twentieth century. But the number of people enthralled by technology per se has always been a small share of the population. For the vast majority, the pre-Internet computer business had surprisingly little to offer in terms of entertainment and/or convenience. Of course, computer games have always been an important exception, but these are best played on dedicated machines, and tend to appeal to a relatively narrow slice of the population, primarily teenage boys. (Although The Sims and a new generation of online games are now changing this demographic.)

Comparative Rates of Adoption

This lack of consumer enthusiasm for computers has carried over into the speed of consumer adoption. While the computer industry has certainly grown rapidly, compared to other major twentieth-century technologies, the rate of computer acceptance at the consumer level is only average at best, especially given today's vastly greater societal wealth and much more efficient mass-market distribution capabilities. Table 1-1 provides a quick statistical comparison.

The data clearly show that radio and television have enjoyed by far the most rapid rate of consumer acceptance. Consider that volume sales of radio receivers to consumers began in 1922, yet by 1932, 62 percent of U.S. homes had at least one radio. Similarly, after a long initial gestation period, television caught on even more quickly. Between 1948 and 1958, TVs went from being in less than 1 percent of U.S. homes to being in roughly 85 percent, despite relatively limited programming. These rates of new media adoption are particularly impressive given that, adjusted for inflation, radios and TVs during these two respective periods cost roughly the same as PCs did in the 1980s and 1990s, and more than many PCs do today.

In contrast, significant PC sales to consumers began in the late 1970s, and today (some twenty-five years later) they are in a little more than half of U.S. homes. Progress on this front has been quite steady over the years, but at the current rates, it will still be a long time before computers reach the virtually 100 percent saturation that radios, TVs, and telephones all have. Today, the few Americans who don't have a TV are mostly making some sort of lifestyle statement. In contrast, there are still a great many people who simply have no real interest in either PCs or the Internet, but are not at all averse to using other electronic media.

Not surprisingly, those technologies that required significant new physical infrastructure—electricity, telephones, and automobiles—tended to initially grow more slowly than television and radio, which could rely on broadcast signals to cover large geographic areas. Obviously, a great deal of expensive and time-consuming work was required to wire and pave much of the North American continent. But even in the face of these obstacles, the rates of consumer acceptance for these infrastructure-intensive technologies rival those of the PC industry.

For example, despite the enormous logistical and technical challenges involved in building power systems and delivering electricity to the home, the use of electricity in urban areas went from 8 percent of U.S. homes in 1907 to 85 percent in 1930, far faster than PCs have been adopted. Given the scale and even danger of the work required and the initial shortage of electricians and other resources, even in retrospect this represents a stunning achievement. Rural electrification, of course, took much longer and eventually relied on significant government support, particularly in the 1930s.

As with television, telephones had a relatively long ramp-up time (in this case between 1876 and 1900), but even afterward the rate of growth was considerably slower than the other major electronic inventions. For example, it wasn't until 1945 that more than half of all U.S. households had at least one telephone line installed. Given how essential telephones are today, this pattern might seem surprising. Overall, there appear to be four main reasons for this relatively long launch period:

1. Unlike radio and television, telephones took on increasing value as more and more people acquired them, and therefore the initial customer sales were considerably tougher. In modern language, because of its strong *network effects,* the telephone industry faced a significantly tougher *critical mass* challenge.[1]

2. As with electricity and roads, a great deal of telephone infrastructure had to be put in place, but with telephones there were also serious compatibility problems. Before the establishment of the unified Bell System between 1905 and 1920, telephones from competing telephone companies typically couldn't talk to one another, even within the same town. This created the so-called "both phone" problem. Seventy-five years later, incompatible e-mail

systems would create much the same frustration until Internet messaging standards became pervasive in the mid-1990s.

3. The evidence suggests that in the first half of the twentieth century, telephones just weren't as appealing to most consumers as electricity and radio. The literature regarding the early use of telephones shows much higher levels of consumer skepticism, especially in small towns where it was still relatively easy for people to talk to each other face to face.

4. As with electricity, telephone companies also faced serious challenges in profitably serving rural areas and eventually relied on government subsidies to extend the national telephone network into remote geographic regions.

Because of its strong critical mass effects, the true value and power of telephones really didn't emerge until most consumers and businesses had regular access. It would not be surprising if the Internet eventually exhibits a similar pattern. As we will see numerous times throughout this work, a system used by 100 percent of the people is much more than twice as powerful as one used by 50 percent. Many of the technology applications presented in chapter 4 and throughout part 2 were chosen because of their ability to drive societywide usage of IT-based systems. Such pervasive availability has always been the hallmark of a truly successful technology, and it remains an essential Internet industry goal.

Putting IT in Perspective

In summary, the technologies of the first half of the twentieth century were often considerably more successful than computers in capturing the imagination, enthusiasm, and spending of consumers. Despite lower levels of societal affluence and less efficient distribution systems, radio, television, and electricity were all adopted more rapidly than PCs by U.S. consumers. The evidence on these points is quite clear and consistent. As we will see later in this chapter and throughout this book, these patterns tell us a great deal about the nature of computers and the challenges involved in establishing widespread IT usage.

Of course, when confronted with these somewhat discomforting or at least challenging statistics, many computer industry advocates understandably are quick to say, "Never mind PCs, what about the Internet?" After all, it is true that consumer use of the Internet rose from virtually zero to nearly half of U.S. homes in the eight years from 1994–2001. Doesn't this put it among the fastest-growing media technologies of all? While it is certainly possible to argue that the Internet deserves to be near the top of the list, the logic of this claim is flawed and ultimately unconvincing.

One reason the Internet could grow so quickly among U.S. consumers (and, for that matter, businesses) was because so many of the necessary PCs and telephone lines were already in place. Consequently, Internet usage was for many computer owners more like a major new application (or a greatly improved form of the online services previously available from CompuServe and others) than an entirely new technology. Thus, comparing the Internet with industries such as television, telephony, radio, and electricity, which had to start essentially from scratch, is not particularly fair or valid. The much more appropriate comparison to these earlier technologies is clearly with PCs themselves.

And if you are thinking that it was the explosion of computers in business that really makes computers the fastest-growing media, consider the following. The use of computers in business began in the mid-1950s, yet didn't become truly pervasive until the late 1980s, more than thirty years later. The Internet did not so much create new business computer capabilities as it made it much easier to take advantage of the computer's inherent possibilities. Extensive computer networking had been occurring for more than a decade before the widespread availability of the Internet. Overall, the vast scope and extent of business computing is now far more impressive than the actual adoption rate.

Establishing New Industries

Another central concern of this book is the way that important new industries are formed. By definition, every industry needs to be launched in some way, and, historically, this market launch period has almost always had long-lasting structural implications. In reviewing the early years of the industries discussed so far, there are three themes that emerge as particularly relevant to the formation of technology-based markets: an initial reliance on vertical integration, the dominant role of strong individuals, and the timely support of governments.

Just about all of these industries faced classic chicken-and-egg problems. Why would a consumer buy a TV or radio if there were no television or radio programs? Why would a company develop television or radio programs if consumers didn't have a TV or a radio? Why would a consumer acquire telephone service if no one they knew had a phone? While today, we often use fancy terms such as positive feedback cycles, critical mass, network effects, virtuous circles, healthy ecosystems, and the like, this basic chicken/egg dilemma in launching new technology markets is now more than a century old.

In virtually all of these cases, the solution to this problem, at least in the United States, has been for industries to be created by vertically integrated companies, which are capable of delivering a sufficiently complete product or service. Essentially, one or more lead companies has taken the initiative and assumed the substantial risks involved in resolving the chicken/egg dilemma. From the consumer's perspective, this approach ensured that one could, for example, get both electricity and electrical appliances that actually worked together. Perhaps the most succinct early expression of this need for close product integration came from none other than the Wizard of Menlo Park, Thomas A. Edison:

> It was not only necessary that the lamps should give light and the dynamos generate current, but the lamps must be adapted to the current of the dynamos, and the dynamos must be constructed to give the character of current required by the lamps, and likewise all parts of the system must be constructed with reference to all other parts, since, in one sense, all the parts form one machine. Like any other machine the failure of one part to cooperate properly with the other part disorganizes the whole and renders it inoperative for the purpose intended.[2]

Perhaps because building a vertically integrated company is inherently risky and often required total management commitment, in each case, the vertically integrated market leader and its CEO were largely inseparable, often for literally decades. For example, in electricity, Edison, and what eventually became General Electric, provided everything from power plants to appliances. With telephony, what eventually became known as AT&T, first under Alexander Graham Bell and then Theodore Vail, built telephones and switching equipment, installed telephone wires and provided telephone services. With television, David Sarnoff and RCA took the lead in developing commercial broadcast equipment, home receivers, and related programming.

The computer industry has repeatedly followed this same vertically integrated model. Prominent IT industry examples of early stage vertical integration include punch card equipment, mainframes, minicomputers, technical workstations, video game players, the early PCs and online services, and, more recently, handheld computers, many wireless services, and to some extent, AOL. The vertically integrated model has consistently been the simplest and most reliable way to put together a useful new IT industry product or service. Later we will see that the fact that the Internet did not begin this way helped lead directly to many of its unusual strengths and weaknesses.

In short, most major technology-based industries have started off being vertically integrated. Importantly, all of the industries discussed in this chapter are now primarily horizontal in nature, meaning that the vertically integrated model has at some point been replaced by a system in which different companies focus on particular parts of what eventually becomes an industry value chain. However, different industries have made this transition at very different rates and for very different reasons. In chapters 2 and 3, we will see how this pattern has shifted back and forth through the mainframe, PC, and Internet eras. Indeed, the interplay between vertical and horizontal forces will recur throughout many of the customer-centric applications covered in this book. It is especially relevant to today's ongoing debate regarding the impact and importance of Web Services.

The Often Essential Role of Government

In Europe, national governments played a much more direct role in launching information technology markets. The telephone, radio, and television industries were often viewed as public services to be owned and operated like postal mail. Indeed, the launch and management of these key twentieth-century industries has historically been one of the defining differences between the U.S. and the European economic models. Clearly, there have been significant pros and cons with both approaches. The U.S. model has tended to create a more successful set of global market suppliers, while the European markets have tended to expand more slowly, but, arguably, more equitably.

However, the strong historical role of the public sector in Europe and elsewhere has made it easy to overlook the important contribution that government has also made to technology usage in the United States. Over the last hundred years, there have been many times when the timely intervention of the federal government has helped to overcome barriers that industry participants could not easily resolve. The four most important of these contributions have been: sponsoring research and development, establishing standards, subsidizing universal service, and coping with monopoly market power. Consider the following brief examples:

1. **Regulating electricity.** The early electrical power plants that served individual cities and towns were one of the best examples of what economists like to call a "natural monopoly" (at least they were before deregulation). It simply was inherently wasteful for a community to try to accommodate more than one electrical supplier. This soon led to a heated debate as to whether these systems should be publicly or privately owned. In the United States, there was extensive experimentation with both approaches, especially during the formative 1880–1920 period. In general, the private approach moved more quickly and tended to prevail (at least in the larger urban markets). However, in the anti-monopoly atmosphere immediately before and after World War I, public sentiment ran against the idea of unrestricted private control of society's increasingly critical power systems. During the 1920s, and for decades thereafter, the model of a government-regulated but privately owned monopoly took hold and allowed the electrical power industry to expand rapidly and relatively smoothly.[3]

2. **Radio spectrum management.** In the early days of radio, there was no mechanism by which to assign specific frequencies to specific broadcasters. As the use of radio transmission grew, the interference caused by overlapping signals became so great as to be nearly intolerable, threatening the viability of the industry itself. The Radio Act of 1912 had previously established that the airways were in fact public property and that their stewardship was a

legitimate government function. But it wasn't until 1927 that the Federal Radio Commission (FRC) was formed with a charter to oversee the radio industry. The FRC took on the task of licensing radio spectrum, and the radio industry soon flourished (although one key consequence was that many amateur radio operators lost out to corporate broadcast interests). In 1933, the FRC became the Federal Communications Commission (FCC). The FCC has been overseeing U.S. spectrum allocation ever since; it remains a critical yet controversial government function.[4]

3. **A uniform television signal standard.** Like radio, television also faced significant standards battles that the participants could not easily resolve. The government-empowered National Television Systems Committee was instrumental in establishing the interlaced broadcast signal standards that still support both the black and white and color television transmission. In both cases, settling the standards issue was essential to the rapid industry growth that followed, since U.S. consumers could be assured that all TVs would receive all U.S. television broadcasts.[5] Government has also played a critical, if often controversial, role in cable television operation, licensing, and copyrights, alleviating what could otherwise have been a paralyzing stalemate between the interests of broadcasters and cable operators.

4. **Building a nationwide telephone system.** Although in the telephony industry there was no one defining moment of government intervention, public policy facilitated the growth of the U.S. telephone systems in many important ways. The controversial patent (#174,465) granted to Alexander Graham Bell was essential to the rise of the company that eventually became AT&T. Perhaps more important, the U.S. government and AT&T eventually came to a complex (and sometimes unstated) compromise whereby AT&T was allowed to acquire or otherwise eliminate most of its independent (and usually incompatible) competitors. In exchange, AT&T accepted various levels of government oversight and largely stayed out of emerging businesses such as radio, film, television, and computers. As with electricity, a regulated, constrained monopoly, along with rural subsidies, proved to be the optimal way to deliver near-universal telephone service.[6]

5. **Computers.** National governments around the world, particularly in the United States, the United Kingdom, and Germany, funded much of the initial development of computers, mostly for military and scientific purposes. Additionally, the U.S. federal government, along with the research and university communities, was instrumental in the development and launch of the Internet. As we will see in chapter 2, were it not for the unintended consequences of this public-sector research, the evolution of the computer industry would likely have been radically different. Chapter 10 will discuss the many ways that governments are participating in today's Internet-driven IT industry.[7]

In sum, while the public sector has certainly made its share of mistakes, it has contributed significantly to each of these major twentieth-century innovations. As we will see in chapter 10, this largely positive legacy will need to continue if the IT industry is to effectively address new challenges in areas such as national security, wireless data spectrum allocation, copyrights, patents, privacy, antitrust, taxation, and many forms of international coordination. Government has always been a major player in technology markets, sometimes as they are launched, sometimes as they grow, and sometimes after they mature. Especially after the events of September 11, 2001, continued government involvement in the IT industry seems assured.

Why Computers Have Taken Longer to Catch on

As noted earlier, among all of the technologies discussed in this chapter, only computers and electricity are primarily general purpose in nature. Over the years, many people have suggested that it is this very same general-purpose capability that is at the heart of the usage difficulties that computers have always presented. Radios, TVs, and telephones (along with vacuum cleaners, stoves, etc.) are dedicated devices that are relatively easy to use. And there has always been a school of thought that computers will eventually evolve in the same direction, turning into what are often referred to as dedicated "information appliances."

The marketplace, however, has generally voted otherwise, and with a few important exceptions such as video games, calculators, and very small devices such as pagers and cell phones, dedicated information appliances have not been widely successful. The reason that efforts to market dedicated word processing, e-mail, or Internet machines have almost always failed is partly because such restrictions are technically somewhat artificial, but mostly because customers really do want to perform multiple tasks on a single machine.

This same phenomenon appears to be occurring again in the hand-held computer market, where those applications that need some sort of computer screen—such as for Internet access, e-mail, e-book reading, and stand-alone Palm Pilot-style applications—will increasingly be accessible via a single general-purpose device. This is why the current handheld competition among Palm, Blackberry, Pocket PC, and screen phone-style devices is becoming so interesting. In contrast, there will always be a substantial market for very small and therefore largely dedicated cell phones and MP3 players where a larger display surface and keyboard are not generally required.

One of the unintended consequences of this preference for general-purpose devices is the unending need for additional hardware capability. While the computer industry understandably takes great pride in the rate at which it has improved the performance of its products, the truly distinguishing feature is that continual and rapid improvements in computing power are still so badly needed. Looking back, it's remarkable how little TVs, radios, and wired telephones have changed over the years, and by and large, this is considered to be a good thing by consumers. While there have been many improvements and innovations, the stability of the television, radio, and motion picture platforms has led to standard modes of usage and a common base of programming, enriched by some seventy-five years of accumulated work.

In contrast, one of the downsides of "ever-improving" computer platforms is that most of the software written for mainframes, minicomputers, and the early generations of PCs has been eventually thrown away. Imagine if today's TVs were only capable of showing programs developed in the last five years. Yet even today, many advocates of various Internet technologies recommend that customers throw away their legacy systems and replace them with more modern Web-based technologies. Many customers will eventually come to agree with this assessment.

Computers typically need rapid and regular improvement because programming computers to do useful things is still so fundamentally hard, and therefore there is a continual need for better approaches. Indeed, the very idea of computer software should be viewed as one of the most difficult, and ultimately remarkable, undertakings of humankind. Essentially, just about every business process and many human interactions need to be converted into highly specific machine instructions. It's a mind-boggling challenge that continues to consume an ever-higher share of the world's brainpower, with no end in sight. Indeed, it's not hard to imagine that the tens of millions of programmers now being trained in India, China, and elsewhere will eventually be seen as an essential worldwide resource. There's seemingly no limit to how much software the market can consume.

Aggravating this software challenge is the fact that ever since its beginnings, now some sixty years ago, computer programming has been an extremely difficult, demanding, and even torturous process that most people would rather not get involved in. These same painstaking difficulties also explain why so many software development efforts fail and why even successful software projects tend to have numerous hidden bugs. The computer science community has been talking about the need to improve and guarantee software quality for more than forty years, and is seemingly no closer to finding a solution. It's a problem that may never completely go away.

As if these challenges were not enough, the very idea of "information processing" was, throughout the twentieth century, a relatively new field, with few proven precedents. Whereas the early television and radio programmers could leverage the base of experience from theaters, music halls, vaudeville, sports, and other domains, the computer industry did not have a comparably strong base of real-world activity to pattern itself after. Most of the industry's roots were in the relatively modest domains of numerical calculation, record keeping, and typewriters. While these have always been important to businesses, they have never meant a lot to most consumers. Only relatively recently has the IT industry expanded into more entertainment oriented areas.

Even today, there are still great and unending debates regarding the risks of information overload and how to best estimate the true value and necessity of various types of information. This sense of uncertainty wasn't nearly as pervasive with earlier innovations. People immediately understood the value of an electric iron that was lighter and warmed up much more quickly than a heavy metal one that required a separate heating source. No one had to explain why using a radio to listen to the World Series would appeal to baseball fans. But how many people intuitively understood that automated accounting systems were a major, or even a significant, societal improvement? Today, the same questions are being asked about technologies as diverse as e-learning, instant messaging, and wireless data services. Just how valuable are they?

The point is that it has always been implicit in the nature of information processing that establishing value would be more difficult than for televised news or entertainment, lighting homes, or replacing horses with cars. And it is this essential difference that provides the simplest explanation why IT industry progress has tended to develop more slowly than other major technologies. Stated directly: The challenge for the computer industry has always been that its work is both considerably more difficult and initially considerably less appealing to consumers than the benefits provided by other major twentieth-century innovations. Despite great progress, the industry remains in an uphill struggle with a never-ending series of difficult challenges.

What has kept the industry going is the belief that eventually the value of all of this programming and hardware improvement will become clear. All experience says that this will only happen industry by industry and application by application. As we have seen with batch processing, online databases, office automation, personal productivity tools, enterprise resource planning (ERP), customer relationship management (CRM), data warehouses, e-mail, intranets, extranets, e-commerce, and e-learning, computers can only prove themselves over considerable periods of time. Clearly, there is still a way to go.

With the arrival of the Internet, the possibilities do seem to be coming at us at an accelerated rate. But history says that the promise of IT is almost always farther off than it initially appears. As the mountaineers like to say, one should never mistake a clear vision for a short distance. Looking ahead, much will depend upon how well the IT industry addresses a number of difficult near-term and long-term challenges. The good news is that history has proved time and again that, given sufficient perseverance, many of the industry's goals will eventually be realized or even surpassed. This time, however, IT customers will have to provide the required leadership, and this leadership is only now being seriously tested.

CHAPTER TWO

Learning from a Supplier-Driven
IT Industry, 1950–2000

CHAPTER 1 used the history of twentieth-century innovation to put the growth of the IT industry into a broader technological perspective. We saw that it has been almost intrinsic in the very nature of software-dependent, general-purpose information machines that new uses of IT often prove difficult, making rapid and successful customer adoption the exception, not the rule. It's a lesson that is easily forgotten, and thus most of us tend to overestimate the rate of IT industry change, both past and present.

While looking at other industries provides a useful wide-angle perspective, the IT industry has its own unique and intriguing history. As someone who has been assessing the evolution of the IT business since the late 1970s, I've often been asked how one can tell which parts of the IT industry's past are still relevant. Since history sometimes repeats itself and sometimes does not, this has always been a difficult question, but as the market shifts from a supplier to a customer focus, it is becoming particularly tricky. Nevertheless, the question should not be dodged. Correctly applying the lessons of the past has often been an effective way to predict and communicate future IT industry change.

More subtly, because so many aspects of the past are still very much with us, we are all greatly influenced by the IT industry's history whether we want to be or not. Consequently, the first half of this chapter will focus on those lessons from previous computing eras that are still highly relevant to the IT industry of today. While some readers may find this material familiar, these ideas will be used in subsequent chapters as almost a shorthand language with which to explain various trends and dynamics, and therefore they need to be clearly understood. In the second half of this chapter, I'll argue that the unquestioned belief that history *would* repeat itself was a major cause of the Internet bubble. Thus, taken together, this chapter will demonstrate both the application and misapplication of the IT industry's historical patterns.

Let's start by looking at the following seven factors, each of which has been broadly influential throughout this industry's past, and will be shown to be relevant to today's customer-driven industry.

1. The realization that long-term IT developments are anything but inevitable

2. The overriding power of pervasive standards

3. The ongoing competition between the new and the old worlds

4. The importance of simple applications

5. The constant presence of monopolies and antitrust

6. The critical interplay between vertical and horizontal market forces

7. The power of underlying economic fundamentals

Long-Term Developments Have Been Anything But Inevitable

It never ceases to amaze me how unpredictable and often random major IT industry turning points have been. Although the relentless emergence of new technologies might seem to suggest otherwise, ultimately it's been the specific decisions of individuals and groups that have shaped much of the IT industry. In *Waves of Power,* I described in detail what I see as the three critical industry Big Bangs—IBM's S/360 mainframes, the IBM PC, and the Internet. As the brief summary below shows, each was anything but inevitable.

The IBM S/360 Mainframe

The main reason IBM has always dominated the mainframe business is that from 1920–1955 it built up an overwhelming, near-monopoly presence in the tabulating equipment marketplace. This dominance was due to the drive, initiative, and occasional ruthlessness of Thomas Watson Sr., who may never have entered the tabulating equipment business at all had he not been at the center of an antitrust controversy at his previous employer, the National Cash Register Company, now known just by its initials, NCR. Later in life Watson Sr. didn't appreciate the potential value of electronic computers. But fortunately, his son, Tom Watson Jr., did, although even he had no idea how important the 1964 introduction of the S/360 family of computers would become. Although IBM had high hopes for these machines, its initial sales estimates were low by nearly a factor of ten.[1] Nearly forty years later, the basic design of the S/360 family remains the foundation of IBM's mainframe computing products, with no clear end in sight.

The IBM PC

Volumes have been written about IBM's decision to build an open architecture PC based around the products of Intel and Microsoft. But the bottom line is that relying on another company's technology was something IBM just didn't do at the time. Had a renegade group within IBM not been allowed to pursue this strategy, the history of the IT industry in the 1980s and 1990s would have been radically different. At a minimum, there may never have been a single dominant PC standard, and Intel and Microsoft would probably never have become the giants they are today. As we shall see, the unexpected arrival of these new industry forces soon overwhelmed much of the existing IT industry order.

The Internet

The Internet is almost certainly the greatest single act of accidental intrusion the IT industry has as yet experienced. By now the story of how both the Internet and World Wide Web emerged is well-known and has been recounted in many other works. For our purposes it is sufficient to point out that the Internet and the Web were never developed for their current commercial purposes; both were intended for government and research use. Equally important, their development occurred largely outside of both the government's official standards-setting bodies and the IT industry's leading hardware, software, and telecom vendors. Essentially, the Internet and the Web were both un-planned and unprecedented one-time gifts bestowed upon the IT in-dustry by the public sector and research communities. In all probability, no IT supplier would have ever intentionally developed them in quite the same way.

The main lesson here is that when the IBM mainframe, IBM PC, and the Internet first emerged, virtually no one foresaw their long-term consequences. Yet the development of these technologies turned out to be the three biggest events in the history of computing. This strongly suggests that the evolution of today's customer-centric value chain will have similarly decisive moments that are not fully appreciated at the time. It's only in retrospect that industry turning points seem so huge, and often even inevitable.

The Strength of Pervasive Standards

Looking back, few features of the IT industry are more impressive than the permanence of certain industry standards. As noted above, the roots of IBM's mainframe architecture are now nearly forty years old, and only the retirement of qualified mainframe programmers might someday lead to a major decline in mainframe usage. Similarly, the dominance of Intel and Microsoft on the desktop is now moving into its third decade, with only the slimmest chance of any serious alterna-tives taking hold. Likewise, the key Internet standards have most of their roots in the 1970s and 1980s and will certainly be in place for many years to come. These standards have merely become stronger the more people have used them. Without standards, many IT markets would simply be too confusing, too small, and too risky.

The flip side is that technologies that don't achieve a sufficient level of standardization tend to fade away. Probably, the best example of this is the minicomputer industry, which repeatedly failed to develop a standard version of the Unix operating system and suffered the conse-quences. Had it been able to do so, it is likely that Microsoft might never have gained such a strong presence in the enterprise server mar-ket. It's also likely that there would have been little or perhaps no need for Linux. Indeed, the open-source movement might well have focused on something different, perhaps even the desktop operating system. Such are the turning points of history.

While the staying power of standards hasn't changed, their formation certainly has. In the past, the key standards in the mainframe and PC industries were controlled by individual suppliers. Today, many important standards are developed and managed within the public domain. It's hard to overemphasize that this change was not the inevitable result of competition and technology evolution; instead, it was due to the largely accidental emergence and subsequent public-sector nurturing of the Internet. Once again, the initial model of market formation has proved crucial.

The emergence of long-lasting standards has also been essential to the growth of the point-of-sale, automatic teller machine (ATM), and credit-card industries, as we will see in chapter 4. New industrywide standards could emerge to enable similar forms of IT industry expansion, including developments as diverse as online advertising formats, Internet payment systems, business exchanges, interoperable learning objects, and industry-specific metadata, all of which are explored further in part 2. A sure bet is that the importance of standards is not about to diminish; the focus is just shifting toward more customer-defined domains.

However, one of the great ironies of the IT industry is that even though standards are often the key to survival, suppliers often do their best to resist them. While the example of the minicomputer vendors and Unix is perhaps the most important of these, it is certainly not the only one. Consider that in the early days of its mainframe business, IBM often fiercely resisted the efforts of companies trying to build complementary products. In many cases, these third-party software, storage, printer, and plug-compatible computer suppliers had to go to court to try to get the IBM mainframe interface information they needed. In retrospect, this all looks a bit strange, since the availability of third-party products has clearly been an important reason why IBM's mainframes have remained so much more popular than those of its rivals. Today, the support of third parties is viewed as an essential part of a healthy business ecosystem.

Nevertheless, similar standards battles continue. Witness the never-ending and unproductive spats between Microsoft and Sun Microsystems regarding Java support or those between Microsoft and AOL over instant messaging. In these cases, lack of standardization and the perceived short-term interests of suppliers have clearly retarded the long-term growth of the market. And while it is true that a company's short- and long-term interests can often be very different indeed, it appears that IT suppliers have too often erred on the side of short-term considerations.

One of the great questions going forward is how these debates over standards will play out in increasingly customer-defined domains, where similar short- and long-term conflicts are now taking place. It seems safe to say that the ability to generate new and widely adopted standards will be an easy way to measure future industry progress for vendors and customer alike. For many years, customers have complained that IT suppliers have done a poor job of building interoperable products. But over the next few years, customers will have a chance to see if they can do this any better. In parts 2 and 3, we'll see why they probably will.

Competition between the New and the Old

Anyone who follows the IT industry has almost certainly come across the phrase *disruptive technology*. This term was made popular in 1997 by Clayton Christensen in his influential book *The Innovator's Dilemma*. However, before this particular phrase caught on, I and many other industry commentators had discussed the same general phenomenon. Included among some of the earlier descriptive terms were *the push* (or *attack*) *from below, paradigm shift, market cannibalization,* and no doubt other phrases now forgotten. Christensen's great contribution was to give this important concept both a much more elegant name and the formal theory to support it.

These terms emerged to describe a distinct pattern that has repeatedly occurred in the IT industry. In market after market, new technologies have been pioneered by new companies rather than the existing major players in seemingly closely related businesses. Examples have been found in just about every IT sector, including minicomputers, PCs, technical workstations, small disk drives, data communications equipment, many types of printers, and much of the software associated with these products. It has arguably been the IT industry's single most prominent competitive dynamic.

This pattern has typically unfolded in three main ways. Sometimes, the new technology has been much less expensive but not sufficiently powerful or reliable enough to meet the needs of an established company's core customers, and thus the technology has been dismissed as a toy not to be taken seriously. At other times, the new technology has been understood to be a serious competitive threat, but rather than adjust to it, the established companies hoped to either ignore or actively undermine it. Perhaps most commonly, the initial markets for new technologies have been seen as simply too small to gain the attention of a large enterprise seeking to significantly expand its near-term revenues and profits.

In all three cases, the results have generally been the same. The new technology wound up being developed and sold by new start-up companies, typically serving new customers and new application segments. Over time, however, as the technology matured, it became superior to previous computing methods, and therefore began to replace earlier systems and applications, resulting in a rapidly growing and eventually large market. Unfortunately for the established companies, by then it was often too late to respond. The start-ups had developed almost insurmountable business momentum, and a new generation of market leaders was established.

However, while this pattern has repeated itself many times, there have always been important exceptions, especially IBM's early dominance of the PC industry. More recently, during the dot-com boom, it's pretty clear that the triumph of the new over the old, while clearly an important possibility, shouldn't have been taken for granted. Indeed, as we shall see, the overreliance on this belief became one of the root causes of the Internet bubble.

The Importance of Simple Applications

A common mistake that IT market forecasters make is spending too much time pondering the various forms of IT exotica: advanced technologies such as artificial intelligence, software agents, parallel processing, supercomputers, speech recognition, robotics, and data mining. The reality is that these advanced systems almost never move the IT industry forward in a major way. The real key to driving a large IT industry expansion has almost always been to take seemingly mundane applications that the average person can easily understand, and develop them as completely as possible. Importantly, these applications have typically been identified quite early in each major cycle of growth.

For example, during the mainframe era, the IT business was driven by a core set of widely needed services such as transaction processing, databases, and general enterprise record keeping. With PCs, a handful of basic applications—word processing, spreadsheets, databases, presentation graphics, desktop publishing, and eventually, Internet access— have created a global market of more than a hundred million PCs sold each year. This pattern was repeated again during the early years of the Web, where e-mail, browsing, searching, linking, publishing, and transaction processing were sufficient to drive an explosion in IT usage.

Looking forward, this suggests that many of the key customer-centric applications have probably already been identified. This is why much of part 2 will focus on relatively familiar topics such as improved searches, online music, advertising, online payments, health care, e-learning, government services, and community interaction. An accurate assessment of these activities will likely tell us all we need to know about the next five years or so of IT usage. One of the main reasons that the growth of the IT business has temporarily slowed is that many important uses have been set in motion, but other than e-mail and search, relatively few are pervasively used. Once these core uses are universally in place, it's much easier to add more intellectually ambitious services.

The Constant Presence of Monopolies and Antitrust

In a business characterized by a core set of applications, a few longlasting standards, strong levels of customer lock-in, and supplier-driven change, it's perhaps not surprising that antitrust concerns have always been an important part of the IT industry story. The roots of this influence run all the way back to 1913, when NCR, which had a monopoly share of the U.S. cash register market, was found guilty of unlawful restraint of trade and violations of the Sherman Antitrust Act. Tom Watson Sr. was among those convicted, and he soon left NCR to join and eventually run the Computing-Tabulating-Recording Co., which in 1924 he renamed as International Business Machines (IBM).[2]

Of course, Watson Sr. and IBM went on to have their own antitrust troubles. There have been three great U.S. suits. The first was settled in 1932 when IBM agreed to end its practice of "tying" IBM equipment exclusively to IBM-made punch cards. The second was settled in 1956 when IBM agreed to sell, as opposed to just lease, its tabulating equipment. As part of this settlement, IBM also agreed to stay out of the emerging computer services business. The third case was dismissed in 1981 as being "without merit" thirteen years after it was initially launched by the Department of Justice (DoJ). More recently, in May 1998, DoJ began its case against Microsoft, which as yet remains unresolved.

The overall message is clear. Strong supplier leadership has always been part of the IT industry, and the dominant players have usually attracted considerable antitrust attention. This pattern seems likely to spread to customer IT initiatives as well. In fact, this has already proved to be the case in areas such as airline reservations, credit-card processing, and ATM networks, as we'll explore further in chapter 4. More recently, similar issues have emerged for market exchanges and other forms of interbusiness cooperation. Perhaps the bottom line is that almost any company that gets more than half of any particular market is likely to attract federal government antitrust attention. Even eBay has been looked at. Overall, this oversight has done more good than harm, at least in my view.

On the other hand, the IT industry has often benefited from having strong market leaders that can provide a clear sense of direction. Perhaps the best ongoing example of this is the PC industry leadership of Microsoft and Intel. Because of their overwhelming positions, these companies have been able to virtually guarantee the acceptance of new products merely by withdrawing their predecessors from the market. Similarly, in its day, IBM set the price/performance standards for the rest of the mainframe industry. While such control clearly has its downside, it has often given the marketplace a predictable path forward. Information technology is often confusing, and customers tend to appreciate the simplicity of having a strong market leader. That's why the "herd effects" are often so strong. In many ways, the IT industry has had dominant suppliers because that is what many IT customers really want. This need for clear direction and strong leadership will be seen again in many customer-led markets.

The Critical Interplay between Vertical and Horizontal Integration

Because of the immense impact of the IBM PC, few IT industry topics have been more important than the interplay between vertical and horizontal market forces. Being vertically integrated typically means building most of the key computer hardware and software components in-house, and taking an integrated system to the marketplace. In contrast, in the horizontal model, companies focus on particular aspects of a wider industry value chain, such as semiconductors, storage devices, software, or distribution. The differences between these two approaches in the mainframe and PC eras are conceptually pictured in figure 2-1.

While many readers are no doubt aware of the huge changes that took place between the vertically integrated mainframe and horizontally layered PC eras, the story is actually a bit more subtle than it is often portrayed. Indeed, we will see that a mistaken sense of this dynamic was another root cause of the Internet bubble. In this section, we'll simply provide a brief overview of the ebb and flow of the vertical/horizontal issue across the mainframe, minicomputer, and PC eras.

FIGURE 2 - 1

The Shift to a Horizontal Value Chain

In the mainframe market model, companies such as IBM, Sperry, and others built much of their own hardware and software, which over time became supported by various third-party suppliers of storage, printers, software, and other products and services. In contrast, in the PC model, companies tended to specialize in a single area. Some of today's PC market leaders are listed in the figure as examples. There is no company listed under services because there is currently no major company specializing in this area. The once large PC training industry has largely gone away.

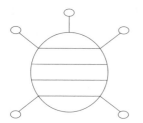

Mainframe Industry Model

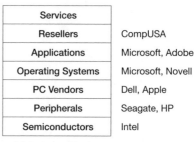

Services	
Resellers	CompUSA
Applications	Microsoft, Adobe
Operating Systems	Microsoft, Novell
PC Vendors	Dell, Apple
Peripherals	Seagate, HP
Semiconductors	Intel

PC Industry Model

This will set the stage for showing how an overreliance on the PC industry mind-set led directly to many of the strategic miscalculations of the dot-com era.

The early computers of the 1950s were so primitive and complex that suppliers such as IBM, Univac, and Burroughs had to build, sell, and service their own systems and applications, with little outside help. I like to characterize this go-it-alone period as the "pre-value–chain era." It was the dominant computer industry model, and as was the case in other major industries, it didn't change quickly or easily. Indeed, the first movements toward a more horizontal structure didn't begin until the late 1960s, when specialized companies emerged to improve upon or compete with specific mainframe vendor offerings, especially those of IBM.

Among the key areas of added value were storage (Memorex), terminals (Telex), software (Applied Data Research), services (EDS), financing (Comdisco), and eventually the mainframe processors themselves (Amdahl). All became important parts of the mainframe ecosystem, and proved that specialized IT suppliers could be successful. However, it's important to note that it was IBM's 1969 "unbundling" of its hardware, software, and services pricing that made much of this possible, a decision at least partially due to mounting government antitrust pressure.

The path toward a more specialized horizontal industry took several additional small steps during the minicomputer era. Many minicomputer suppliers used third-party semiconductors, disks, and printers, and steadily moved toward being more like system assemblers than vertically integrated manufacturers. Additionally, the minicomputer industry gave birth to two of today's horizontal giants. Oracle, then called Relational Software, began in 1977 as a supplier of database software for Digital Equipment and eventually other minicomputers. EMC began in 1979 as a minicomputer add-on memory supplier. However, ultimately, the minicomputer industry failed to become as horizontal as it could have been had it agreed upon a truly standard version of Unix.

This slow march toward a horizontal structure continued through the early years of the PC era. Although both the early PCs and technical workstation suppliers tended to use microprocessors, disks, and displays from other vendors, they still developed proprietary systems and often used their own operating systems. All evidence suggests that were it not for the unexpected and unpredictable way that IBM entered the market, the purely horizontal approach would have taken much longer to emerge, and possibly would never have happened at all. But of course it did, and the industry structure and mind-set was fundamentally changed.

IBM's open PC standards made it relatively easy for other suppliers to assemble IBM-compatible machines. As the demand for these products grew, they created large new markets for just about every aspect of the PC—batteries, disk drives, displays, keyboards, mice, memory chips, graphics processors, software, distribution channels, modems, support, training, maintenance, and so on. This resulted in an extraordinary burst in innovation and product refinement. The Compaqs, Dells, and Gateways of the world then integrated all of this activity into a complete system package, which kept things relatively simple for the customer.

Since all of this innovation was being channeled into what was now a proven value chain, the annual PC industry price/performance improvements from 1981–1995 were stunning, certainly unlike anything ever seen in the mainframe and minicomputer worlds. Perhaps even more important, as both Intel and Microsoft expanded into the enterprise server and software markets, they tended to take the horizontal model with them. By the early 1990s, it was the dominant model for the entire IT industry. In 1991, while researching this issue at IDC, I labeled the process of moving from a vertically integrated to a horizontally structured computer industry "dis-integration."

In addition to being more efficient, the focused, horizontal industry structure was ideally suited to the investment of unprecedented amounts of venture capital. Each layer of the value chain could now receive its own level of funding, something that couldn't easily happen in the vertically integrated world. For the first time, money could flow into specific areas according to each area's potential profitability. This had the important effect of making it much easier to start new companies, further accelerating innovation, competition, and efficiency.

For all of these reasons, many people falsely concluded that the horizontal model had won a final triumph. This was actually quite odd because during the second half of the 1990s, companies such as AOL and Palm were proving that the idea of vertical integration wasn't dead after all. Both companies used this approach to gain an important edge in their marketplaces, an edge now being challenged by more specialized horizontal competitors.

The bottom line is that vertical and horizontal forces are continually redefining their relationship. Many IT markets start off vertically integrated, then tend to become horizontal. Although timing this change can be difficult, the shift usually stems from market growth itself, which often generates conflicting economies of scale within the vertically integrated model. In the aftermath of the dot-com bubble, many e-commerce markets have also become more vertically integrated. However, Web Services appear to have the potential to once again set powerful horizontal forces in motion, as do the various forms of industry consortia. Once again the competitive consequences will likely be profound.

The Power of Underlying Economic Fundamentals

In addition to heightening competition and innovation, the shift to the horizontal model during the PC era had another important and long-lasting effect. As businesses became more specialized, the underlying economics of each activity rose to the fore in a way that was impossible in the old vertically integrated world. Essentially, the hardware, software, services, and telecom businesses each have their own distinct economics, and once separated, they began to evolve in very different ways, resulting in very different industry structures. The easiest way to see this is by examining the marginal and average cost curves of these four sectors, as shown in figure 2-2.

In this figure, there are four distinct average cost curve patterns because hardware, software, services, and telecommunications typically have their own distinct marginal costs. As the figure indicates, software average costs fall the most quickly, because software has very low marginal costs. For example, while the cost of developing an initial software product can be quite high, the marginal cost of producing an additional unit is very low—a CD-ROM, a diskette, or when online close to nothing at all—so the average cost curve falls steeply, continually, and essentially asymptotically.

The hardware average cost curve also shows a sharp downward pattern, at least up to a point. The cost of making an initial unit of computer hardware is typically quite high (possibly as high as or higher than an initial unit of software, depending on the specific product). But as additional units are built, volume manufacturing efficiencies drive both the marginal and average cost curves down sharply.

31

FIGURE 2 - 2

Underlying Economics—Key IT Markets

The lines on this figure show the average cost per unit sold. In standard economics, the average cost of a good is determined by dividing the total cost of production by the total volume of production. Economic theory (and basic mathematics) says that the shape of any product's average cost curve is determined by the marginal cost of producing that product with marginal cost being defined as the cost at any particular point on the production curve of producing one additional unit of volume.

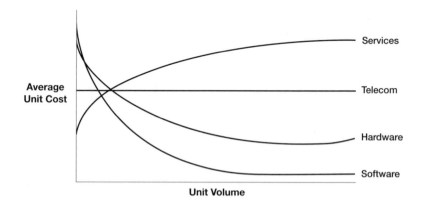

However, at some (not easy to define) point, these scale economies slow, eventually cease, and arguably even slightly reverse themselves. For example, if Dell were asked to make all of the PCs in the world, it is not at all clear that its costs would continue to go down. Consequently, in theory, the average cost curve eventually flattens, and perhaps even turns up a bit.

Conversely, so-called professional (meaning human) services such as consulting, contract programming, and training exhibit a third distinct pattern. While the initial cost of providing an in-person service can often be quite modest, marginal and thus average costs tend to rise as projects become larger and more complex and as more business overhead is required. This explains why the big consulting companies such as IBM and Accenture also tend to be the most expensive. Thus, the services industry average cost curve tends to rise moderately with volume. However, it can be argued that once sufficient volumes of business are achieved, efficiencies can reemerge so that the curve might theoretically flatten out, and perhaps even begin to dip back downward.

Finally, network costs tend to expand linearly, meaning that the cost of adding a new user to the network doesn't change all that much as the network expands. For example, imagine that there are three people in three different physical locations, two of whom are connected. In this situation, the cost of connecting the third person to the network isn't necessarily any different than the cost of connecting the first two people. Thus, the average cost is actually equal to the marginal costs, meaning the telecom average cost curve is essentially flat. This makes it difficult for any one telecom supplier to gain a major cost advantage based solely upon size, a reversal of the long-held view that telecommunications was a "natural monopoly." Essentially, the natural monopoly view became obsolete the moment that interoperability became a realistic competitive option.

As someone with only a modest undergraduate background in economics, it never ceases to amaze me how these few basic principles, taught in just about every introductory economics course, can effectively explain the structure of such large and seemingly complex market segments. Consider the following:

1. Software has essentially infinite scale economies and therefore software markets such as operating systems, databases, and major applications are often highly concentrated.

2. Hardware has significant but ultimately finite scale economies and therefore mature hardware markets such as PCs, servers, disk drives, and printers tend to support a handful of relatively large players.

3. Professional services have relatively flat but subtly changing economics and therefore the industry consists of a great number of players of just about every shape and size.

4. Networks have linear costs and thus tend to have many national and global players. It is this fundamental lack of decisive scale economies that explains why there are still several thousand Internet service providers (ISPs) in the United States alone.

These simple principles are sufficient to explain most of the IT industry's underlying competitive structure. As we shall see in chapter 3, the underlying economics of customer-driven, Web-based businesses essentially make up an important fifth major class of IT activity.

When History Doesn't Repeat Itself

While all of us are perhaps only too familiar with the collapse of the dot-com industry, I would like to propose a single statement that I think sums up what happened, and suggests the need for new industry perspectives: *Investors and most other dot-com participants wrongly assumed that the Internet business would be just like the PC business, only bigger and better.* In other words, they bet heavily on the idea that recent IT industry history would repeat itself, failing to realize that a successful shift toward customer-centric innovation would require a different set of value-chain dynamics. More specifically, the belief that history would repeat itself was based upon three main concepts, each of which was largely incorrect. In general, the market believed that,

1. like the PC business, the Internet industry would be best served by a highly horizontal value chain,

2. like software and microprocessors, individual Internet markets would each have their own dominant supplier, and

3. just as PC vendors made the minicomputer industry obsolete, a new class of dot-com suppliers would replace much of the established economic order.

While there is no need to revisit the dot-com collapse in great detail, a few examples in each of these three areas will show how much IT industry dynamics have changed. Making this case is still necessary because, although the dot-com bubble burst nearly three years ago, much of the pre-bubble mind-set remains surprisingly intact. Revealing the flaws behind this thinking will set the stage for defining the more accurate set of industry dynamics and perspectives to be presented in chapter 3.

Horizontal Limitations

As noted earlier, horizontal markets can be much more innovative and efficient than vertically integrated ones. During the Internet boom, it was often predicted that just as most of the IT industry became horizontal in the 1980s, much of the wider economy was about to do the same. Many of these predictions cited the work of English economist Ronald Coase as a key part of their underlying theory. More specifically, Coase's 1937 article "The Nature of the Firm" enjoyed a boomlet of interest. In this article, Coase argues that the relatively high transaction costs of dealing with the outside world are the main reason that firms exist and why many firms choose to do things in-house. (In 1991, Coase was awarded the Nobel Prize for economics.[3])

Applying Coase's theory seemed natural enough. Clearly, the Internet enabled information to flow much more freely between firms and, in many cases, it has greatly reduced transaction costs. Thus, the theory went, businesses should become increasingly specialized. While the logic here is sound and in the very long term should prove to be correct, in the short term it tends to overlook the fact that information flows and transaction costs vary greatly depending on the relative state of market maturity. More pointedly, there is still little historical evidence that highly horizontal approaches are well-suited to effective new market launches, a topic that Coase wasn't directly concerned with.

The reality is that in the PC industry there were proven markets for just about every piece of the industry value chain. With the Internet, there was no such thing; there mostly were just interesting and often well-funded ideas. Some of these ideas were certainly much better than others, and specialized, horizontal companies such as Amazon, Yahoo!, eBay, Earthlink, and Google have clearly succeeded. But the great majority of dot-coms were depending on value chains that just weren't there. That's why I like to refer to this period as one of "premature disintegration." This reality was largely ignored by investors and venture capitalists, who more than any other group bought into the parallels with the PC industry. Below are four of the more prominent examples of how the market expected the highly horizontal market to take hold.

1. Specialized telecommunications companies such as Covad and Northpoint assumed they could piggyback upon an existing telecom infrastructure that was owned by their competitors. Not surprisingly, and despite FCC wishes to the contrary, the local Bell companies had every incentive to make their rivals' lives as difficult as possible, the very opposite of a PC-like ecosystem.

2. Many independent business exchanges assumed they could quickly gather the support of Fortune 1000 corporations, even

for sensitive business practices such as reverse auctions. This was the logical equivalent of Compaq or Gateway trying to tell Intel and Microsoft how to run their businesses.

3. Most "pure-play" Internet content companies were totally dependent on completely unproven forms of online advertising, especially increasingly ineffective banner ads.

4. Countless dot-com companies assumed they could rely on partners for revenues as opposed to selling their products themselves.

Of course, one of the great ironies of all of this is the fact that the single most successful Internet company, AOL, chose a very different strategy. The company rejected the trend toward specialization. Instead, it maintained many aspects of a vertically oriented model, including a custom user interface, exclusive content, proprietary services, and, until the late 1990s, actual network transmission. This strategy also explains why AOL has been able to single-handedly launch important new services such as Instant Messenger (IM). In short, AOL was one of the few companies that took advantage of the market not being ready for the widespread shift to a highly horizontal approach. Today, the key question is whether AOL's vertical approach can maintain its edge in the market. Increasingly, this is beginning to appear unlikely.

The Often Futile Search for Gorillas

The PC-industry mind-set was flawed in a second important sense. To the great disappointment of investors, each major Internet industry sector was not about to create the equivalent of a new Microsoft, Intel, or Cisco. Other than eBay, major Internet businesses have not taken on monopolistic tendencies; many have not even created a highly profitable, market-leading "gorilla," to use the influential author Geoffrey Moore's popular expression.[4] Instead, as is the case in financial services, retail, Internet access, and other sectors, Internet markets have often been highly competitive. Only AOL, eBay, and Amazon have managed to maintain a dominant position in their respective markets, and only eBay has been able to sustain monopoly-like levels of profitability.

This unwarranted reliance on history had particularly calamitous consequences in the telecommunications industry. For example, one of the most common conceits of many Internet enthusiasts was that just as microprocessors helped drive the PC industry, communications bandwidth would drive the Internet era, and therefore providers of telecom and cable television-based services were presented with a future of almost limitless opportunity. The first half of this statement is true; it's the second half that was based on an important misunderstanding.

The problem with this analogy was always that what made Intel and Microsoft so special was not just that their technology was important. It was their near-monopoly market control. However, other than in the local loop, there was never a realistic scenario for bandwidth suppliers to gain a similarly strong market position. Thus, from virtually the beginning of the Internet boom, the real analogy was not between bandwidth and microprocessors; it was between bandwidth and memory chips, another brutally competitive, capital-intensive commodity business. This mistaken analogy wound up costing the telecom industry more than $1 trillion in lost paper wealth, with much of the sector on or over the edge of bankruptcy.

Similarly strong competition has emerged in many e-commerce, dot-com, and content marketplaces, which are characterized by direct and often brutal competition. While these businesses are still in their early stages, consider the following evidence.

1. In online stock trading, no single company has emerged to dominate the business, which is now a mix of pure-play companies such as E*TRADE and pre-Internet companies such as Schwab, Fidelity, and many others. The simple act of processing stock transactions will eventually become a commodity, like getting cash from an ATM. More value-added services will be required to ensure survival.

2. No single supplier has come even close to dominating the e-mail services business. The mix of network giants such as AOL, AT&T, and Microsoft's MSN, along with dedicated ISPs such as Earthlink, specialized Web-based services such as Hotmail (owned by Microsoft) and Yahoo!, and software packages such as Microsoft's Exchange and Lotus Notes (owned by IBM) would seem to ensure a highly competitive future, although Microsoft's position is certainly impressive.

3. In the travel industry, major initiatives such as Expedia, Traveloc-ity, Priceline, Orbitz, and many others are all vying for the same consumer dollar.

4. Google has already cut deeply into Yahoo!'s once dominant posi-tion in the search engine business, just as Yahoo! once surpassed AltaVista. Similarly, new competition for Google is now beginning to emerge.

5. While a single B2B market exchange such as Covisint may well dominate a specific sector such as automobiles, the fact that the major exchanges are becoming increasingly controlled by their participating member companies means that single-vendor mo-nopoly power is unlikely.

6. Today, there are dozens of media companies with more than $1 billion in annual revenues, all of which are on the Web to some degree. Even from a pure dot-com perspective, the presence of gi-ants such as Microsoft, AOL, Yahoo!, CNET, and many others, makes it unlikely that any single company will gain anything close to Internet content control.

As noted above, only eBay has what might be considered to be a near monopoly position. The reason is that the auction business takes the fullest advantages of the power of Metcalfe's Law in that the more people who use eBay, the more attractive the service becomes.[5] These powerful network effects have made it difficult for any would-be com-petitors to match eBay's market and service reach, other than in spe-cialty areas. However, the chances of many other new companies repeating the eBay model in other businesses seem pretty slim. As we shall see, increasingly, most new "gorillas" are likely to come from the cooperation of existing market leaders.

The Triumph of the Old Guard

Last but certainly not the least of these misconceptions was the wide-spread belief that the new would once again triumph over the old. Be-fore and during the Internet bubble, this was a concept that was often accepted as gospel in the IT industry, and reached its greatest manifes-tation in January 2000 when AOL announced its plan to acquire the media giant Time Warner. However, by the mid-1990s, it had already become apparent that this idea was anything but an ironclad law.

Companies such as Microsoft and Intel know what they did to IBM and Digital and have been determined ever since that they won't fall victim to a similar fate. Similarly, companies that survived the mistakes of the past—such as IBM and Hewlett-Packard (HP)—have clearly learned their lessons. Overall, the IT industry has become much more acutely aware of the potential impact of disruptive technologies and has become more adept at managing them. Today, IBM and HP are among the PC and Unix server market leaders, and Microsoft dominates the Internet browser market. Other major examples include Sun, which during the 1990s made a remarkable 180-degree transition from a supplier of technical workstations to high-end commercial server company, and AOL, which transformed itself from a struggling proprietary online services vendor to an Internet industry giant.

Clearly, the idea that the new would triumph over the old was still a real possibility, and should have been a major topic of debate. But it should never have been taken for granted. Yet this is what much of the dot-com industry did in markets such as stock trading, banking, retailing, real estate, furniture, mortgages, publishing, toys, health care, and many other areas. For largely irrational reasons, great stock was put behind the so-called first-mover advantage, even though the IT industry has repeatedly shown that the early market leaders don't necessarily retain their positions. After all, the early PC industry leaders included Radio Shack as well as long-forgotten companies such as Commodore, Osborne, and Kaypro. Similarly, Visicalc and WordPerfect were once PC software market leaders.

Today, in an environment where cash rules, the old guard is being besieged in a very different way, this time by once high-flying dot-coms hoping to be acquired. Overall, the highly horizontal approach has given way to a period of consolidation, with established companies increasingly taking control.

Which Brings Us to Today

While much of the above has been critical of many aspects of the Internet's boom and bust cycle, this assessment would be incomplete without an explicit affirmation of the extraordinary amount of hard work and value creation that occurred. There have been few better examples of the United States' ability to embrace and drive economic and social change. And while much of the recent media focus has been on the industry's speculation and greed, we shouldn't forget the extraordinary energy and courage displayed by so many Internet entrepreneurs, who often worked day and night to pursue their dreams. It's this widespread willingness to go out on one's own and risk everything that often distinguishes the U.S. economy from those of other major nations.

The sad thing is that so much of this energy flowed into a flawed industry vision. This is why it is still so important to come up with a new and more accurate sense of our times. In the aftermath of the dot-com collapse and a sluggish IT business, we all need a fresh way of seeing, thinking, and communicating that doesn't automatically conjure up the disasters of the recent past. However, although it's now been several years since the dot-com bubble burst, the industry has yet to adopt a new and shared vision to replace the flawed frameworks of the past. Instead, in the face of strong economic pressure, our business has understandably tended to shrink its horizons and act as if a wider industry perspective is somehow no longer necessary.

By now, I'm sure you realize that I disagree. Over the rest of this book, I will argue that unless the IT industry embraces some sort of shared long-term vision and direction, the use of technology could either drift aimlessly or continue to squeeze diminishing returns out of proven areas of investment. In chapter 3, I will argue that the idea of a truly customer-driven IT industry value chain is the best way to fill this void. Adopting the view that our industry is now increasingly driven by its customers can help a wide range of IT industry participants gain a more positive perspective on where our industry is and where it is headed. It's a very different mental map, but I think it's one that we can quickly get used to. Once adopted, many of the IT industry's current barriers seem more manageable, and the long-term promise of the industry seems more likely to be fulfilled.

CHAPTER THREE

Envisioning a Customer-Driven Industry

CHAPTER 2 ended with the claim that the IT industry needs a new way of seeing and talking about itself. It's been my experience that when trying to communicate important new concepts, visual models are usually more effective than even the most energetic text descriptions. Therefore, in this chapter, I'll present the transition to a customer-driven industry through a series of figures and tables. These images will provide the conceptual background with which to frame the specific examples presented throughout part 2. I consider them to be my basic IT industry mental map.

Perhaps the most direct way to show how things have changed is to simply look at the sorts of value creation that major IT customers and suppliers are or will be working on, as illustrated in table 3-1. By comparing these two lists of challenges, the differences between the customer and supplier worlds should become clear. Don't worry if some of the terms are not immediately familiar; everything in the left-hand column will be explained more specifically over the course of part 2. The terms in the right-hand column are not really the focus of this work but can be easily explored further via the Web and elsewhere.

As the title of table 3-1 suggests, the two lists are limited to those areas of IT activity that could eventually create significant amounts of new IT usage. That's why major but established markets such as electronic mail and supply chain management are not included on the customer side, and things like denser disk storage and memory chips are not shown on the supplier side. It's not that these activities aren't important, it's just that they are no longer major new applications frontiers. They already have all the momentum and critical mass they need.

TABLE 3 - 1

Major New IT Industry Frontiers

Customer Frontiers	Supplier Frontiers
1. Online music and radio	1. Speech and video recognition
2. Online video, film, images, etc.	2. Wireless video and imaging
3. Advertising techniques and formats	3. Broadband enhancements
4. Content subscriptions/micropayments	4. 2.5, 3G wireless Internet
5. Business and consumer billing	5. Wifi, spread spectrum
6. Internet payment systems	6. Infrared, Bluetooth
7. Exchanges, auctions, and catalogs	7. Digital Rights Management
8. Industry cooperation/consortia	8. Authentication, sign-on
9. Health care restructuring	9. Instant messaging
10. Internet auctions, reverse auctions	10. Voice over IP
11. Business partner support and integration	11. Web conferencing
12. Enterprise content management	12. Storage Area Networks
13. Embedded product identification (RFID)	13. Gigabit Ethernet
14. e-Logistics	14. Blade servers
15. Industry metadata/taxonomies/ontologies	15. InfiniBand I/O
16. Value-added Semantic Applications	16. Nano- and biotechnology
17. E-Learning content and objects	17. Multifunction handhelds
18. Premium learning accreditation	18. Profiling software
19. K–12 online learning successes	19. Content management software
20. Expert system databases	20. Taxonomy software
21. Community content and ratings	21. XML, SOAP, et al.
22. New open-source movements	22. Business Process Outsourcing
23. Synchronous communication interest	23. Humanless data centers
24. Peer-to-peer resource sharing	24. Electronic ink
25. GPS applications	25. Flat panel, tablets
26. Consumer skills, education, and training	26. Audio/video editing software
27. Consumer time and enthusiasm	27. Enterprise Content Management
28. Self-publishing and blogs	28. XML databases
29. Online games and contests	29. Web Services
30. Voting and registration	30. DVD recorders
31. National identification standards	31. Robotics
32. "Low-friction" security	32. Collaborative software
33. Spectrum allocation and management	33. Wearable computers
34. Public information services	34. Home networks
35. Integrated government databases	35. TV, Internet integration
36. Antitrust, regulatory, and tax policies	36. Fiber optics
37. Copyright and patent law	37. Grid computing
38. Privacy and consumer protection	38. Radio Frequency ID
39. Many forms of e-commerce	39. Low orbiting satellites
40. Business funding and commitment	40. Venture-capital funding

By including forty items on each side of table 3-1, there is an implicit message that there are plenty of opportunities in both the customer and supplier worlds, and that one could easily expand either list. In other words, the issues shown are meant to be representative, not comprehensive. Similarly, since each side consists of the same number of items, I am also implying that it is not the quantity of frontiers, but rather their nature that sets them apart. Stated simply, the issues on the left tend to be ones for which traditional IT supplier leadership will not be sufficient. It's mostly up to customers to create these types of new application platforms, societal systems, and supporting policies.

Significantly, the items on the left contain a mix of business, education, consumer, and government opportunities. This sets up much of the structure of part 2 of this book. At this point, suffice it to say that over the course of this industry's history, business computing has been by far the dominant sector, while both consumer and educational usage have often struggled. Clearly, if the IT industry is to reach its full potential, a major expansion into these latter two areas will be required. Additionally, a considerable number of government issues have been included to support the view that over the next decade public policy will become an increasingly important IT industry factor.

Additionally, table 3-1 should make it clear that by no means am I implying that supplier innovation will cease or become unimportant. The list on the right is impressively diverse and powerful, and these technologies will clearly be necessary for many of the envisioned customer systems shown on the left. Some readers may even think that these supplier challenges are in fact the key issues in the IT industry today. Later in this chapter, and over the course of part 2, I hope to convince you otherwise.

Value-Chain Implications

While table 3-1 presents many specific information technology activities, it is important to put these challenges into a broader IT industry context. In the following sections, I'll present five images that highlight my sense of the current situation. While some of these explanations will include rather complex analysis and logic, I hope you can stay with me; it will only be a few pages before things become more concrete again.

Let's start with the long-term picture presented in figure 3-1, which integrates the shift to a customer-driven industry with many of the themes and patterns presented in chapter 2. This picture provides about as complete a view of the IT industry's value chain evolution as any one figure can. If this figure makes sense to you, you have a good sense of the IT industry's structural development. Note how each generation of change has been associated with the addition of some important new industry suppliers. No doubt the customer-centric era will as well.

From this perspective, a customer-driven value chain is really just the latest stop on a half-century continuum of change. Figure 3-1 suggests that there have actually been seven structural orientations over the last fifty years. There are the four generally recognized eras—mainframes, minis, PCs, and Internet, with each linked by various interim stages. On average, these phases last eight years (fifty years divided by six stages), which is certainly a reasonable expectation for the thoughts and models presented in this work. After that, new centers of gravity will probably emerge. In other words, the shift to a customer-centric business is not an end to IT industry evolution; it's just the focus of our particular time.

You might be curious about the last image in figure 3-1 with the odd-looking circle with a question mark inside of it. This is intended to suggest that more vertically integrated models are once again returning, largely as a correction to the excessive dis-integration of the dot-com period. Certainly, this is the case in those areas undergoing significant consolidation such as telecommunications, e-learning, exchanges, and many content marketplaces, topics to be explored further in part 2. Additionally, in chapter 6 we will see that the tension between vertical consolidation and specific Web Services will be another major important example of the competition between integrated and dis-integrated forces.

The use of a timeline also helps clarify when the customer-centric era actually began. It's really a somewhat strange situation, but one that highlights how far off base the mental models of the past have actually been. Technically, the customer-centric era could be said to have begun way back in 1995, when the commercial use of the Internet actually began and customers first started creating value for other customers.

FIGURE 3 - 1

IT Industry Structural Evolution Timeline

This figure summarizes the evolution of the IT industry over the last fifty years. Circular shapes are used to reflect vertically integrated models and layered designs reflect horizontal value chains. Those images that use both shapes indicate a mix of both vertical and horizontal forces. In addition, this figure also identifies the major vendors that have emerged during each period.

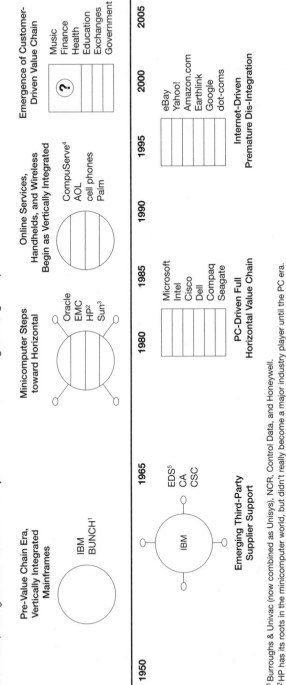

[1] Burroughs & Univac (now combined as Unisys), NCR, Control Data, and Honeywell.

[2] HP has its roots in the minicomputer world, but didn't really become a major industry player until the PC era.

[3] Sun, like the PC companies, was driven by microprocessor power, but has remained largely vertically integrated.

[4] CompuServe was acquired by AOL in 1998.

[5] EDS stands for Electronic Data Systems, CA for Computer Associates, and CSC for Computer Sciences Corporation.

Certainly, this is what Amazon, eBay, E*TRADE, Yahoo!, and others were doing, and it was clearly a significant break with the industry's past. As I mentioned in the introduction, I've been kicking around the idea of a shift to a customer-centric industry since early 1997, but during the dot-com boom, it didn't seem to be having any significant industry effect.

It wasn't until after the collapse of the dot-com bubble that the effects of this change began to take hold. It was only then that it became clear that the model of venture-funded dot-com start-ups was not sufficient to fulfill the Internet's promise, and would have to be greatly scaled back. Instead, new methods of systematic customer value creation are needed. In this sense, the dot-com phase can be viewed as a huge diversion away from the real impact of the Internet, which is the shift toward a customer-driven industry. The IT industry is now trying to figure out how to get back on the right track, after a wild but ultimately very expensive multiyear detour.

An Expanded Marketplace

While figure 3-1 provides a chronological perspective, figure 3-2 zooms in on the current period. This picture best reflects today's situation. According to this view, in the supplier-driven past, the IT industry value chain consisted of various vendor products that were brought to the market via several types of direct and indirect distribution channels. These were then supplemented by a wide variety of IT supplier services such as consulting, systems integration, outsourcing, and so on. Today, however, those customer activities designed to create value for other IT customers are now the dominant part of the picture. From this visual perspective, figure 3-2 makes three main points.

First, with the addition of these new customer activities, the value chain is simply much larger than it was in the supplier-driven era. Second, customer activities are now at the very top of the value chain. This is important since the top of the value chain has always carried with it some specific leadership responsibilities. And third, as a new layer in the value chain, customer activities will, like hardware, software, and services, tend to have their own distinct set of underlying economics; this is of great importance to any customer organization doing business

FIGURE 3-2

Envisioning a Customer-Driven Value Chain

Since the arrival of the Web, customer activities have taken over the top of the IT industry value chain, both replacing and overlapping with IT supplier services and significantly increasing the overall size of the IT business. But as the shaded area suggests, the lines between customers and their services firms are sometimes blurry.

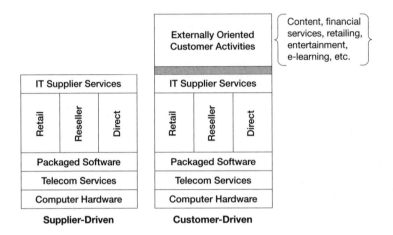

online. Let's look more closely at all three of these implications, starting with the issue of overall industry size.

An Extended Value Chain

The image on the right side of figure 3-2 is much larger than the one on the left because it now includes certain new types of customer spending. Customers have, of course, always spent a great deal of money on their computer systems, and this activity has always been inherently more difficult to measure than the spending that companies allot to IT suppliers. However, there has been a general rule of thumb that for every dollar a company spends with a vendor, it probably spends at least another on its own people and processes. Among the major traditional types of internal IT expenses are systems design, programming, installation, maintenance, training, and operations management. In addition, it's clear that many employees who are not IT personnel at all

47

spend a major part of their time on IT-related activities. This time and expense is particularly difficult to measure, and therefore often isn't.

However, this traditional customer spending on IT should not be viewed as part of the formal IT industry value chain. Over the years, most of this activity has consisted of internal business applications such as payroll, human resources, inventory, accounting, document management, internal communications, ERP, CRM, and the like. This work typically means little to customers outside of each particular enterprise, and therefore does little to drive overall market demand. For example, how one company uses its payroll software usually has no effect on another company's IT spending. It's important to realize that, before the Internet, these non-value–chain IT activities typically constituted well over 90 percent of most companies' total IT spending. External applications were generally restricted to Electronic Data Interchange (EDI) and various partner-specific systems.

With the growth of the Web, however, customer IT investments shifted toward more of an external focus for applications such as public Web sites, e-commerce, and online business partnerships. Internal IT activity is, of course, still huge and still accounts for as much as 80 percent of all customer-spending activity. Indeed, in the aftermath of the dot-com bubble, many companies have returned to much more of an internal focus. However, over time, the importance of external activity will continue to rise. And while calculating the exact balance between internal and external priorities is inherently difficult and subjective, I would argue that the two types of tasks are heading toward a rough balance, a situation depicted in figure 3-3.

The point is that most of this external activity is, by definition, aimed at creating value for other IT customers and thus is now part of the formal IT industry value chain. This is why the overall IT industry is now so much larger than it was in the supplier-driven past. In addition, as shown back in figure 3-2, the boundaries between internal and external applications are blurring. Companies are coming to realize that information that was traditionally viewed as internal—such as customer records, product information, and price lists—can also have important external value, hence the high industry interest in using the Web to "expose" internal information assets to both partners and customers. This will be an important theme throughout part 2.

FIGURE 3 - 3

Internal versus External Orientation, 1980–2010

This figure provides a conceptual depiction of the fact that in recent years, there has been a huge change in IT customer priorities. Despite the retrenchment from 2001–2002, externally oriented projects are increasingly coming to the fore.

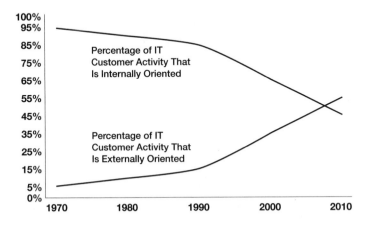

There is also a second, more traditional way of viewing the size of any industry value chain. From a classical economic value-added perspective, the top level of a value chain is, by definition, typically larger than the sectors below it, because each layer tends to subsume the value created in the layers that are beneath it. For example, the net value of all the components inside a PC is slightly less than the value of the PC itself, which includes the value of the integration provided by the final PC assembler. Similarly, most large systems integration contracts tend to subsume the value of all their various hardware, software, networking, and personnel components.

These effects will only become stronger over time. Indeed by the end of this decade, the proportion of the chain accounted for by customer activities will be considerably larger than it is today, a forecast depicted conceptually in figure 3-4, which also reflects the increasing overlap between the supplier and customer worlds. This type of blurring will be discussed further throughout part 2.

FIGURE 3 - 4

Long-Term IT Industry Value Chain Composition

Customer value creation will eventually surpass that of IT suppliers, although in many industries these lines will be difficult to draw as specialized IT service companies develop a strong, industry-specific focus.

A New Class of IT Industry Economics

Perhaps the most theoretically challenging aspect of the shift to a customer-driven value chain stems from the fact that customer activities will tend to have their own unique set of economics. In chapter 2, we saw how the shift to a horizontal PC industry released the underlying economics of the hardware, software, services, and telecom sectors. As indicated in figure 3-5, customer activities now comprise a fifth major class of IT economics.

The importance of this fifth class is hard to overstate. We know that the economics of all four of the previous types of IT activity have all been highly predictive of the eventual structure of these huge and seemingly complex industries. This pattern strongly suggests that if we can identify the underlying economics of customer-based businesses, we should be able to forecast what sorts of new competitive structures will tend to emerge. And since these new structures will cut across so many important sectors, such an analysis might well tell us a great deal about the nature of the twenty-first century economy.

FIGURE 3 - 5

Web Business Economics

Using the same marginal cost analysis used in figure 2-2, it appears that the established IT segment that Web-based businesses most clearly resemble, in terms of costs and competitive structure, is actually the computer hardware business.

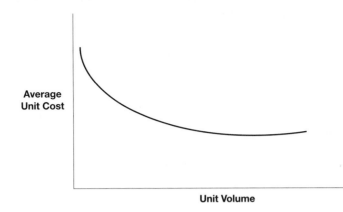

Perhaps because the rewards of this line of analysis are potentially so great, the challenge seems more complex than in previous eras. Someday, everything might look much more obvious, but from today's perspective, customer activities appear to be a complex mix of existing economic forces. For example, like a telecom service, the cost of operating an online business tends to go up linearly with usage as new capacity is needed. But unlike such services, the value for most customers does not typically go up exponentially as new users are added. More often it remains flat, meaning that the value that one person obtains by visiting a Web site is often not affected by how many other people visit that site. (Clearly, sites such as eBay or services such as instant messaging that rely on community interaction are important exceptions.)

In this sense, customer activities are more like software programs in that the value one gets from using an application is usually not fundamentally affected by other people's use of that program. However, Web-based businesses are unlike software programs in that they don't tend to have near-zero marginal costs and they don't tend to have high levels of customer lock-in.

Oddly, because so many Web-based businesses have both significant, but not unlimited, scale economies, modest network effects, and relatively low customer lock-in, the IT market they most closely resemble is actually that of PC hardware, an historically low margin area. Today, huge parts of the IT hardware business, including PCs, displays, disk drives, and memory chips have large revenues, but often very low margins, a situation sometimes referred to as "profitless prosperity."

This entirely abstract deduction is actually strongly supported by current marketplace realities. As described in chapter 2, markets as diverse as content, stocks, e-mail, e-commerce, search, and travel are all highly competitive. The main areas where a single company has proven dominant are in the various forms of industrywide consortia, successful first movers such as Amazon, and the special case of eBay. But these examples are still much more the exception than the rule, and therefore tough competition seems to be the dominant economic model for many online businesses.

However, these economics and their resulting market structures are still in their early stages. Consequently, the overall degree of concentration for Web-based markets will likely remain an important area of attention, research, and theory. In the end, many Web businesses should prove to be more like media companies than hardware vendors. More broadly, the establishment of clearly recognized economics will be an important sign of industry maturity.

The Importance of the Top of the Chain

In addition to greatly increasing the IT industry's overall size and creating a new set of industry economics, the emergence of a customer-driven chain is significant because customer activities now control the very top of the IT industry value chain. By definition, the top of the chain has always been the most important determinant of customer usage and demand. As shown back in figure 3-2, this position has previously been occupied by various types of IT suppliers. Sometimes it's been pure-play services companies such as EDS, but equally often it's been the major hardware, software, and networking firms. These are the four main types of organizations that have brought advanced information technology to the customer.

Overall, this close cooperation between customer activity and various IT vendor services will determine the leadership that the top of the value chain provides. This is why, looking ahead, it is becoming increasingly useful to begin to think of banks, insurance companies, entertainment companies, publishers, manufacturers, and other traditional IT customers as if they were a new form of IT supplier. All of the above are now in the business of systematically creating IT value for other IT users, much as software and services companies have done in the past.

What exactly does it mean for customers to begin to think and act more like IT suppliers? While in some ways, information technology is just another industry sector, it has, as does every industry, its own distinct requirements, patterns, tendencies, and emphases. Below are seven of the more important aspects of IT industry leadership over the last few decades, all of which remain significant today:

1. **Risk.** For nearly forty years, the IT industry has been defined by the willingness of companies and especially of entrepreneurs to take substantial risks. IT suppliers know that most new companies and products will not succeed, and a high tolerance for failure has been part of the industry's entrepreneurial culture. IT customer organizations have often been much more risk-averse in their IT activities. This has been especially so in the 2001–2002 climate.

2. **Reward.** One reason that the IT industry has been willing to assume relatively high levels of risk has been the potential for huge rewards. Many IT segments have exhibited strong winner-take-all, or at least near all, tendencies. The industry has also showered its winners with high non-monetary rewards in terms of publicity, reputation, and influence. These rewards have historically been harder to replicate with customer-driven IT activities.

3. **Perseverance.** As shown throughout this book, building useful computer applications has often proved difficult, and therefore considerable time has been required in even basic areas such as databases, transaction processing, and customer service systems. In many cases, demonstrating substantial payback can easily take several years, necessitating high levels of confidence and perseverance. This certainly conflicts with the short-term IT strategies of the post-bubble era.

4. **Hype.** Although this term is usually used in a pejorative fashion, a considerable amount of industry, media, and investor hype is often necessary to mobilize customers and resources. This is especially true given that many IT products are initially immature and take time to establish themselves. During these early stages, effective public relations is very important to maintaining momentum through the often long product adoption cycle. Ultimately, there is a fine and sometimes indistinguishable line between hype and true faith and enthusiasm, but whatever one calls it, active marketing will be required for many of the industry-specific systems to be discussed in part 2.

5. **Cooperation.** As the very different stories of the minicomputer and PC industries have shown, the ability of an industry to coalesce into an effective value chain has often spelled the difference between growth and decline. Looking ahead, many forms of IT industry advancement and restructuring will require extensive customer cooperation. Some important historical examples will be presented in chapter 4.

6. **Standards.** History clearly shows that many IT markets are primarily defined by how standards are set, who controls them, and how effectively they evolve. There is little reason to expect that this will change. However, whereas most IT standards were once set by suppliers and are now set by standards bodies, in the future many will also need to be set by customers themselves. How effectively this process evolves will say a great deal about the speed of IT industry advancement.

7. **Start-Ups.** For most of the IT industry's history, new technologies have been pioneered by new companies, and the threat from new rivals has often been an essential part of overall industry change. With the demise of so many dot-coms, the strength of this challenge has been considerably weakened. In theory, this could significantly slow future rates of change. The establishment of major new customer-driven platforms will often require difficult reengineering and restructuring, which may not happen unless there is serious pressure from somewhere. More than any other single issue,

it is this potential lack of start-up pressure that could allow overall technology usage to stagnate. It's one of the often-unrecognized downsides of the dot-com collapse.

Again, the factors just mentioned are not unique to the IT industry, but they have been particularly important in launching new technology markets, which in some ways is what the IT industry has been all about. One can consider these seven aspects as an easy means of evaluating the health and dynamism of IT value-chain leadership at any point in time. Are risks being taken? Are customers showing commitment and enthusiasm for change? Are meaningful new standards being developed and implemented? Is there pressure to change coming from somewhere? Unless the answers to these questions are mostly yes, the pace of industry expansion will likely slow. How these questions are being answered in key business, education, consumer, and government sectors will be the main focus of part 2.

Putting the Other Candidates in Perspective

While reading the preceding text, I'm sure many readers have sat back and thought some version of the following "Wait a minute. What about wireless technologies, high-bandwidth network services, biotechnology, and nanotechnology? Aren't these going to be the driving forces of the IT business? And aren't these still primarily supplier-driven issues?"

Indeed, as the timeline in figure 3-1 suggests, it is important to see today's customer-driven industry as being dominant for only a particular period of time. The Internet and related technologies have generated a set of concepts and capabilities that are now rippling through various industries. But it's certainly not hard to imagine a day when the essence of these changes has been largely determined, and the industry focus shifts to other topics. In fact, there is little doubt that this will eventually be the case. The only real question is when the next shift will occur, and it seems reasonable that the ideas described in this book will be dominant for the remainder of this decade. To put this view in perspective, let's look at some of the other major forces that have the potential to reshape the IT industry.

What about Wireless?

In many ways, it is tempting to see wireless communications as the natural heir to IT industry leadership. After all, the flow between mainframes, minicomputers, PCs, Internet, and mobile systems seems smooth and natural enough. All of these technologies have had very similar patterns of innovation, entrepreneurship, and change. Clearly, wireless systems have also followed the traditional path of supplier leadership, complete with early stage proprietary systems and vertical integration, followed by an increasingly horizontal model. From the perspective of most IT suppliers and venture capitalists, it's easy to believe that wireless voice and data, wireless home networks, nationwide wireless Internet (Wifi) networks, Bluetooth, and other systems really are the IT industry's Next Big Thing. They clearly have tremendous long-term potential.

But from a broader demand-creation perspective, the story of wireless has its limitations. It seems clear that, unlike mainframes, PCs, and the Internet, mobile systems are not going to become the dominant computing platform anytime soon, and they are unlikely to fundamentally alter the way that businesses and other organizations are run. In other words, despite all that can and will be done with mobile systems, the wired Internet will remain the more important economic force. To fully appreciate these distinctions and limitations, consider today's three main areas of wireless activity:

1. **Replacing/complementing traditional wired voice services.** Wireless systems have become a real alternative to traditional telephone service, and will, at a minimum, be an important check on today's near-monopoly local telephone service pricing. More likely, the growth of wireless telephone services will eventually have vast consequences for the very structure of the voice services industry (assuming, of course, that mobile phones continue to be seen as medically safe devices that don't give off brain-damaging signals).

2. **Improving connectivity.** Wireless home networks, Bluetooth, and Wifi are all important technologies that should eventually make it much easier to access computer devices and Internet services from almost anywhere. Once the many kinks have been worked out, they should be capable of making IT usage much more ubiquitous.

3. **Enabling new application platforms.** Handheld devices, Global Positioning Systems (GPS), Radio Frequency Identification (RFID), Ultrawideband, video phones, and smart mobile products are all important new market platforms, and will result in countless new applications and services.

But as important as these areas of activity are, from this book's perspective what's really noticeable is how few of these uses for wireless technologies are likely to truly transform existing businesses and industries. Of the three types of activities mentioned, only the final group represents an important new application frontier. The first two can be categorized as significant expansions in existing types of IT usage. Wireless phone calls are still just phone calls, and Wifi Internet access at Starbucks is still just high-speed Internet access. No new forms of usage are really being established; we're just getting much better mobile support and possibly better price/performance.

Establishing new types of uses for information technologies is very important because otherwise we might merely be creating a surplus of Internet and communications options—wired, cable, wireless, voice, e-mail, voice mail, pagers, text messaging, instant messaging, and so on. Without new uses such as video and photo messaging, we could reach the point where innovation begins to generate diminishing returns, a topic examined more closely in chapter 9.

Even for these new applications, the very nature of small mobile devices limits the handheld market, at least in the near term. While voice recognition might someday make keyboards unnecessary, and special glasses might simulate a full view display, we're many years away from widespread use of these approaches. For now, no matter how skilled we get with our thumbs and Blackberry-style devices, small screens and difficult data entry make handheld products a supporting, but not primary, device. Today's new generation of foldable mobile keyboards can certainly help, but don't really solve the problem.

For example, if forced to make a choice, how many of us would give up our PCs and keep our Palm Pilot, Pocket PC, or screen phone? Not many, I think. And it is this inherent subordination that makes it hard for wireless systems to become the IT industry's overall center of gravity. The relatively slow acceptance of wireless data services in the enterprise (outside of niche applications among the high end of traveling workers such as Wall Street professionals) and the general lack of consumer excitement regarding so-called digital wallets also seem to confirm this.

Finally, while GPS and RFID (more on this in chapter 4) systems could have great long-term importance, these will also be highly dependent on customer-created standards. For example, the Uniform Code Council (UCC) and the European Article Numbering (EAN) International group in Brussels are working to develop standards that will make RFID an international supply-chain standard, much as the UCC did with bar code point-of-sale systems three decades ago. Similarly, GPS developments are heavily influenced by the U.S. government, and it's the European Union that's looking to develop an alternative European-controlled GPS-like system. Consequently, both of these technologies are actually part of the larger customer-driven pattern.

What about Plain-Old High-Bandwidth Services?

If you asked most IT suppliers what's held the business back in recent years, the slow rollout of high-bandwidth consumer services would likely be the most common answer. Clearly, such networks would make many new services possible, and as we shall see, barriers in this area played an important role in bursting the Internet bubble. Today, just about every advanced or developing nation wants to make sure that it has the right dynamics in place to assure the build-out of this critical part of the IT industry's infrastructure. Lack of consumer bandwidth is certainly a major industry limitation.

That said, it's easy to exaggerate the importance of this one factor. Most businesses, educational institutions, and government agencies have all the bandwidth they need, and could get more if necessary. The extensive use of videoconferencing, Voice over IP, instant messaging, and Applications Service Providers will often require substantially more network capacity, but lack of bandwidth is not the main reason these new types of services have yet to widely catch on.

Additionally, increasing consumer bandwidth won't do anything to overcome many of the challenges to be discussed in this work such as Extensible Markup Language (XML)-based interoperability, shared industry systems such as exchanges, a restructured health care industry, e-learning, or enhanced government services. Indeed, even in the consumer realm, higher bandwidth won't directly solve the larger questions of unauthorized music and video distribution, the reluctance to pay for content, or the value of online advertising. In the short term, it would actually make the music and video problem much worse.

Of course, one shouldn't take this too far. At some point, a critical mass of high-bandwidth consumer services will be reached, triggering new and more positive dynamics. It's entirely possible that the IT industry is closer to this than many realize. While today only about 10 percent of U.S. households have high-speed services, it would not be surprising if penetration of 15 to 20 percent was sufficient to create the required critical mass. Eventually, these new services might be compelling enough to attract the 50 percent of consumers who don't use the Internet at home at all. That's why bandwidth is so important in the long run. However, as long as the key consumer applications remain bogged down with copyright concerns, high-bandwidth services will likely remain only a relatively small if highly visible part of the overall IT industry story.

What about Bio- and Nanotechnology?

Sometime in the not-too-distant future, both biotechnology and nano-technology will start to make today's processing of data and text seem dull and inconsequential. Certainly, little of what happens on the Internet today can compete with biotechnology's promise of curing diseases, creating new species, and eventually unraveling many of the mysteries of life itself. Similarly, the ability to manipulate the atomic composition of matter via various forms nanotechnology is the sort of general-purpose revolution that arguably only electricity itself has previously delivered.

From an IT industry perspective, these new frontiers are likely to be the answer to the age-old question of how tomorrow's huge increases in processing power and storage will be used. While computer industry people generally talk in terms of gigabytes and increasingly terabytes, in the life sciences, systems that require petabytes, exabytes, and zetabytes (quadrillions, quintillions, and sextillions) are starting to become imaginable. Similarly, the processing requirements envisioned for advanced genetic and protein analysis could easily require the capacities of both future supercomputers and the type of peer-to-peer grids to be discussed in chapter 9. In short, both nanotechnology and biotechnology should ensure that we will never have too much computer capacity.

That said, the widespread influence of both of these areas is still quite a few years off. While significant venture capital is now flowing into both areas, most of this is aimed at long-term investment returns, not the quick fortunes of the dot-com era. If nothing else, the limited pool of talent in these areas, especially nanotechnology, would seem to imply that the build-up will take time, and not become a major IT influence until very late in the decade. But eventually, they will once again use information processing to advance society, and could easily become the IT industry's new center of gravity.

What Happens When Customers Don't Lead

A good way to demonstrate the importance of customer leadership is to show what happens when this leadership is absent. The story of online music demonstrates how customer efforts can be required to move particular IT markets forward, but that such efforts can't be taken for granted. Online music still has the potential to help push the Internet to its next threshold of usage and infrastructure. However, almost four years after the birth of Napster, this goal remains as far off as ever. While this issue has received a great deal of publicity, the larger connection to a customer-driven industry has, as far as I know, never been explicitly made.

Since the Napster story is quite well-known, we need only recount the highlights. In May 1999, Napster was founded by Shawn Fanning after he dropped out of his freshman year of college. This was in the midst of the Internet boom, when it seemed just about anything was possible. Napster made it relatively easy for consumers to swap music files with other Internet users. The system wasn't all that user-friendly, but for computer-savvy teenagers and students it was more than manageable. The idea soon proved wildly popular and attracted tens of millions of users—albeit mostly because it was free. Fanning was suddenly among the most famous of the Internet's many high-profile entrepreneurs.

One of the important unintended consequences of the extensive use of Napster was an increase in the demand for high-speed Internet services. Online music delivery is just too slow over standard 56K telephone lines to be used extensively. Had Napster (or its equivalent) remained a free and fully legal service, IT industry hopes for the rapid adoption of high-bandwidth consumer services would have been much more likely to be fulfilled. Additionally, a large increase in online music usage would have spurred many significant innovations and investments in related markets such as PCs, CD burners, portable music players, and digital home entertainment systems.

However, as we all know, the music industry (to protect its own perceived interests) decided not to allow this to happen. In December 1999, the Recording Industry Association of America (RIAA) filed a copyright infringement suit against Napster. After much legal wrangling, the service was essentially shut down in July 2001. The company has since filed for bankruptcy and been acquired by Bertelsmann. As of this writing, its very existence remains in serious doubt.

The timing of these events closely coincided with the bursting of the Internet bubble. Naturally, this has led to speculation that if the RIAA had accepted Napster's royalty offers or been forced to do so by the courts, the Internet industry story might well have been very different indeed, especially within the telecom sector. While we can never know for sure, it's certainly fair to say that the demise of Napster marked a critical industry turning point, and as we saw in chapter 2, such turning points can have consequences far greater than the participants of the time realize.

Moreover, the broader lesson here is clear. Many segments of the IT industry were desperate for high-bandwidth services to enable a new generation of systems and applications. Yet many IT vendors, with their traditional supply-side focus, spent most of their time worrying about the regulatory aspects of high-bandwidth competition, particularly the so-called open access issue. Too often, they seem to have all but forgotten that the real challenge is to create actual consumer demand, and that this is something they really can't do alone. In the case of online music, IT suppliers were dependent upon what the recording industry decided, and thus far at least, the interests of these two businesses have been at increasingly rancorous odds. The outlook for online music will be revisited in chapter 7.

Looking back, the contrast couldn't be more striking. When the mainframe industry needed better ways to get data into and out of a computer (via display terminals and disk drives), companies could build these devices for themselves. Similarly, when PCs first emerged, they would have been almost worthless without easy to use applications.

Fortunately, the Independent Software Vendor (ISV) community was well equipped to develop the word processors, graphics programs, spreadsheets, and databases needed to make PCs useful. Overall, there were powerful synergies between suppliers of IT hardware and software, whose growth and efforts generally fed upon each other.

Today, however, the majority of demand-creating Internet activity has to come from industries over which IT suppliers have little or no control. As the list of possibilities in table 3-1 suggests, online music is just one of many such examples. A wide range of industries has to make significant changes to take full advantage of today's information technologies. In part 2, we will assess the prospects for customer-driven IT change, and will see that it's currently a very mixed picture. Many online businesses are still in the formative stages, and the long-term pattern of value-chain leadership has yet to be established. This is what makes the coming years such an important period. While it has become almost a cliché to say that market "power" has shifted to customers and consumers, it has often gone unrecognized that with this power comes obligations and responsibilities. Defining the nature of these responsibilities is a key part of this book's overall mission.

CHAPTER FOUR

When Customers Have Taken the Lead

AS WE HAVE SEEN, one of the great accomplishments of the IT industry has been the establishment of long-lasting platforms upon which the industry could build. In chapter 2, we recounted how IT suppliers have historically assumed most of the risk and responsibility for this work. In chapter 3, we explained how and why much of this responsibility is being transferred to IT customers. Since these customer organizations are now the most important creator of new sources of value, they must take the lead in developing many of the platforms needed to move the industry forward.

However, although the efforts of suppliers have defined the bulk of IT evolution over the past fifty years, they are certainly not the entire story. There have been a number of times when customers have taken the lead, and cooperated to establish important new information processing capabilities. These efforts have not been nearly as general purpose as IBM's mainframes, Windows PCs, or Internet standards. Instead they have focused on particular industries or sometimes a particular problem. But within these relatively narrow domains, their impact has been considerable. In each case, they have led to significant industry and even societal change, as well as to a large expansion in IT usage and investment. They have been an important part of the IT industry's success.

Examples of this type of customer cooperation and leadership can be found in a wide range of industries, but they have proven particularly important in consumer-oriented businesses such as retail, travel, entertainment, and especially financial services. Viewed together, these stories tell us a great deal about how new customer technology-based platforms are created and operated, whose interests they tend to serve, and what the general effects are on their respective marketplaces. These are the same questions that many companies face today as they assess their possible participation in various market exchanges, product and/ or service aggregations, and other potentially new forms of standards development, business interoperability, and online partnering.

Interestingly, over the last thirty years or so, these customer-driven systems have not followed a single dominant pattern. Sometimes a single supplier has provided the initial required leadership; other times, a cooperative process has ruled from the start, while still other platforms have only emerged and solidified over time. However, in all of the cases that follow, the same basic critical mass challenges seen throughout IT industry history have been repeated. New platforms often take time to reach the necessary threshold of commitment and capability, but once this level is realized, growth is rapid, the platform is long-lasting, and the respective industry is substantially transformed.

Six Customer Platforms

In this chapter we will look at the rise and impact of six important customer-initiated platforms—bar code scanning, credit-card processing, Automatic Teller Machines (ATMs), airline reservation systems, the ASCAP and BMI music royalty tracking systems, and Electronic Data Interchange (EDI). These are certainly not the only prominent customer-driven examples. The financial services industry in particular has developed many forms of interinstitution interoperability in areas such as funds transfer, check clearing, and stock trading. However, all of the selected examples are representative of long-lasting industry and application-specific systems that have substantially increased the effectiveness of new technology usage. Additionally, each is also now under pressure to change because of the capabilities of today's technologies, often the Internet.

With the exception of the ASCAP story, each of the chosen examples has relied heavily on computer processing. The story behind the formation of ASCAP is included as a reminder of how in the pre-computer era, the entertainment industry managed to effectively address a set of copyright and new media usage issues similar to those facing the music industry today. It is one of the better examples of an industry coming together to systematically address a seemingly intractable problem that was presented by new technologies—at that time player pianos, radio, and recorded music—and allowing these new media to rapidly develop.

While the stories behind each of these six major developments may be familiar, they're included in this chapter to provide a broad and unique perspective on the range of customer-driven market launch possibilities and outcomes. And while all of these stories had their roots in the United States, all have also gone on to become powerful global platforms as well.

From a more personal perspective, back in 1979 my first job in the IT industry was researching the market for just these sorts of specialized transaction processing systems—especially point-of-sale (POS), ATM, credit-card, and EDI systems. Because these systems represented the early intersection of technology and specific industries, I've always had an interest in how these markets evolve. Looking back, much of the industry debate really wasn't all that different from what is being said about e-business today. New business transaction technologies have always generated a considerable amount of hype and controversy, as well as a new set of competitive dynamics.

After looking at each development individually, we'll assess the general patterns that have emerged, with the emphasis on how customer-driven systems appear to have established an effective middle ground between the IT industry's twin poles of de facto single supplier control and the reliance on independent standards bodies. Explicit forms of goal-oriented and industrywide cooperation have usually been the main path forward; it's a model that has worked quite well, and bodes well for the IT industry's future.

Bar Codes—The Development of Industrywide Standards

For much of the twentieth century, leaders in a wide range of hard-goods industries knew all too well that they faced serious challenges in their ability to efficiently manage their companies' inventories. Businesses dealing with large numbers of unique and rapidly changing product items found it almost impossible to keep track of what was and was not in stock without constant and costly manual attention. This problem has been of particular importance to large grocery stores, where the number of available goods is very high, and where consumers randomly select items in real time, but still expect all items to always be in stock.

Ever since electromechanical punch card machines began to be widely used in the early twentieth century, there had been interest in seeing whether there was any practical approach to automating the inventory management and sales checkout processes of large retail stores. Yet for most of the twentieth century, the available technology simply was not up to the task. While experiments with ultraviolet lights and encoded labels were conducted in the 1940s and 1950s, it wasn't until lasers started becoming affordable in the late 1960s that the widespread use of electrical scanning systems became feasible.

Supermarket industry interest in scanning technology became serious in 1969 when the Grocery Manufacturers of America (GMA), which then had nearly two hundred members, met to discuss the need for what was then called an "inter-industry product code." In 1970, the idea of using technology to identify and keep track of individual products began to move forward as a GMA committee was set up to assess the situation and McKinsey released a study describing the substantial savings that could be achieved through the use of retail checkout systems.

To explore the concept further, the grocery industry asked the computer vendor community to develop detailed proposals for the necessary encoding processes and supporting technology. Initially, there were experiments with a so-called bull's-eye label (using a round pattern) developed by RCA, but this system did not prove satisfactory. In 1973, what is now viewed as a highly elegant IBM proposal for a Universal Product Code (UPC) was adopted by the grocery industry. On June 26, 1974, a ten-pack of Wrigley's chewing gum was the first retail product scanned at Marsh's Supermarket in Troy, Ohio. The technology worked, but in order to effectively use it, the industry itself had to take collective action.

As with many technology markets, there was a serious chicken/egg problem. Since most stores did not have scanners, there was not much of an incentive for suppliers to print machine readable bar codes on every product item. Additionally, each company tended to have its own way of categorizing its products. To address these issues, GMA members required that their suppliers register with the Uniform Grocery Product Code Council (which later became the Uniform Product Code

Council and now is known as the Uniform Code Council, or UCC, reflecting the fact that the association's interests now extend well beyond the grocery industry). UCC registration ensured that each supplier had its own identifier so that its products could be accurately recognized. To this day, the UCC oversees the UPC bar code standard, and is governed by the retail industry itself. It now has more than two hundred thousand member companies and is active in a number of related global standards areas.

As suppliers began to put bar code labels on their products, the retail industry became increasingly convinced that the use of optical scanning technology could result in significant checkout counter savings. What came to be known as retail point-of-sale systems began to be rapidly installed by the major supermarket chains, despite price tags that often ran into the hundreds of thousands of dollars per store. Indeed, the growth of these expensive systems created a substantial new business for early POS suppliers such as NCR and IBM. While most of the early benefits resulted from a faster and more accurate checkout process, sophisticated links to inventory and sales tracking systems were eventually developed. Over time, bar code technology was adopted by many other industries, including other forms of retail, manufacturing, health care, and the military, often on a global scale. It is now a pervasive and essential international standard, and it all began with the grocery industry's willingness to address a common need.

Today, scanning systems themselves are feeling the pressure to change. In many large-scale environments, the costs of manually scanning each item is simply prohibitive, particularly in shipping and receiving environments where goods are packed in crates or large truck containers. As mentioned in chapter 3, there is now rising interest in what's known as RFID (Radio Frequency Identification) technology, which attaches a small and inexpensive semiconductor to each inventoried item. The data on this chip can be read by a wireless device that does not need a line-of-sight connection. In theory, this could allow the contents of an entire crate or even an entire railcar to be checked without manually unpacking or even touching the contents. Not only would this be much more cost-effective, but it could have important security uses as well. International container shipments are currently one of the more worrisome security dilemmas.

Looking ahead, the wider use of RFID presents many of the same standards and interoperability issues that bar code systems have so successfully overcome. Once again, the UCC is taking the lead in conjunction with EAN International (European Article Numbering), the key European standards body in this area, formed in 1977. From a broader perspective, the UCC and the EAN have recently pledged to work together in a number of areas of importance to the retail industry, including physical, information, and process standards, especially as they relate to XML. This cooperation could make many forms of global commerce more workable and efficient.

More quirkily, bar codes are now even being used in offices to identify equipment, individual belongings, and even people, especially in offices, such as some at Accenture and other companies with highly mobile workforces, where employees don't have their own desks. Contemporary culture seems to have anticipated this. Witness the recent popularity of bar code imagery with rock bands and clubs, and even a rising number of bar code tattoos. Someday perhaps everything and everybody will have a unique and machine-readable identifier.

Credit Cards—The Importance of Industry Ownership

It is almost hard to imagine today, but for centuries, the very idea of individuals buying goods on credit was considered in most Western nations to be highly suspect, even immoral. Many people believed that the seller was engaged in a form of usury and the buyer in reckless and dangerous extravagance. Individual debt was strongly associated with the poor, and even the debtor's prison. However, in the United States, from the middle of the nineteenth century on, consumer credit began gaining in popularity as a way to buy horses, farm seed, pianos, books, sewing machines, and the like. Still, the social stigma didn't completely fade away until the 1920s, when loans became the preferred way of financing automobile purchases, then the ultimate in consumer prestige. Acceptance of the idea of buying on credit in Europe was generally even slower.

The first actual charge cards in the United States date back to 1914, when Western Union started offering its best customers the option of deferring their payments. In 1924, a similar service was offered by the General Petroleum Corp. for gasoline and other automobile related services. In the 1930s, AT&T, the railroads, and other businesses also began to offer deferred payment cards. However, this steady growth was brought to an abrupt halt by World War II, when the congressionally enacted Regulation W greatly restricted the use of charge cards, ostensibly as an effort to limit wartime inflation. During these first three decades of activity, U.S. banks were almost completely absent from the charge-card industry picture.

However, after WWII, the pace of events significantly quickened as consumers began to buy more expensive consumer durables—such as cars, furniture, and major kitchen appliances—and both business and vacation travel within the United States picked up sharply. This created the need for a simple nationwide payment system. Toward this end, Diners Club was launched in 1949, and during the 1950s a number of banks, especially in the New York City area, began to enter the charge-card business. Perhaps the most important year was 1958, when American Express, Hilton hotels (Carte Blanche), Bank of America (BofA), and Chase Manhattan all got into the market.

The blue, white, and gold BankAmericard proved particularly popular, and BofA began to license its card capabilities to other banks in the United States and eventually around the world. BofA initially did this under the name of National BankAmericard, Inc., under the leadership of the now legendary Dee Hock. In the early 1970s, NBI and Hock, with the technological assistance of TRW, led the way in installing electronic authorization and processing systems, which simplified previously paper- and phone-based methods. (This work was greatly aided by the emergence of magnetic stripe technology, first widely used in the late 1960s in the London and San Francisco subway systems.) In 1976, NBI was renamed Visa. Eventually, BofA gave up its controlling interest and today, Visa is jointly owned by its more than twenty thousand member banks.

The origins of today's MasterCard are quite similar, if a bit less glamorous. During the 1950s and early 1960s, regional bank franchises emerged where a major bank in each city would accept payments from certain merchants that the group had agreed to work with. In 1966, a group of seventeen banks formed a federation of reciprocal credit card acceptance. The group's initial motivation stemmed from the many impracticalities and high costs of each bank operating its own proprietary credit-card system. Initially, this group was named the Interbank Card

Association, which in 1969 was changed to the more marketing-oriented name of Mastercharge, which itself was changed in 1979 to MasterCard. Like Visa, MasterCard is also now owned and managed by its twenty thousand member banks.

If you think it is odd that both Visa and MasterCard have twenty thousand members, it really isn't. Today, just about every major bank is a member of both organizations, although there is no overlap among the two firms' boards of directors. Even so, this is certainly an unusual competitive situation and one that over the years has attracted considerable and ongoing government oversight and consumer complaints. Many observers, including at times Hock himself, have expressed concern and regret that the two organizations don't have different members. If they did, many argue, they would have a much greater incentive to compete directly. Strangely enough, it was government pressure in the mid-1970s that forced Visa to allow its bank members to offer Master-Card as well.[1]

This system has been allowed to function in this way because member banks do compete with each other in terms of their specific credit card–service terms, fees, and interest rates. Additionally, the still important role of American Express, the Discover card, and many business-specific cards also ensures a certain level of credit-card industry competition. While both consumers and retailers have complained about the power of Visa and MasterCard in areas such as commissions, late fees, interest rates, and international surcharges, the two companies have generally used their power carefully. However, the current legal challenge coming from Wal-Mart and other retailers appears to be a serious one. The plaintiffs hope to end Visa and MasterCard's ability to tie the use of their credit and debit cards and are seeking huge past damages.

But from a broader economic perspective, these competitive concerns pale when compared to the extraordinary impact that national and now global credit cards have had on businesses, consumers, and society. Although there is certainly a well-documented downside to consumers' extensive reliance on credit-card debt, the ease, flexibility, efficiency, and security of credit (and now debit) cards greatly exceed the capabilities of previous cash, check, and money order systems. Looking forward, the credit-card industry clearly has the necessary critical mass to eventually launch enhanced services based on smart cards and other technologies, including the Internet. However, thus far at least, efforts to move beyond magnetic stripe technologies have proven difficult. Many have argued that it's Visa and MasterCard's overwhelming market control that makes the emergence of new technologies so difficult. Perhaps this is why both Europe and Japan have tended to show more interest in more modern card and payment technologies.

From an IT industry perspective, as with bar codes, the credit-card industry has been a major driver of computer industry technology and growth. Today, there are literally millions of credit- and debit-card authorization devices, each plugged into some of the world's most sophisticated computer networks, and backed by giant and redundant data centers. These systems have become increasingly interoperable around the world, all based on simple and inexpensive magnetic stripe technology. Because of their flexibility, convenience, and built-in consumer protection, they have even become the dominant form of payment on the Internet, and thereby have made much of the e-commerce industry possible. They are a great example of industries working together in a mutually beneficial way to take full advantage of a powerful new IT capability. The question going forward is whether this record of payment system innovation and cooperation will be successfully extended.

Automatic Teller Machines—Controlling a New Technology

The story behind the now ubiquitous ATM reveals another distinct market pattern. This time, the question was how an industry would respond to a significant new invention. In 1968, engineers at Docutel, a company that made baggage handling equipment and other specialized systems, developed the first ATM, which was installed at New York's Chemical Bank. The early ATMs were typically either inside of or attached to an existing bank facility and were intended to lower individual bank teller transaction costs, since the cost of disbursing funds or accepting deposits via a machine was considered to be less than when using human tellers. Initially, each bank operated its own ATMs, a model that lasted through the 1970s and into the early 1980s.

However, banks eventually began to realize the consumer appeal of having ATMs distributed throughout their regions as opposed to just attached to existing branches. This idea was appealing to both the many small banks (which could now better serve their customers) as well as larger banks, which were aggressively expanding geographically as long-standing regulations and restrictions on inter- and intrastate banking were eased. The number of ATMs a bank could offer became an important competitive factor, both in obtaining and retaining consumer accounts.

As banks began to install their own off-site ATMs, it became clear that sharing machines could be much more cost-effective than having every bank deploy its own ATMs, sometimes ridiculously close to one another. The increasing sophistication of online computer networks made such sharing possible, as long as the banks could agree upon the necessary formats and standards. Fortunately, magnetic stripe technology had already matured through its extensive use in the credit-card industry. As long as each ATM could correctly read the ATM cards issued by each participating bank, computer networks could do the rest by essentially switching each ATM transaction to the appropriate bank. Despite a few bumps along the way, the banking industry managed to avoid any serious interoperability problems.

During the 1980s, the rise of first regional and then national ATM networks drove the ATM industry to new heights, and radically changed consumer banking to the point that, increasingly, many of us only rarely set foot inside an actual bank office. As with Visa and MasterCard, the nation's banks managed this transition relatively smoothly and maintained full control over the newly emerging systems, repeating the credit card industry's pattern of joint ownership and operation. Today, the two major ATM networks in the United States, Cirrus and Plus, are actually owned and managed by MasterCard and Visa, respectively. As explained earlier, both MasterCard and Visa are jointly owned by the same set of roughly twenty thousand member banks.

In short, the banking industry managed to take full advantage of two major new innovations—credit cards and ATMs—without ceding control to any other entity. However, Cirrus and Plus (like Visa and MasterCard) have tended to take on lives of their own, and have acted in ways not always in the long-run interest of all of the bank members. For example, ATM networks have shifted from being merely a way to cut costs to becoming their own source of revenue, as various fees and new services such as selling stamps are added. Looking forward, the concept of cooperatively created entities eventually outgrowing the intentions of their founders is likely to become an important e-commerce pattern in areas such as business exchanges, new forms of aggregation, and other cooperative endeavors.

However, as with credit cards, these concerns are relatively minor in terms of their overall market impact. The main story occurred in the 1980s, when large ATM networks became another major technology-based platform, one that both consumers and the banking industry continue to benefit from. As new payment schemes struggle to reach critical mass on the Internet, the lessons of the ATM and credit-card businesses are important to keep in mind. Looking ahead, the key question is whether the banking system will once again manage to co-opt and control the use and proliferation of new payment technologies. This topic will be addressed in chapter 7.

SABRE—IT as a Competitive Advantage

Whereas the stories of bar code technology, credit cards, and ATMs have shown how industries have come together to solve a shared problem, the history of airline reservation databases reveals a different pattern of technology-market evolution. Here, it was the all-out competition between two large and powerful rivals that led first to a single supplier's advantage and then to an interoperable industrywide system. Although the SABRE story has been told many times elsewhere, it is still one of the best examples of how to use IT for competitive advantage. Perhaps more important from this work's perspective, the SABRE system is the only example in this chapter where a single company has managed to maintain long-term market control.

The roots of this story go back to 1954, when, legend has it, American Airlines CEO C. R. Smith happened to sit next to a high-level IBM salesperson, coincidentally named Blair Smith, on a flight from New York to Los Angeles. (Some say the shared flight detail has been added over time, but it does make for a better story.) Apparently, C. R. Smith explained his company's complex ticket processing needs; thirty days later, Blair Smith and IBM responded with an initial proposal. However, five years later, the two companies were still just talking; the required technologies simply were not yet available.

Serious joint development began in 1959–1960 and was called the Semi Automatic Business Environment Research project, which mercifully was shortened to SABER and later to SABRE. An initial system was implemented in 1962. Over the years, the close work between IBM and American on the SABRE project pushed many of the frontiers of information processing, including telecom line concentrators, front-end communications processors, online disk storage, high-volume transaction processing, and mainframe operating system capabilities. Eventually, Delta, United, PanAm, and other airlines developed similar systems, often also in conjunction with IBM. These independent developments continued into the early 1970s, when American's system started to lag behind the competition, especially United.

It is here that the story gets interesting. Bob Crandall became the newly appointed head of American's marketing group. With a background in computing, Crandall had a good sense of what IT could do, but was dismayed at the state of American's system. Working with the head of data processing, the now-famous Max Hopper, Crandall and his team fought for increased funding and substantially upgraded SABRE. They then began marketing the system to U.S. travel agents. Initially, Crandall hoped to convince all of the U.S. airlines to develop a single, industrywide system based upon SABRE. But United was the overall airline industry leader, and it was confident that its Apollo reservation system was superior. It declined to support Crandall's initiative, and thus the two companies began to compete head on in the airline reservation system marketplace, a battle mostly won by SABRE.[2]

Because of its unique and powerful position with travel agents, SABRE eventually came under significant and ongoing antitrust scrutiny in both the United States and Europe. American was eventually forced to accommodate other airlines more equally, rather than, for example, giving its flights preference on the reservation agent's computer terminal display. Nevertheless, during the 1980s and early 1990s, SABRE provided American with many significant marketing and financial advantages, which is why in its day it was perhaps the signature example of using IT for competitive advantage.

Today, there are five major airline reservation systems, SABRE, Apollo, Galileo (owned by Cendant), Amadeus (founded in 1987 by the major European Airlines), and Worldspan (mostly Delta and Northwest). However, SABRE still accounts for roughly half of all North American bookings. In 2000, after nearly forty years of evolution and controversy, American (now part of AMR) spun-off SABRE as a separate, publicly traded company. Perhaps more tellingly, in 2001, American,

United, Delta, Continental, and Northwest came together to create Orbitz, a cooperative Web site for air reservations and other travel services. Orbitz will compete with existing services such as Expedia (now part of USA Networks, Inc.), Travelocity (70 percent owned by SABRE), and increasingly, Priceline, and other discount travel services.

Not surprisingly, a system such as Orbitz that is jointly owned by the airlines has led to serious antitrust concerns from competitors, who fear that Orbitz will get preferential airline treatment. Right now, it's too early to say what will happen, and since the online travel reservation business still has very low market penetration, and several powerful non-airline players, the market is being allowed to evolve on its own, at least for now. Close industry coordination can easily be seen by others as a form of illegal collusion. Such controversies are part of nearly every successful highly cooperative platform.

ASCAP—Making Copyrights Work

To listen to the brouhaha over Napster and subsequent forms of online music, one would think that the music industry has never had to accommodate a new technology before. Obviously, in a century that saw the rise of radio, television, vinyl records, audio tapes, VCRs, and CDs (as well as a huge expansion in live concert performances), this is not the case. In their day, these new technologies and businesses were viewed as just as threatening as Internet-based music is today. Yet somehow society managed to find a way to make these new technologies acceptable to artists and the business interests of the times. How this initially happened is a revealing and, surprisingly, not very well-known story.

Prior to 1909, U.S. copyright law was based on a very strict view of what was meant by a legal "copy." This was perfectly understandable given the technologies of the 1800s, but became increasingly problematic as new forms of encoded music emerged in the early years of the twentieth century. For example, in the important 1908 case of White-Smith Music Pub. Co. versus Apollo Co., the Supreme Court ruled that, based on existing law, the perforated rolls used for player pianos were not actually "copies" of songs, and therefore companies developing such products were not in violation of existing law. In other words, businesses and individuals were free to reproduce a copyrighted work in another format, as long as the original form wasn't directly and exactly copied.[3]

The Copyright Act of 1909 changed that, and expanded protection to encompass new forms of encoded media. It basically gave the original composer of a work the right to make the first recordings of his or her creation; but after that, other performers could legally make recordings or other uses in exchange for a contractually agreed-upon fee. This was an important change that greatly increased the legal rights of composers. However, the idea still needed to be put into practice. In February 1914, a group of leading composers, including John Philip Sousa, Irving Berlin, and Victor Herbert (*Babes in Toyland*) founded the American Society of Composers, Authors and Publishers, a nonprofit organization better known as ASCAP. There were initially about one hundred ASCAP members, mostly in the New York City area.

ASCAP sought to develop an efficient way for composers to be compensated for the subsequent use of their work, with the full backing of the U.S. legal system. Initially, the focus was on printed music sheets, where a royalty of one cent per sheet was collected. Over time, however, this system was expanded to include musical recordings, radio and television broadcasts, and live performances. Participants in these businesses were asked to pay an annual license fee that enabled them to use the works of ASCAP members. ASCAP then developed a sampling system, whereby it estimated the relative frequency of usage for each member artist, and distributed its pool of royalties proportionately.

ASCAP was virtually the sole arbiter of U.S. music royalties until 1940, when the broadcast industry, concerned about ASCAP's near-monopoly power and frustrated by some of its rules, set up its own system. A group of some six hundred broadcasters met in Chicago in 1939 and went on to set up Broadcast Music, Inc. (BMI). BMI grew rapidly because of its general openness to any songwriter, and its willingness to include country, blues, and R&B. A third organization, SESAC (which initially stood for Society of European Stage Authors and Composers, but is now just SESAC) was set up in 1930 to protect the rights of foreign composers. However, SESAC eventually expanded into jazz, gospel, Latin American, Christian, and other musical areas then neglected by ASCAP and later BMI.

Over the years, there have been many complaints about these organizations, particularly ASCAP, whose secretive calculation methods, strict usage policies, and sometimes heavy-handed legal enforcement, have made it somewhat of a pariah to many, especially nightclub owners and other small businesses. However, the royalty system ASCAP created achieved its overall mission. New outlets for music and other forms of entertainment were allowed to develop without a costly permissions process, but in a way that both the original creators and their copyright holders generally found acceptable.

Had this not been the case, it is entirely possible that copyright holders might have shut down radio broadcasts in the 1920s in much the same way they shut down Napster in 2001. ASCAP's sampling-based royalty allocation scheme has proved sufficient to do the job, but the emergence of such a system was by no means inevitable. It required both timely changes in copyright law and the efforts and cooperation of some of the leading figures of the time. It remains to be seen if both copyright law and the music industry will find a similar solution to support the online distribution of music and other copyrighted materials, a topic discussed in chapter 7. Ironically, the music industry's recent efforts to collect what many consider to be excessive royalties from the nascent Internet radio industry has pretty much brought the issue back to where it was more than seventy-five years ago.

EDI—The Challenge of General-Purpose Solutions

Whereas bar codes, credit cards, ATMs, SABRE, and ASCAP were all major successes that have had many visible and long-lasting societal implications, Electronic Data Interchange (EDI) is an example of an important technological concept that has only partially lived up to its envisioned potential. While thousands of companies and government agencies still use EDI technology, it has never managed to truly revolutionize commercial transaction systems, and has been mostly restricted to relatively large organizations. The reasons why remain instructive.

The roots of EDI go back to the late 1960s. Rail, trucking, air, and sea transportation companies, along with their supporting infrastructure of shippers, brokers, forwarders, and others, needed to reduce the amount of slow and expensive paperwork. Consequently, the initial EDI standards were developed by the Transportation Data Coordinating Committee (TDCC) and consisted of some forty or so transaction sets designed to enable IT vendor independent computer-to-computer information exchange. This work became the basis for the broader EDI standardization efforts of the American National Standards Institute (ANSI). In the 1970s and 1980s, as these standards were developed, EDI usage expanded considerably, and many imagined a bright future for this approach. However, from their earliest inception, certain problems and limitations with EDI repeatedly occurred. The three most prominent of these were:

1. EDI systems tended to be relatively expensive, requiring custom software support and implementation, and often the use of specialized telecommunications services from so-called Value-Added Network (VAN) providers. Consequently, EDI capabilities were only rarely used by small and even many medium-sized businesses, which often lacked the required skills, and didn't have the transaction volumes needed to efficiently amortize high EDI start-up costs. Since most large companies also must deal extensively with many small and medium businesses, this meant that while EDI could reduce a firm's manual processing costs, it couldn't eliminate them.

2. Many business transactions proved to be more complex and more rapidly changing than predefined EDI systems could easily manage, and thus a certain amount of manual intervention was still required in most companies, again negating at least some of the potential gains. This was especially the case in fast-moving industries where new offerings inevitably required modifications, which formal standards processes such as ANSI's could not easily keep up with.

3. While TDCC and ANSI standards often seemed clear on paper, during implementation a number of "interpretation" issues arose, and thus many EDI systems were not as fully interoperable as their designers had hoped. This lack of 100 percent clarity has often been a problem with de jure IT industry standards. In these situations, there is no real enforcement mechanism to assure EDI interoperability other than testing each transaction on a case-by-case or company-to-company basis.

For these and other reasons, EDI never became a ubiquitous nationwide or worldwide platform in the way the other technologies described in this chapter have. This partial success was not really the fault of the people involved. The challenge of automating the vast array of business transactions was simply much more complex than the other systems discussed in this chapter, which focused on a specific activity or type of transaction.

Indeed, many of the problems that EDI systems have faced remain serious obstacles, even for today's advanced e-commerce systems. Perhaps the most important lesson is that focused, application-specific systems have a much higher likelihood of success than more all-encompassing ones. Today, proponents of technologies such as XML and Web Services, for example, hope to greatly improve the ease of business-to-business transactions, but still face a wide range of new and arguably even more complex challenges. Seamless business-to-business automation remains an elusive industry goal.

Conclusions

The examples we've covered in this chapter are certainly not the entire list of the important customer-driven IT-enabled platforms. One could add the great bank funds transfer systems, online stock exchanges such as the Nasdaq, a wide range of IT-related manufacturing standards, and others. But whether one uses the shorter or longer list, one of the most immediate observations is how many of these systems are related to financial services, and conversely, how few come from other major sectors such as insurance, health care, education, and other areas. Exactly why the financial services industry seems so much more adept at developing these large transactional systems is not immediately obvious. Certainly, banks are not typically thought of as being especially innovative or open to partnering.

Financial transactions seem to have become the most automated type of activity for several reasons. First, financial exchanges are by far the most numerous type of transaction, and therefore they offer the greatest potential for improvements in efficiencies and consumer convenience. Second, most payment systems are also relatively predictable and repeatable with fewer of the variances seen, for example, with EDI systems where actual goods are often being described. More fundamentally, unlike most goods and services, money itself is usually a clear and absolute standard, ideally suited to system interoperability. In short, financial transactions appear to be the most common because they are the simplest to implement and offer the clearest rewards. However, as the cases of both smart cards and Internet micropayments suggest, this doesn't mean that the acceptance of new financial systems is always easy or inevitable.

While the differences between these various technologies and industries are important, the key is identifying how these innovations compare to the way the IT industry has traditionally advanced. Here, the comparisons are actually quite striking. As mentioned in chapters 2 and 3, the IT industry has tended to progress through one of two diametrically opposed models. Either a single vendor such as IBM, Microsoft, Intel, or Cisco sets the pace, or, as in many Internet businesses, a vendor-neutral third party group such as the World Wide Web Consortium (W3C) or the Internet Engineering Task Force (IETF) has developed the required standards. As we saw in the Unix market, direct supplier-to-supplier cooperation has typically been much less successful.

In contrast, and as shown in table 4-1, our selected customer-driven initiatives reflect more of a middle ground. Only in the case of airline reservations (and to some extent Visa), has the strong single-vendor approach been the dominant model. Similarly, only in the partially successful EDI business has the neutral standards-body approach been tried. In the four other areas, a mix of industry-specific customers, suppliers, and standards groups have contributed significantly. For example, in the bar code industry, it was the major grocery stores working closely with IBM. In the ATM and credit-card businesses, banks initially worked independently, but then evolved toward vast shared-system capabilities. In the ASCAP example, an entirely new nonprofit organization was created to solve a problem that music composers could not really solve for themselves.

In the end, there seem to be four main cooperative system market launch models

1. De facto—single vendor leadership as in airline reservations,

2. De jure—standards-driven systems such as in bar code and EDI systems,

3. Emergent systems—as in ATMs and credit cards, which only became interoperable over time, and

4. Third-party services—such as with ASCAP.

TABLE 4 - 1

Customer-Led Patterns of the Past

Perhaps the most noteworthy aspect of this table is how long ago most of these systems began and that only one, SABRE, is still run by a for-profit company.

	Year Launched	Initial Management	Current Management
ASCAP	1914	Artist members	Nonprofit organization
Visa	1958	Bank of America	Bank members
SABRE	1962	American Airlines	Independent company
ATMs	1968	Individual banks	Bank members
EDI	1969	Transportation Association	ANSI
Bar Code	1974	Grocery Association	Retail Trade Association

Of these, the second and third approaches are the most common, accounting for four of the six examples in this chapter.

In chapter 3, seven common characteristics of IT supplier leadership were presented—risk, reward, perseverance, hype, cooperation, standards, and start-up companies. It's interesting to see how each of these themes has played out through this particular set of historical customer-driven examples. This comparison will provide our first objective evidence as to how supplier and customer leadership might differ.

For example, because of the extensive use of cooperative models, many of the risks, rewards, and perseverance issues were spread evenly across the industry's main participants. This cooperative approach also largely eliminated the need for start-up companies, which, with the important exception of ASCAP, were not part of the initial market launch. In fact, new companies such as Visa, MasterCard, Cirrus, Plus, SABRE, Nasdaq, and others typically have come out of the end of the process, not the beginning, a complete reversal from the way the IT business has traditionally evolved. As we will see in our discussion of the music industry, business exchanges, e-learning and other areas, this will likely be a very important future industry pattern.

In terms of hype, technologies such as bar code scanners, ATMs, and credit cards were all, in their day, major and popular media stories, and this publicity played an essential role in overcoming consumer fears and building enthusiasm. Perhaps most important, in all of the cases, except perhaps EDI, once critical mass was achieved, the benefits and underlying economics of these automated transaction systems became compelling, and thus these systems greatly benefited their industries as a whole, with relatively few long-lasting account control or other competitive problems.

Even when there were initially significant benefits to a single player —such as American Airlines and the Bank of America—these benefits faded over time. In five of the six cases, the basic platforms are now owned by either the industries that created them or some independent nonprofit body. This is entirely unlike the mainframe and PC business, where one supplier often owned everything, but it is also unlike the Internet situation, where neutral standards bodies tend to dominate, often with seemingly no real point of control. Because these customer-created systems are both tightly managed by their participants and generally equitable to the players involved, it would appear that customers have, at least arguably, often found a better way to develop and launch new IT-based platforms. However, the one downside is that, as shown by the examples of credit cards, ATMs, airline reservations, and ASCAP, successful industrywide cooperation will almost inevitably result in ongoing antitrust scrutiny.

Overall, the stories presented in this chapter suggest that good news lies ahead. Customers have repeatedly built major new technology-based systems without relying predominantly upon the IT supplier community. Importantly, many of these systems—especially ATMs, credit cards, and ASCAP—have affected just about every U.S. consumer. These types of societywide systems remain important IT industry goals. As we shall see, the emergence of the Internet has created the opportunity for many more such systems to be spread across a much wider range of industries and applications. The challenge now is to reproduce the successes of the past but on a much broader and more rapid scale. These challenges will be the principle topic of part 2.

II

A Customer-Driven IT Industry

CHAPTER FIVE

Business Attitudes and Resources

GIVEN THE prevalence of engineers and programmers, one would think that the IT industry would be among the most rational of businesses. But to me it's pretty clear that the single most important factor in the IT industry's health is the overall customer mood, often referred to as "business confidence." Indeed, sometimes I think that much of the history of computing can be summed up as follows: Computers are so confusing and complicated that customers operate in a constant (if not always conscious) state of wariness and even fear. In this climate, it's only natural that IT buyers often seek safety in numbers. The result is powerful "herd effects," which manifest themselves in two main ways: unusually high supplier concentration and recurring boom and bust cycles.

Many customers understandably find comfort in choosing the same supplier as everyone else. While economies of scale, network effects, and software lock-in are also important factors in explaining IT supplier concentration, the herd effect has always been an essential aspect of the IT industry's tendency to have very strong, often single-vendor leadership. As the saying goes, at various times no one has ever been fired for buying IBM, Digital, Microsoft, Cisco, or Oracle. Many supplier decisions have to be lived with for so long that career safety has often been an overriding human factor. This is why FUD (Fear, Uncertainty, and Doubt) has always been such a powerful and widely recognized industry force.

More important for our purposes, these herd effects also extend to the willingness of customers to buy computer products and services, and thus they directly explain much of the industry's cyclical behavior. When confidence in IT is high, so is buying, and when this confidence slumps, so does the market. Consequently, global business confidence in IT has always been a critical industry success factor, especially during tough economic times. This is particularly so today, as customers are increasingly being asked to take on the type of risks more traditionally associated with the IT supplier community.

Of course, in many ways the trillions of dollars in business IT investments over the last forty years is evidence of substantial customer confidence and commitment. No one invests in IT unless they believe they will get something useful in return. But today's situation is fundamentally different. Businesses are being asked to create IT value not just for themselves but for their customers, their industry, and even for society at large. In most cases, the required systems, applications, and services can't be bought from any one supplier. Instead, they must be established by the industry participants themselves. The situation gives new meaning to the phrase "a confidence game."

Evolving Business Attitudes toward IT

Over the last twenty years, there have been two great U.S. IT booms, from 1982–1985 and from 1992–2000. Each of these expansions was followed by a significant slump, the first of which began in 1986 and lasted until 1991. During that period, I happened to be in charge of computer industry research and forecasts for International Data Corp. (IDC), which was then and is still now the principle source of industrywide IT statistics. Thus, I had a front-row seat for that particular market downturn. It was then that I first began to appreciate the importance of business confidence. The story has great relevance to the current period.

It's easy to overlook the fact that during the 1970s and 1980s, perhaps the single biggest debate in the IT industry was whether computers really did increase worker productivity, and whether there really was an adequate Return On Investment (ROI) for business IT expenditures. This issue became particularly acute during the second half of the 1980s, when many U.S. business leaders were forced to face the following dilemma: By just about every measure, U.S. companies had invested in and developed much more sophisticated information systems than their Japanese rivals, but in industry after industry, U.S.

companies seemed to be losing ground, and no one was really sure what to do about it.

Remember that in the late 1980s, many, perhaps even the majority, of business leaders came to believe that Japan had developed a superior form of global capitalism. Books such as Ezra Vogel's *Japan as Number One* (1979) and former U.S. trade representative Clyde Prestowitz's *Trading Places* (1988) were best-sellers. In 1989, the Nikkei average of Japanese stocks reached forty thousand, while the Dow was just three thousand. From our perspective, perhaps the most noticeable aspect was that while Japan was investing heavily in automated manufacturing systems, its use of IT in office-oriented, white-collar productivity systems was far less than that in the United States. Much of the Japanese business culture was still based on face-to-face meetings.

Given Japan's apparent success, it was only natural that both business and academic leaders would begin to seriously question the value of large and sustained investments in office-oriented information systems. Thus, not surprisingly, U.S. corporate investment in IT sagged considerably from 1986–1991 despite a reasonably good overall economy. Things reached such a depressing point that a number of prominent IT industry leaders as well as much of the investment community began to seriously and sometimes publicly doubt the long-term prospects for the business. Everyone was wondering whether modest single-digit IT industry growth was becoming the new norm.

For example, I can remember being in meetings with some of IBM's top strategic planners in the late 1980s and early 1990s. It's hard to imagine now, but IBM executives were seriously wrestling with the view that perhaps IT was not really such a great business after all, and that top management might be wise to prepare IBM for a low-growth and lower-profitability future. Similar sentiments were being expressed within the executive chambers of other industry leaders. Looking at the evidence then available, the customer enthusiasm regarding the value of computers often just wasn't there, and there seemed to be relatively few new areas of exciting usage.

The troubling doubts about productivity, ROI, and the future of IT really didn't really end until the 1992–1994 period when the U.S. economy began to grow rapidly, and it first became clear to the business community that the threat from Japan had been greatly exaggerated. Suddenly, streamlined U.S. companies were regaining the edge in a wide range of industries and IT began to receive a significant share of the credit. The difficulties in measuring ROI were never fully resolved, but the once-heated productivity debate almost completely faded away. (Although it has resurfaced following the 2001–2002 downturn.) CEOs and CFOs began to believe in IT again, and strong customer investments resumed.

The initial mass-market availability of the Internet in 1993–1994 coincided with this increasingly favorable view of IT. In retrospect, it appears that it was a growing economy, the powerful combination of outperforming Japan and other economic rivals, the newfound belief in the power of IT, the advanced technologies displayed in the Gulf War, and the seemingly infinite possibilities of the Internet that combined to produce the long IT boom of the 1990s. Had the Internet emerged in the late 1980s, when IT was viewed much more skeptically, the market reaction would likely have been significantly more muted.

Perhaps it was the fortuitous coming together of these five forces that made it so easy for us to forget one of the main messages of IT history. Doing important new things with computers is almost always hard, and major waves of innovation usually take a long time to prove themselves. The IT enthusiasm of the 1990s seemed to have temporarily blinded many of us to the IT industry's highly cyclical past and the long list of implementation barriers that lay ahead. In other words, business attitudes toward IT had swung full circle. In the late 1980s, they were too pessimistic, and during the late 1990s, too optimistic. Such is the power of business confidence and the resulting herd effects.

The Situation Today

Today's business attitudes are nowhere near as pessimistic as they were in the last downturn. Despite the dot-com meltdown, the belief in IT productivity has generally held firm, and advanced technology is still seen as an important U.S. competitive edge, particularly because the fundamentals of the U.S. economy—despite some debilitating scandals and other setbacks—still look strong compared to those of its main twentieth-century rivals. As long as the United States has the most competitive economy among major developed nations and is the most advanced user of technology, business leaders are likely to conclude that these two facts are related. Nevertheless, the current downturn has once again led to a renewed emphasis on productivity and ROI. Fortunately, most of the discussion is much more positive than in the previous downturn.

For example, a widely publicized 2001 study by McKinsey revived the productivity debate by arguing that, although the overall increases in U.S. productivity have been significant, nearly all of the real gains have been limited to six key sectors: retail, wholesale, securities, telecom, semiconductors, and computer manufacturing.[1] Since three of these businesses are part of the high-tech industry itself, the study isn't particularly positive about the impact of IT on the rest of the economy. Nevertheless, the study predicts continued future overall productivity improvements.

This sort of evidence is important not so much for the numbers themselves, but because of the way they help shape peoples' (especially CEOs and CFOs) minds. My own view is that, as it is generally defined, the very idea of measuring IT productivity is hopelessly flawed as an individual company decision-making tool. Nevertheless, the strength of our belief in the overall ability of IT to significantly improve worker productivity is still an important part of the customer decision-making process. These two broad and seemingly contradictory statements clearly require further explanation.

The reason that traditional productivity measurements are largely irrelevant to individual company decision making is that they take no account of improvements in quality and functionality. The seriousness of this problem can be demonstrated by the following simple example: Suppose there are just two automobile makers, both of which make cars that cost $1,000 each. Now let's also suppose that a new engine design is developed that costs exactly the same to build and install as previous engines but is twice as reliable and has twice the power. According to traditional productivity metrics, using this new engine results in no automobile industry productivity improvement, since the cost of the inputs needed to make a $1,000 vehicle has not changed.

However, clearly if one company didn't use the new engine, it would suffer disastrous competitive consequences. Thus, while the gains from a new technology may show up only in hard-to-quantify areas such as quality and function, in the real world these dimensions are every bit as important as the dollar value estimates that current productivity data are based upon. That's why the whole concept of a "productivity paradox" has always been so flawed. The problem was not that investments in IT did not improve productivity; it was that the productivity measurement tools were so clearly insufficient. Consequently, broad-based productivity statistics should be almost completely irrelevant to individual company decision making, which must respond to competitive opportunities and pressures, regardless of how well they can be measured.

This explains why studies such as McKinsey's can show no productivity gains in industries such as banking and insurance, even though it is basically impossible to run these businesses without sustained IT investments. Consider that banks have been spending heavily on IT since the 1960s, and it's entirely possible that these investments have never resulted in any traditional productivity gains, as an economist would measure them. But no one would argue the seemingly logical conclusion that banks that haven't invested in IT should be just as productive as the banks that did. One couldn't even begin to conduct such a comparison because any bank that didn't invest in IT is almost certainly no longer in business. Again, there is no logical link between traditional IT productivity data and the need to make significant IT investments.

Consequently, the only place where IT productivity statistics have real meaning is at the level of national economic data, where they can help distinguish how much of our economic growth comes from efficiency gains versus increased labor or other inputs. But even here, the statistical challenges are so daunting that even the economists directly involved are often reluctant to state their conclusions too forcefully. More important, the inability of virtually all of our national economic statistics to effectively take into account increases in quality and service means that our standard economic numbers often significantly understate society's actual economic progress. (Then again, given that spending money on prisons is included in the Gross National Product [GNP], while spending time teaching one's own children to read isn't, the actual meaning of GNP numbers is pretty suspect anyway.)

Yet despite all of these caveats and drawbacks, the idea of IT productivity is so entrenched in people's minds that studies such as McKinsey's or the occasionally supportive words of the Federal Reserve chairman still matter a great deal. They help shape business thinking regarding the value and wisdom of IT investments, and, as we have seen, such confidence has often proved critical. Thus, as long as people believe productivity statistics are meaningful, none of the shortcomings described above makes their importance any less real. We should all hope for as many positive studies and comments as possible. They are a proven way of helping us keep the necessary customer faith.

The ROI Perspective

It is also useful to extend this line of analysis to the issue of IT ROI. Certainly, many types of IT spending can be justified by the direct costs savings they can generate, and today this is a major area of IT customer focus. In tough economic times, most companies understandably give priority to money-saving measures such as cutting procurement costs, consolidating servers and storage, improving internal application integration, or using Web conferencing or e-learning to cut back on travel and training expenses. In a down market, it's easy to make internal cost savings the top priority, and to use hard one-year-or-less ROI data to rank and choose among various possible IT projects. Understandably, everyone wants to be able to show that they are making a direct contribution to the business.

However, to be useful as a long-term decision-making tool, ROI calculations must also factor in the more difficult to quantify value of quality and service improvements. If these more intangible measures are not part of the calculation, strict ROI analysis will have the same flaws as the productivity data described earlier. Additionally, many industry participants have come to realize that a great deal of supposedly hard ROI data does not stand up to close scrutiny. While consultants throw around terms such as Net Present Value, Payback Period, and Internal Rate of Return, in many cases these metrics are vulnerable to clever, subjective, and even inadvertent, statistical manipulation.

Fortunately, most businesses have come to realize this, and while projects with sufficient direct cost savings typically receive the most rapid approval, it is generally understood that they can't comprise a company's entire IT agenda. But during tough times it's particularly important to keep in mind that any company that uses IT only in areas of direct cost savings will eventually go out of business. Sometimes companies have to forget the formal ROI numbers and simply "Rely On Instinct." More typically, getting a sponsoring business unit to sign off on a new project is usually pretty good evidence that a proposed IT initiative will deliver sufficient value, whether such value can be accurately measured or not.

Businesses Have the Necessary Resources

Many readers might ask how IT customers can play an aggressive leadership role at a time of significant budgetary constraints and an uncertain economic environment. This is a fair enough question. After years of double-digit growth, IT spending in 2002 is estimated to be only around 2 percent. Given this, this particular market pullback is actually steeper than the one that began in the United States in the second half of the 1980s, when the IT agenda was not nearly as expansive as it is today. Understandably, many CIOs and other IT industry leaders have talked about the need to go back to basics, and to put the brakes on many new e-business ideas and projects.

However, unless the economy turns out to be far worse than expected, the actual IT budget reality is not nearly as bad as these numbers might suggest. Although annual growth rates of just a few percentage points may sound depressing, they come after so many years of double-digit growth that there is still an enormous amount of money available. Indeed, the frequent hand wringing regarding inadequate IT funding reminds me a bit of being a taxpayer in my home state of Massachusetts. During the long boom from 1992–2000, Massachusetts state tax revenues increased far faster than anyone ever expected. Not surprisingly, this money was spent almost as fast as it came in. Then in 2001, state tax revenues finally slowed, and suddenly "drastic cuts in essential services" had to be made. This despite the fact that 2001 tax revenues were still far higher than anyone back in, say, 1995 would have ever imagined.

In many ways, IT budgets are in a similar situation. IT managers get used to certain levels of funding and then find any change difficult to adjust to. Today's IT budgets are actually far higher than anyone ever expected them to be. Total internal and external IT spending on computers, telecommunications, and related staffing is now more than $1 trillion per year in the United States alone. One can easily argue that the modest increases of 2002 are coming on top of 1997–2000 spending levels that were significantly higher than warranted. From this perspective, today's actual budgets are not low at all. If you had asked a typical IT director in 1997 whether the current 2002 or 2003 budget would be adequate, he or she would have been impressed. This is why the current drop-off can be numerically steeper than in previous downturns without necessarily being as drastic. It's not as if IT departments are without significant resources.

Additionally, only about 15 to 20 percent of today's total IT spending by large and medium-size companies is e-business related, with the rest being spent on legacy and other largely internal systems. Consequently, even small shifts away from internal projects toward external initiatives can make significant additional funds available. Consider a hypothetical environment in which e-business applications account for 20 percent of a company's total IT spending. Simple arithmetic says that for such a firm, a 5 percent reduction in non-e-business spending can fund a 20 percent increase in e-business investment without any change in total company expenditures. In short, a small shift in priorities from internal to external projects can make a huge overall difference. Many companies are trying to address the funding issue in this way.

There are three other important reasons why current funding should not be as big a problem as many in the industry have claimed. First, roughly half of all company IT spending goes to salaries, mostly for programmers and related software professionals. The salaries of most technical professionals went up rapidly during the dot-com boom, as talent shortages resulted in a strong seller's market and frequent bidding wars. With the demise of so many dot-coms, this is clearly no longer the case, and salary pressures have declined significantly across much of the United States. In a global economy that is often more concerned with deflation than inflation, overall salary levels could trend downward for several years without reversing all of the big gains of the dot-com boom. This will be especially likely if the use of offshore technical talent in countries such as India continues to grow.

Second, IT budgets shouldn't be as debilitating a factor as some have argued because many of the most important IT projects of the next few years are not necessarily cash intensive. Implementing new industry standards, cooperative systems, Web Services, and many other important new applications will not necessarily require huge investments in new hardware, software, and networks. Even in the case of business exchanges where significant new spending is often required, the costs can be shared by a number of participants. One of the surviving benefits of the Internet bubble is that a great deal of IT infrastructure has been put into place. This means that many new applications may not require large new capital investments.

Finally, if dedicated IT budgets do prove inadequate, there is always the option of getting additional funding from other company divisions such as product development, sales, and marketing, which usually have the authority to transfer resources from traditional offline activities to e-business alternatives. This is already a major source of IT funding and makes the potential supply of money almost unlimited. The bottom line is that the United States is now a $10-trillion economy. The only truly limiting factor is our overall confidence regarding what can be done with IT. If business leaders really want to find the money, they should be able to do so.

Of course, none of this is meant to minimize the challenges in the IT industry today. Companies face a bewildering array of IT possibilities and decisions. Additionally, in the post-September 11 environment, considerably more IT spending is being allocated to back-up systems and operational security, and this spending is clearly affecting the resources available for other IT projects. For example, a number of companies are looking at entirely "peopleless" data centers, which could continue operation even in the face of a biological or chemical attack. Such capabilities will require substantial new investments.

Nevertheless, unless today's low-single-digit budget increases persist for several more years, as they did from 1986–1991, the absolute level of funding should not be the IT industry's biggest concern. With some exceptions, the real questions have to do with individual company strategies, confidence, and commitment. During the last downturn, IT customers may have had their doubts, but the supplier community kept innovating, and thanks to improved U.S. competitiveness and then the Internet, eventually strong growth returned. The question today is whether customers will continue to innovate through the current downturn. As of this writing, short-term thinking is clearly the dominant pattern.

However, from a longer-term perspective, the picture is significantly more positive. While the Internet era is proving once again that new computer advancements rarely happen quickly, history tells us that problems during this initial launch period are perfectly normal, and that the second decade of a new platform will likely be much more impressive and lucrative than the first. This is perhaps reason enough for a strong sense of overall industry optimism. The issues faced by the IT industry today are no more daunting than those of the past. Of the many barriers to growth that exist today, very few seem insurmountable, as long as the necessary confidence remains in place.

Economic and Product Cycle Issues

Given the inevitable lag time in producing a book such as this, writing about the overall business climate has its perils. Although this book does not in any way seek to forecast the growth and health of the U.S. economy (let alone the global one), it does make the case that in order for the IT business to fulfill its potential, certain changes in customer behavior need to occur. Clearly, any progress the IT industry makes on the frontiers described in this book will have significant market growth implications. However, since the growth of the IT business is also affected by the health of the overall economy, technology issues alone can never be decisive. A broad economic recovery would clearly give the IT industry a significant boost. (Then again, in the event of renewed domestic terrorism or a major war, any such trends become, at least temporarily, irrelevant.)

In addition to the strength of the economy and prevailing business attitudes toward IT, supplier product cycles have historically been the third major determinant of IT industry growth. Indeed, there was a time when these cycles were actually the most important industry force. However, the theory of this book predicts that the relative importance of vendor activity should decline in a customer-centric era, and this certainly appears to be the case.

For example, from the 1960s through the early 1980s, IBM mainframes constituted such a dominant portion of the IT market that the introduction of new IBM machines tended to drive new cycles of industry growth. After a year or two, this growth typically ended as those machines aged and customers began anticipating a replacement generation. Major new generations of minicomputers and PCs, along with the emergence of LANs, were also all examples of product-led growth, which was either fueled or tempered by the overall economic environment and current customer attitudes toward IT.

In contrast, the Internet boom began not because of any supplier product, other than arguably Internet browsers, which were mostly free. Instead, the Internet was an unexpected gift from the public to the commercial sector. Ever since, the importance of new products has receded. Over the last two years, many high-profile IT supplier efforts to stimulate IT sales have increasingly given the impression of someone pushing eagerly on a rope. New products and technologies simply haven't gotten the market response they once did. This is certainly the case in traditional IT sectors such PCs and servers, where the release of Windows XP, new Pentiums, and new server operating systems have been largely taken in stride, and can no longer be counted on to create significant new customer demand.

But these supplier limitations also seem to have spread into new technology domains as well. Clearly, telecom vendors hoped that rapidly improving network bandwidth would provide the sort of impetus that ever-improving PCs once did. However, because of the lack of compelling applications, most consumers have not felt an urgent need to upgrade their home-based Internet services. Similarly, whereas the packaged software industry created much of the new value that mainframe, minicomputer, and PC customers required, the importance of applications software has been surpassed by customer-created Web-based offerings. More recently, major supplier initiatives such as Microsoft's .Net have had little direct connection to increased customer spending activity.

In short, supplier ability to drive IT usage has declined significantly, and thus, almost by definition, the fate of the IT industry is in customers' hands to a much greater extent than ever before. This certainly does not mean that, barring customer breakthroughs, the IT industry is destined to remain in a serious slump. But it does mean that sustained long-term double-digit growth is unlikely without the overtly positive actions of major IT customers. In essence, there are now three main market growth variables: the economy, customer leadership (broadly defined to include government, educational institutions, and consumers), and supplier product cycles. The first is basically unpredictable; the second is on the rise, and the third is steadily shrinking in importance. Consequently, it follows that over the next five years or so, IT customer dynamics will emerge as the most fruitful area of IT industry analysis.

CHAPTER SIX

Web Services and
Semantic Applications

THE KEY THEME of this book has been that the leadership required by the IT industry has usually been provided by suppliers, but this burden is now shifting to customers. In the following chapters, I'll provide many specific examples of where this leadership is needed. But perhaps the most telling example of this shift is the unprecedented degree to which customers are now shaping the evolution of information technology itself. This change will be the focus of this chapter.

Consider that two of the most significant Next Big Thing concepts on the Web today are Web Services and Semantic Applications. Both are potentially major advances in the way IT is used, and both will be a key part of the business, education, consumer, and government analyses that follow. In this chapter, I'll explain what these concepts are and why they are so important. But the primary purpose will be to show why the transition from Web Services to truly Semantic Applications will mark a major handoff between the supplier- and customer-driven worlds. For the first time, the establishment of major new computer capabilities is becoming primarily a customer responsibility.

During what will be a sometimes complex analysis, Web Services will be portrayed as part of a long tradition of major supplier-led initiatives, each characterized by a great deal of promotion and hype, along with many important new acronyms and standards. In contrast, Semantic Applications will be shown to be predominantly a customer challenge, with vendors playing a supporting but more secondary role. This difference is telling since, despite all the hype, Web Services should really be seen as just a stepping-stone to the larger goal of developing truly intelligent Semantic Applications. This type of multiphase transition has been a common industry pattern, as shown in table 6-1.

Similarities and Differences

Given that Web Services and Semantic Applications are actually two steps along the same path, it's not surprising that they both have a lot in common. Both ideas signal a Web community that is beginning to take on much more advanced information management challenges. Whereas much of the work on the Web to date has been a matter of delivering text and images to relatively dumb Internet browsers, both Web Services and Semantic Applications will require much higher levels of information and application standardization. This increasing focus on content and usage will inevitably push the Web itself deeper into specific customer domains, with important implications for the structure and dynamics of a wide range of industries.

For example, one of the more immediate benefits of Web Services is to make it easier for enterprises to rapidly enhance and integrate their IT applications without extensive in-house programming. Enthusiasts see a world in which highly flexible internal, business partner, and third-party applications can easily talk to one another, both accelerating innovation and lowering costs. From this perspective, Web Services are designed to alleviate many of the headaches involved in developing,

TABLE 6 - 1

Stages of IT Industry Standards

Previous IT platforms have had to go through several iterations and often a decade or more before they reached their full potential. XML and its subsequent uses in Web Services and Semantic Applications will likely follow the same pattern.

	PC Operating Systems	Internet Communications	Content/Application Platforms
1st Generation	CP/M	ARPANET	XML
Growth Generation	MS-DOS	FTP, Gopher, WAIS	Web Services
Pervasive Generation	Windows	HTTP, HTML	Semantic Applications

updating, and integrating business applications, but without necessarily transforming the actual customer or end-user experience.

In contrast, the need for Semantic Applications stems from the fact that, just as different protocols and operating systems have made computers incompatible in the past, so do different terminology, definitions, and languages retard information interoperability today. In order for text and data to flow seamlessly between applications and organizations, a new generation of content-oriented standards needs to emerge. Such standards could make Web usage much more systematic and predictable, more like a structured database transaction than today's search and browse metaphor. While Web Services can make many IT processes more efficient, truly semantic systems can result in an entirely new range of capabilities. Additionally, unlike most Web Services, Semantic Applications can also create an important new set of information-based assets.

In both cases, significant new capabilities will clearly be required. Both Web Services and Semantic Applications are based on the Extensible Markup Language (XML), which has already emerged as a platform likely to be every bit as important as Microsoft Windows and the core Internet standards of HTML, HTTP, and TCP/IP. XML and its many supporting concepts will make it possible for applications and information to effectively communicate. Not surprisingly, these new platforms are being heavily promoted by many of today's leading IT suppliers. From a vendor perspective, Web Services can be seen as the next phase of computer network design, much as client/server computing was in the late 1980s, and Internet networking in the 1990s.

Yet in many ways this aggressive supplier promotion is misleading. The reality is that both Web Services and especially Semantic Applications are highly customer-centric in nature in that they represent major new Web capabilities, but require only modest investments in new technology. Unlike previous generations of Web development, these next phases won't require huge new spending on servers, routers, and bandwidth. Sometimes, they won't even require major new investment in software. Typically, a customer's biggest expense will be for its own information management efforts. In other words, the key to both concepts is not so much their underlying technology, but the basic IT practices that customers are being asked to master. In this way, they are much more of a "customer implementation frontier" than the traditional "supplier technology frontier." Let's see why by looking at each of these two concepts more closely.

Defining Web Services

Although the term *Web Services* might be familiar to many readers, it still needs to be carefully defined. Unfortunately, the phrase has been used to describe a wide range of different things. Much of the definitional problem stems from the word *services* itself, which is without doubt the most overworked word in the IT business. Even before the Internet, the extensive use of this word had become problematic. Consider the widespread use of terms such as professional services, maintenance services, processing services, value-added network services, carrier services, disaster recovery services, outsourcing services, training and education services, and many more "services" types.

The Web has made this problem even worse. We now have the so-called XSPs—Internet Service Providers, Application Service Providers, Managed Service Providers, and so on. In addition, there are Web hosting services, messaging services, wireless Internet services, and a vast range of other activities that have all at one time or another been grouped under the heading of Web Services. No wonder we sometimes get trapped in our own terminology. Clearly, both the word *services* and the phrase *Web Services* must be used carefully or precise meanings will be lost. (That's why this phrase is capitalized throughout this book, reinforcing that a specific definition is being used.) Believe it or not, I've even heard industry participants talk about the "Web Services services" business, meaning companies that provide services to Web Services companies.

In light of all of this, what does the market mean by its current emphasis on Web Services? Today, there seem to be three main types of activities that are often referred to as Web Services, all of which are different, although, as with many things on the Web, they are somewhat interrelated. Let's look at each of these, and then define how this term will be used for the rest of this work.

1. **Replacing packaged software with Web Services.** This is a broad industry trend that has been recognized and commented on since at least 1996, hence all of the hype regarding Applications Service Providers (ASPs). Clearly, in some market segments, ASPs have replaced the need for packaged software for both technology services and business applications. For example, e-mail, Web-based teleconferencing, and instant messaging are all areas in which,

instead of buying a software product, customers can use various third-party services. Similarly, business application companies such as Salesforce.com and Employease provide Web-based alternatives to packaged software for CRM and HR applications, respectively. The ASP approach is clearly viable and will certainly grow, but it's not really new and in many areas has yet to take hold, and therefore it can't really be seen as the IT industry's Next Big Thing.

2. **The Web as a service utility.** This is the most philosophical of the three main uses, and this idea has also been around for quite some time. Since at least 1995, many industry leaders have been forecasting that—as with the electrical power, water, and telephony grids—companies will increasingly move away from the idea of owning and operating their own technology environments. Instead, they will acquire processing power, storage capacity, and communications bandwidth as needed from various service providers who will build and operate large IT infrastructures designed to support many customers. However, while some movement in this direction is inevitable, the utility analogy is only partially valid. Computers are not just like water or electricity, which one turns on and off. They also resemble automobiles in that they are something that most of us need to learn to operate and use for our own ends. In short, there is a lot more going on than just plugging in, and therefore a major shift toward the utility model remains unlikely.

3. **Web Service components.** Finally, Web Services can be defined as interoperable Internet modules. For example, at its Web site, IBM defines *Web Services* as "self-contained modular applications that can be described, published, located and invoked over a network, generally the World Wide Web."[1] Sometimes this definition sounds similar to the ASP concept described above, especially since similar applications are often used as examples for both concepts. However, the Internet component definition takes the ASP idea one step further by requiring that Web Services can be easily integrated with other Web-based systems. In contrast, most ASPs operate essentially as stand-alone services, although this may well change over time, at which point ASPs and Web Services could often be one and the same.

It is this interoperable component definition that is now being heavily promoted by major suppliers such as IBM, Sun, and Microsoft, as well as specialized players such as Bowstreet, Iona, and many others, and it is this definition that this chapter will address. To start, let's explore the sorts of Web Services applications that seem most likely to emerge and how these might transform the structure, composition, and dynamics of a wide range of industry sectors. We will then show how Web Services are really just the first step toward an increasingly semantic World Wide Web.

Web Services Applications

Much has been written about the difficulties in effectively implementing Web Services. The three biggest concerns seem to be that suppliers will once again fail to deliver the promised standards and interoperability, the required in-house staff will not be sufficiently available or affordable, and there will be serious security challenges. All of these issues are, of course, greatly compounded when dealing with systems that span more than one organization. Not surprisingly, many customers are taking a cautious approach. But while these obstacles are formidable, they also have a reasonably good chance of being overcome. Thanks to organizations such as the W3C, the standards process is much more robust and reliable than in previous IT eras. Additionally, IT professionals have a strong career incentive to master the ins and outs of Web Services just as they have with many previous new software concepts. Finally, there are many useful initial applications for which security is not necessarily a prohibitive barrier. So let's assume that these issues don't get completely in the way. What will customers actually do with all of this new capability?

Some of the Web Services applications that have received significant mention are summarized in table 6-2, where they are grouped into three main categories—internal applications, technology services, and external content/applications services. Of these, the latter two will ultimately be the most important. Although more effective internal integration is the dominant form of Web Services usage today, and can result in both significant cost savings and more rapid application development, internal improvements alone are unlikely to move the industry to new levels of usage. Typically, it's external services that can reshape the way businesses operate and that can create major opportunities for new value creation. External services also tend to have the more powerful and longer lasting industry benefits, as shown in chapter 4.

Of course, many viable external Web Services already exist. Certainly, news feeds and other forms of content syndication meet the criteria of an easily accessed and inserted component, as do various online credit-card processing systems or money transfer services such as PayPal. Similarly, many Web Services boosters have talked about familiar applications such as stock quotations, weather reports, travel information, exchange rate calculations, maps, and directions. But these are all traditional ASP-style services that have been around for almost as long as the dot-com industry itself. They're great for developing consumer portals, but how important are they to most businesses? What we are really looking for are new types of specialized Web Services that can be plugged into existing mainstream business applications as Web-based components.

TABLE 6 - 2

Representative "Web Services"

While some of these services overlap with earlier dot-com–style offerings, the key conceptual difference is that Web Services are designed to be delivered as components that can be easily integrated with other applications.

Internal Applications	Technology Services	External Content/ Applications Services
Integration of Web with legacy systems	E-mail	Online procurement
Exposing internal information assets	Instant messaging	Online auctions
Corporate portals	Web conferencing	Billing services
Intranet infrastructure	Streaming media	Credit evaluation
Merger integration	Voice over IP	e-Logistics
Faster development	Collaboration	Syndicated content
Reusable components	Security/back-up	e-Learning
	Single sign-on	Business intelligence
	Authentication	Mobile worker support
	Integrated search	Portal services

The Need for Structural Change

Taking advantage of these types of Web Services will require that previously integrated business activities be broken down into their particular components. For example, a commonly cited Web Services candidate is a company's billing system. In a Web Services environment, a billing system, complete with collections, could become a separate service provided by a third party over the Internet, and then automatically inserted back into a customer's larger financial reporting system. This would enable a company to take advantage of the latest billing and collection systems, ideas, and tactics, ideally without rewriting any existing application code.

This example suggests that companies hoping to aggressively adopt Web Services, will, as other IT sectors have in the past, need to move from more vertically integrated business processes to an increasing horizontal value-chain approach. In other words, it's possible that eventually all of the services listed in table 6-2 will be provided by specialized companies that focus on billing, procurement, content, auctions, conferencing, back-up, business intelligence, streaming media, instant messaging, and so on. It's a classic example of how new technological models can result in a new generation of companies.

This is why the future of Web Services is so closely tied to the issue of how the Internet will ultimately reshape the dynamics of particular industries. As shown in figure 6-1, the key question is whether these technological advances will eventually lead to a more horizontal structure in many portions of the economy. As explained in chapter 2, horizontal IT specialization can result in many important benefits since companies can focus on their core competencies and third-party service providers can take advantage of much greater IT economies of scale. However, as we saw throughout part 1, the timing and extent of this type of large-scale business or industry "dis-integration" is not easy to predict, and the required changes can often be wrenching. Nevertheless, few IT issues will tell us more about the competitive dynamics of this customer-driven period.

Let's begin with the fact that there are really two areas of potential dis-integration—within the IT department and across the business itself. While these two options are certainly not mutually exclusive, they

FIGURE 6 - 1

The Potential for Customer Dis-Integration

From a structural perspective, the overall impact of Web Services will be determined by the degree to which they replace integrated internal activities with specialized externally provided services.

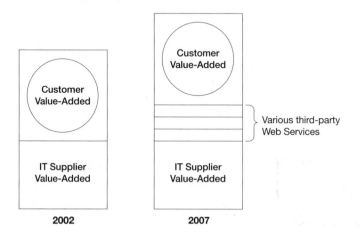

are different enough that they could easily evolve in different ways. We'll start with the potential for change within today's IT department, since this is the most familiar and simpler area of ongoing IT evolution.

Dis-Integration and the IT Department

Web Services will likely continue to push IT departments toward a more horizontal approach because, despite occasionally significant counter-currents, this is where most IT groups and their corporate bosses are already headed. The long-term trend toward outsourcing (and the closely related concept of managed services) has been going on for nearly twenty years and has been driven by a number of factors, including the desire to cut or at least control IT costs, the wish to reduce IT management and staff complexity, and the need for more rapid access to the latest technologies and/or skills.

From a wider business perspective, the extensive use of outsourcing provides the IT industry with much better economies of scale and much more effective leveraging of industry talent. As the years go by, it becomes increasingly self-evident that it doesn't make sense and is probably not even physically possible for every company in every nation to build and maintain its own systems, networks, and IT staffs on a 24/7 basis. That's why the overall case for outsourcing has always been strong; it makes for a more robust and efficient IT industry.

That said, a large-scale shift to Web Services by the traditional IT department is clearly not going to happen overnight, or even over a few years. As with most entrenched organizations, enterprise IT groups have an interest in preserving their own staffs and operations, and thus pure economics are not always sufficient to drive significant change, especially when the economic case is not always completely clear cut. For example, while it once appeared that certain applications—such as e-mail and Web hosting—should be outsourced, many companies are now glad that they kept these functions in-house.

This understandable inertia has been substantially reinforced by the collapse of the dot-com industry, which exposed many forms of outsourcing as being much more risky than previously realized. More pointedly, the demise of the dot-coms has, in and of itself, seriously diminished the prospects for the rapid growth of Web Services. Small, rapidly growing dot-coms without large investments in internal systems and people were the ideal prospects for many Web Services, just as they were for ASPs. But since the buying power of these firms has shrunk so dramatically, it is now the more established companies that will determine the overall rate of both Web Services and ASP acceptance. And it's hard to see why these companies won't take a more conservative approach than the dot-coms would have. Historically, aggressive IT outsourcing has been mostly associated with companies either growing very rapidly or in considerable financial trouble.

Thus, the mostly likely scenario is that while many new Web Services will be outsourced, changes in existing systems will be much more gradual. This suggests that technology-based services such as instant messaging, Voice over IP, and Web conferencing will tend to be provided by specialized providers, and emerge as important new areas of industry growth. However, the dis-integration of mainstream enterprise financial, production, and customer-service applications will take substantially longer, since the advantages enjoyed by external providers are relatively small, and the pain and risks of change are relatively great. This issue is explored further in the section that follows.

Dis-Integration at a Corporate Level

Of course, the potential for Web Services is not limited to the way IT re-sources are managed. Indeed, we certainly wouldn't need all of today's hype and promotion just to raise the issue of technology outsourcing. The real change, if it is to come, will have to be in the fundamental structure of companies and even the economy itself. Many Web Services advocates have argued that by increasing the flow of information and lowering trans-action costs, the Web will eventually create a much more specialized hor-izontal economy in the United States and other technologically advanced nations. According to this scenario, longer, more integrated value chains will become the dominant economic pattern as specific business processes evolve into specialized third-party offerings. This is certainly the sort of long-term mega-trend that is worthy of consideration and debate.

But wait a minute. Haven't we just been here? Didn't we see in chap-ter 2 that a huge part of the dot-com boom was based on the belief that the Internet would rapidly shift many economic sectors to a much more horizontal approach, and didn't we just see that this belief often proved disastrously wrong? In many ways, the most aggressive pro-moters of Web Services are making claims that, at least on the surface, seem quite similar to those of the now mostly defunct dot-coms, includ-ing once again frequent references to the works of Ronald Coase. How-ever, before dismissing this view as a case of déjà vu all over again (to use Yogi Berra's classic phrase), it's important to point out that there are several significant distinctions.

The most important of these differences is that much of the dot-com enthusiasm for the horizontal model was based on the belief that com-panies such as eToys and Webvan would rapidly make their brick and mortar predecessors obsolete. Not surprisingly, Web Services enthusi-asts have largely dropped this now discredited vision and replaced it with the view that, although the old guard has triumphed, it is about to be revolutionized from within. In other words, Web Services enthusi-asts predict that companies will increasingly become a composite of other companies' services, just as PC makers have become the final as-semblers of the specialized components of others, or as companies in many industries have often outsourced much of their manufacturing. This outsourcing of key corporate functions is often referred to as Busi-ness Process Outsourcing (BPO).

This type of transformation is certainly an intellectually interesting vision, and one that in the long term will likely prove more right than wrong. There are clearly significant scale economies and efficiencies that only horizontal specialization can deliver, and ever-improving Web standards are making it increasingly possible for new services to be more easily integrated into a wider company offering. Overall, these forces do seem stronger than those that are pushing the economy in the opposite direction toward a more vertically integrated model. Fifty years from now, IT historians will likely conclude that the rise of Web Services did lead to a more horizontal global economy.

Indeed, unless there is some sort of military or social disaster, it's almost unimaginable that the alternative would prove to be the case. The reality is that industry value chains have been lengthening for literally thousands of years, as information, communications, and transportation infrastructures have evolved. This is why Coase's argument is so fundamentally and undeniably correct. Moreover, there is little reason to think that this pattern is about to suddenly grind to a halt. Thus, the real question is how quickly and extensively this type of horizontal change will occur.

As we have seen, the manner in which major industries have disintegrated into their horizontal layers has varied greatly over the years, but unless there is some sort of decisive government or market event, change tends to happen gradually. This is likely to be the case with Web Services. For example, in July 2002 IDC forecasted that the worldwide BPO market will grow from roughly $700 billion (in 2001) to $1.2 trillion in 2006, a compound annual growth rate of some 11 percent per year. If this rate of change proves accurate, one can legitimately say that the horizontal model is steadily taking hold. And while most BPO efforts do not currently rely on Web Services, the two concepts will become increasingly interrelated over time.

Looking ahead, it's not hard to envision a two step process whereby the initial outsourcing of various processes by individual businesses eventually leads to the emergence of more specialized service companies. This pattern whereby new companies emerge at the end of the process, not the beginning, will be repeated many times over the rest of this work. That's why Web Services are such a good example of how tomorrow's digital economy is now in its formative years.

Defining Semantic Applications

Despite the power of Web Services, emerging standards such as XML and SOAP (Simple Object Access Protocol) are really only capable of facilitating some of the tasks at hand. They are basically just the conduits through which information can flow. To achieve true computer-to-computer interoperability, business terminology itself has to become much more standardized. And it is here that the concept of Semantic Applications starts to emerge. The challenges in this area are often as great as or even greater than those with Web Services, but then again, so are the potential rewards. From this book's perspective, the rise of Semantic Applications is perhaps the strongest evidence yet that the IT industry is becoming truly customer-led. Semantic systems represent a whole new frontier of activity where traditional IT suppliers will play a significant but clearly secondary role.

Given that Semantic Applications will often be built on top of Web Services, it's not surprising that the two concepts share a common technical foundation. Most Semantic Applications work is also based on XML and other Web Services standards, only with some additional rules and structures that enable consistent information definitions and usage. This supporting infrastructure is generally provided through what are known as Resource Description Frameworks (RDF). As with Web Services, there are many Web sites that provide excellent explanations of RDFs, at just about any level of reader sophistication.

Additionally, like Web Services, almost everything having to do with the phrase *Semantic Applications* needs to be defined carefully. In this case, the word *semantic,* which is strange enough to most us, is often used in two different but important ways. Sometimes it refers to "intelligent" Web applications capable of essentially "understanding" each other. At other times, it refers to better ways to manage and use ever-rising quantities of digital information. However, both uses point toward an IT industry increasingly concerned with information and content standards. Indeed, for really the first time, the overall IT standards emphasis is rising above hardware and network infrastructure, and even many forms of software. Increasingly, it's all about the information itself.

This is why the word *semantic* is so appropriate. My thirty-year old *Webster's Seventh New Collegiate Dictionary* defines semantic as "of or relating to meaning in language." Unfortunately, most of us, if we use the word at all, do so in a pejorative sense, such as "let's stop talking semantics" or "enough semantics, let's get to the point." It's hard to think of semantic being used in any other popular context, certainly not any positive ones. Nonetheless, over the next few years many of us will be using this term regularly. To see why, let's start by fleshing out the two main ways that the term *Semantic Applications* is used. We will see that the task of managing content is already well underway and primarily evolutionary in nature. In contrast, the development and use of intelligent applications is still much more speculative, but has the potential to become a major new source of IT value and usage.

Managing content. Whether the base of business information is doubling every six months, every year, or every other year doesn't really matter. It's increasing very fast, and companies have to take steps to maintain control. This is particularly the case for so-called unstructured data: information, primarily text, that has not traditionally been part of any formal database system. Clearly, the Web and e-mail have increased the quantities of unstructured information at an extraordinary rate, and IT suppliers are responding accordingly. For example, leading database companies such as IBM, Oracle, and Microsoft are pushing to be able to manage both structured and unstructured information as a single information repository.

Additionally, over the last few years the concepts of Web Content Management (WCM) and Enterprise Content Management (ECM) have emerged as strategies to control the production, publishing, updating, and accessibility of unstructured content, often merging with traditional forms of document and knowledge management. When used in these content management contexts, Semantic Applications usually refers to the methods, software tools, and services that are used to help classify and manage unstructured enterprise information, typically with the goal of making important information more readily accessible and usable. It's a very active area of new products and service development.

Intelligent applications. In contrast, intelligent applications require that two different computers effectively "understand" each other, a fundamental change from the way the Web operates today. For example, today's

HTML-based Web is conceptually much like the postal system in that the computers that send and receive Web pages typically have no knowledge regarding the content that is being transmitted. In contrast, a truly intelligent Web application could behave as if it actually understood terms such as price, product, availability, name, address, and date. With these types of capabilities and standards, computers should be able to sift through information and process transactions in a much more systematic way.

The idea of widespread semantic standards has gotten a tremendous boost from none other than Tim Berners-Lee, the primary architect of today's Web, and now the director of the W3C. Since the late 1990s, Berners-Lee has been using the phrase *Semantic Web* to describe a Web increasingly capable of interpreting its vast range of content. As we shall see, should this ambitious idea come anywhere close to fruition, all sorts of important new uses would likely emerge, as the hundreds of millions of computers on the Web become capable of really communicating with one another. The range of possible Semantic Web applications is shown by the examples below

1. The greatly enhanced ability to automate specific tasks such as price comparisons that can correctly identify a product and a selected feature set

2. Much more interoperable business-to-business supply chain and exchange applications based around standardized product, sales, and delivery information

3. Improved search systems that could, for example, reliably distinguish a request for a high school photograph of Martin Luther King, Jr. from a request for a photograph of Martin Luther King Junior High School

4. Improved system interoperability, for example, a semantically-enabled Computer-Aided Design and Manufacturing (CAD/CAM) system that could understand the manufacturing requirements of a particular design and link directly to a parts-and-inventory system that could then automatically generate overall materials requirements and their related costs, all from the initial design

5. Greatly improved handling of multiple national languages (even the ability to identify simple fields, such as addresses, product names, and specifications, would be helpful)

In each of these examples, shared terminology that is understood by two or more applications is required. As shown in figure 6-2, this typically requires some degree of content reengineering that gives words and their usage much more specific and unambiguous meanings, a major change from the essentially unstructured and content-neutral way the Web works today. Over the course of part 2, we will see how industry-specific information standards can be of great value in areas as diverse as music, advertising, business exchanges, learning, and government services. They can help transform the use of unstructured information into much more of a transaction-like experience, what I like to refer to as "transactional reading."

Understanding Semantic Terminology

Although managing enterprise content and building intelligent applications would seem to be very different things, they share some common terminology. The main concepts in both areas can be described through four intimidating words, three of which, like the word semantics itself, are derived from ancient Greek, and one from Latin. Since the following terms are becoming increasingly important to many IT

FIGURE 6 - 2

The Shift toward Enhanced Content

In the first phase of Internet growth, existing forms of content were made available via the Web. But increasingly, customers must reengineer content to take advantage of key Internet standards and capabilities.

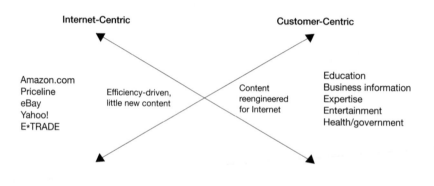

industry participants, it's worth starting off with their actual definitions. (The Greek roots also come right out of the Webster's dictionary cited earlier.[2])

Metadata. This basically means "data about data," from the Greek *Meta,* meaning "among, with, after," and sometimes "change." When meta is used along with the name of a subject or discipline, it usually indicates a new field that deals conceptually with the original one. Metaphysics, metamathematics, and metadata are good examples of this type of usage. XML tags are now the most prominent form of IT metadata, but the use of metadata certainly predates the existence of computers. The traditional library card catalog is an excellent example of low-tech but very effective metadata.

Today, most large-scale metadata creation efforts are automated via software, but manual and/or hybrid systems are still sometimes required. And, while many companies have yet to begin this process, there is a great deal of work being done by international standards groups, industry specific associations, and even open-source communities. Indeed, over time and without much fanfare, a vast new infrastructure of information categorization standards is being built, often with little direct involvement of the IT supplier community. In subsequent chapters, we will see that accurate and consistent metadata will be one of the keys to many new forms of both improved content management and more intelligent Web applications.

Taxonomy. This term traditionally refers to the study of the general principles of classification, and comes from the Greek, *taxi,* meaning "arrangement," and *nomy,* from the Greek *nemein,* meaning "to distribute." Although IT industry use of the word *taxonomy* has grown substantially in recent years, to be honest, the term is rarely used in its proper scientific sense. Widespread use of this term began in biology and the life sciences, where taxonomies are used to rigorously and uniquely classify living species. In contrast, business taxonomies (the most famous of which is the simple topic hierarchies used by Yahoo!) are mostly used to classify documents, which often need to be accessible through multiple paths.

Nevertheless, the word taxonomy is now widely used to describe computer-based systems that use hierarchies of topics to help users sift through information. Many companies have developed their own taxonomies, although there are also an increasing number of industry standard offerings. Additionally, a number of suppliers, including Applied Semantics, Autonomy, Verity, and Semio, provide taxonomy-building software. Today, business taxonomies are mostly used for managing content, but they will eventually drive intelligent applications as well. However, this latter type of usage will often require information to be defined more rigorously and mutually exclusively, in the more traditional scientific sense of taxonomy. This leads us to the idea of ontologies.

Ontology. This is a word that many businesspeople may have heard of but few can actually define. The word stems from the Greek *ont-*, the present participle of *einai*, meaning "to be," and *logos*, the Greek for "word." To philosophers, ontology is a branch of metaphysics focused on the nature of being, certainly among the most rarefied of topics. From an IT industry perspective, the word *ontology* was first used by artificial intelligence researchers and then the Web community to describe the linguistic specifications needed to help computers effectively share information and knowledge. In both cases, ontologies are used to define "the things and rules that exist" within a respective domain. In this sense, an ontology is like a rigorous taxonomy that also understands the relationships between the various classified items.

For example, there are basically five main types of streetlights—red, flashing red, yellow, flashing yellow, and green. These colors could be said to define a simple traffic light taxonomy or classification system. However, each light is also associated with a set of rules—go, stop, slow down. This combination of a taxonomy and its predefined properties results in a simple traffic system ontology. While this distinction is real enough, many IT industry participants do use the two terms largely interchangeably. Some even use the expressions *light* and *heavy ontologies,* the former being just a taxonomy, the latter including both the taxonomy and its associated properties. My own view is that it would be great if we used the word ontology when referring to carefully defined intelligent applications, and taxonomy when we're just organizing and sifting through content. However, since most people can't use either term without feeling pretentious, we're a long way from having this level of generally understood language. To most of us, it's pretty much all still a matter of semantics.

Objects. For those organizations that deal with long documents—such as books, manuals, courses, and training programs—semantic systems also provide a way of managing large numbers of discrete "information objects," which I like to define as the smallest unit of text, image, sound, video, or data that is both useful and self-contained. These "chunks" of content could be advice for dealing with a certain problem, training in a specific area, a self-contained passage from a book or article, a song from a CD, or a useful bit of legal or medical expertise. The process of breaking up a larger collection of content into directly addressable, self-contained objects is often referred to as "content chunking." Easily accessible chunks of content are an essential part of turning today's often imprecise and inaccurate Web searches into a more reliable, transactional experience, especially in education and other fields with many long documents. In this context, taxonomies can be used to help individuals efficiently locate and sift through large numbers of discrete objects.

Emerging Information Standards

One of the amazing things about Semantic Applications is that once one begins to see the world in this way, the need for information standardization begins to appear just about everywhere. Certainly many types of business information could benefit from shared intra-company, intra-industry, and even inter-industry terminology, and today just about every major industry has some sort of standardization effort. Groups such as RosettaNet (electronics), STEP (manufacturing), Acord (insurance), Medbiquitous (medical), Chematch (chemicals), the Open Travel Alliance (Travel), and STAR (automotive) are typical of literally dozens of industry-specific efforts to define unique information standards. Many of these efforts are either formally part of or work in close conjunction with various business exchanges, since shared terminology and information formats will be such an important part of many of these endeavors. The recent merger between RosettaNet and the retail-oriented Uniform Code Council is an important example of the need for broad industry cooperation.

Not surprisingly, there are also equally important cross-industry committees, associations, and consortia. These organizations exist because many terms—such as names, addresses, and phone numbers—tend to be used in just about every business, and therefore cross-industry standardization is also very important. Among these groups are the ebXML (Electronic Business XML) efforts of OASIS (Organization for the Advancement of Structured Information Standards) and the so-called Dublin Core Metadata Initiative (that's Dublin, OH, by the way). The W3C is also heavily involved through its overall XML and Semantic Web support. Of particular long-term interest is the Defense Advanced Research Projects Agency's (DARPA) so-called DAML (DARPA Agent Markup Language) project. As the group most directly responsible for the initial funding that led to the Internet, DARPA's work is always worthy of special attention. DAML is envisioned as an extension to both HTML and XML, designed to support the inclusion of ontologies.

International organizations, including even the United Nations (through its Universal Standard Products and Services Classification, UN/SPSC), the International Standards Organization (ISO), and the IEEE (through its Standard Upper Ontology Study Group) are also getting involved. Many of these organizations are working together in one way or another. Indeed, if anything, there are too many overlapping groups, which is why lead customers in particular business areas are still so important. Many companies will be more than happy to have a clear path to follow. Unlike most IT vendor standards, customer-created metadata standards themselves are not typically seen as a major competitive battleground. On the other hand, as we shall see in the music, education, and other industries, the effective *use* of these standards can become an important area of competitive advantage.

In general, however, there is not a lot of money to be made in these areas right now. Nevertheless, participants believe that standardized business terminology will eventually emerge as essential industrywide platforms, upon which new services will be built. The fact that it is now human language itself, not computer programs, that needs to be standardized lends a level of both intellectual interest and potential long-term significance. While effective development and implementation are by no means guaranteed, given the current momentum, there is good reason for a long-term sense of optimism.

Implications for Industry Leadership

From the larger perspective of this work, Semantic Applications, even more than Web Services, are principally areas for customer responsibility. Indeed, the eventual emergence of more intelligent applications will mark a decisive shift toward a customer-driven industry. Whereas IT suppliers are actively promoting Web Services, only customers can really build Semantic Applications. For example, the General Accounting Office has recently suggested that federal agencies might want to hold back on advanced XML implementations until an overall government standards and terminology strategy is clearly in place.

This public sector example reflects the fact that in order to take advantage of higher levels of business interoperability, it is customers that have to agree on and accept (and possibly develop) shared taxonomies and ontologies. They then have to implement these new forms of rules and syntax in a consistent and disciplined fashion for structured and unstructured data alike. Ideally, this industry terminology should be easily adaptable to new uses, widely available to relevant participants, and, ultimately, translatable into multiple national languages. All of this will require considerable time and energy, which are really just proxies for cost and commitment. As noted at the outset of this chapter, we are increasingly looking at implementation, not technology frontiers.

More broadly, the need for much more formal labeling and language suggests a new phase of IT industry focus. Whereas the PC and Internet industries were once described as the "revenge of the nerds," looking ahead, the emphasis on detailed classification and information management might well be described as the "revenge of the librarians." Semantic systems present a different set of challenges and require a different set of business skills. The need for fancy words such as semantics, taxonomies, and ontologies, with all of their ancient Greek connotations, suggests a world of more rigorous thinking and information handling, a significant cultural change from today's mostly free-wheeling Internet.

Importantly, much of this work will have to take place industry by industry, which makes it even more difficult for suppliers to influence the overall pace of change, other than through their services organizations. More pointedly, each industry will have to establish its own semantic dynamics in terms of business cooperation and value-chain leadership. This means that the rate of individual industry change could vary widely.

As explained in chapter 4, industry-specific standards have historically come about in one of three main ways. First, as with POS and EDI technology, an industry can jointly establish key standards and implementation goals that address a commonly recognized problem. Second, as with ATMs, companies can take their initial steps for their own strategic use. Then, once a technology has proven itself, more ambitious shared systems can eventually emerge. Third, as with Visa and SABRE, a strong market leader can launch a new system that others feel compelled to follow. Additionally, in areas such as defense, financial reporting, and health care, government-mandated standards and practices are another potentially powerful driving force.

All four of these customer-driven dynamics will play significant roles. But from the perspective of this work, the point is clear. The more that IT activities become focused on content and industry-specific standards, the greater the shift away from a supplier-driven industry. And while neither Web Services nor Semantic Applications will quickly become pervasive, and while both may never completely fulfill all the promises of their proponents, they are strong evidence that a customer-driven IT industry is now emerging. In the end, customers will have to decide which new standards, applications, and systems are worth implementing, and on what timetable they will be built. In this sense, they are increasingly setting the overall pace of IT industry innovation.

CHAPTER SEVEN

Where Business Leadership Is Needed

THERE CAN BE little doubt that of the four major sources of customer IT value creation—businesses, educational institutions, government, and consumers themselves—the most important of these groups is businesses. Not only are small, medium, and large businesses the largest sources of IT expenditures, but corporations are also the one customer segment with the most significant ongoing experience in creating the IT platforms and standards that have defined so much of the industry's progress. And although Web Services and Semantic Applications hold a great deal of future promise, the most pressing question is what businesses will do within the confines of today's dynamics.

Obviously, one chapter can't come close to covering the vast range of today's business computing challenges. Modern IT usage now touches virtually every part of business activity, and the list of critical enterprise systems only gets longer over time. Among the major challenges are ERP, CRM, data warehousing, intranets, legacy financial and transaction processing systems, corporate messaging, network management, enterprise content management, business-to-business (B2B), business-to-consumer (B2C), and business-to-employee (B2E) portals, XML and Web Services, security, and disaster recovery. These core systems must be continually enhanced and maintained. CIOs, like CEOs and COOs, need to have a deep strategic and operational knowledge of just about every important company effort.

In this chapter, we will focus on just a few important areas. Each selected topic has the potential to be a major new source of industrywide and even societywide demand. By focusing entirely on new sources of demand creation, there is an implicit message that too many organizations instinctively opt for the seemingly safer path of squeezing ever more efficiencies out of existing internal systems and supply chains. History shows that the biggest and more permanent improvements will come from the demand side of the business, and that these are the systems that truly change an industry. Over the remainder of this chapter, five such possibilities will be explored.

1. Creating new entertainment value via metadata-driven content

2. Establishing effective online advertising

3. Managing cooperative B2B exchanges and online commerce

4. Restructuring the health care industry using technology

5. Developing new Internet-based payment systems

Importantly, these topics are not particularly advanced or exotic applications. Most could be effectively addressed using technologies that are already available. As noted in chapter 2, it has always been the relatively basic applications such as transaction processing, database management, word processing, e-mail, and search which have led to broad increases in societal usage. This pattern will almost certainly hold true in the current period. This means that the search for new application areas is usually much less important than the effective exploitation of ideas that are already in place.

Thus, our focus in this chapter is on what it will take for these already identified applications to fulfill their inherent potential. Today, all five of these have gotten off to a pretty slow and/or rough start, but taken together they provide a sense of the sorts of progress that could sustain a significant industry expansion.

Example #1—Enhanced Content via Metadata

In chapter 3, we saw how the recording industry's decision to shut down Napster (as understandable as it was) had the effect of greatly reducing the demand for high-bandwidth consumer services, and thereby contributed significantly to the bursting of the Internet bubble. Sadly, not much has happened since to improve the situation. All manner of new and rapidly changing free online music services have sprung up and proliferated, and the music industry is once again trying to shut them down, in what increasingly looks like a losing battle. While the recorded content of the future can perhaps be protected, the existing base of CDs cannot. According to the Recording Industry Association of America (RIAA), CD sales were down 10 percent in 2001, a trend it attributes to free online services and related home CD burning. Although the RIAA's views are hardly objective, they may very well be right. Clearly, a great deal of music copying is taking place.

Overall, the music industry is still getting the worst of both worlds. It can't stop unauthorized copying, and its own online services are not attractive enough for most consumers. Both Pressplay and MusicNet have thus far been panned by the marketplace. Compared to free services, they offer less choice of music, are more difficult to use, and cost about $10/month. As many in the music industry have noted, all these services really have to offer is guilt-free listening for those who would otherwise be concerned about copyright violations. Not surprisingly, demand has been less than impressive. Even the companies involved admit that these services need to be substantially improved.

While many people understandably see this issue as simply one of free versus for-fee music, there is also an important demand-creation perspective. To go back to the Semantic Application discussions in chapter 6, there is almost limitless potential for new value creation if the music industry could systematically take advantage of its own information assets. There is clearly a need for a comprehensive online music industry database that consumers can easily search and partners can easily supplement. If this occurred, the music industry could become one of the first great examples of metadata-driven transformation. Thus far, however, the music industry remains an example of what can happen when customers don't lead and bottom-up alternatives start to emerge.

This story starts with the fact that in the pre-Internet era, the recording industry did not envision the need to embed metadata on most CDs, and thus there was no easy way for computers to identify and search for particular songs. Consequently, this information needed to be compiled from scratch. In the mid-1990s, California-based Gracenote (then CDDB) came up with a clever way of using CD track time information to identify particular songs, which could then be mapped back to actual song titles, artists, and related services such as lyrics, upcoming concerts, news, and other information. This system has become the basis for a whole new range of music industry services. Gracenote now has some eight thousand partners around the world, including many of the leading players in the audio hardware and Web businesses.

Overtime, Gracenote expanded its metadata categories into areas such as musical genre, language, years, and liner notes. To do this, it enlisted the support of the music-listening community through its voluntary metacredits program. This approach enabled significant but certainly not comprehensive coverage, as well as good although far from perfect data quality. It's a classic open-source approach, but with one big and controversial exception: Gracenote owns and seeks to profit from this asset rather than share it freely, as would be the case in a true open-source model. Not surprisingly, this has led to much public criticism, some legal action, and even new true open-source and other rivals. This story also suggests three important metadata and online services lessons:

1. **Top down versus bottom-up metadata.** Had the recording industry taken the initiative, it could have done this sort of metadata work on its own and developed a much more systematic, comprehensive, and accurate database. But since it didn't, the bottom-up approach of Gracenote and others emerged to fill the void. The established music companies have missed the opportunity to develop and own an extremely important new industry asset. This is something they should have been doing, even if they weren't ready to put their music online. This lesson is applicable to many content industries.

2. **Lost potential.** Although the bottom-up approach may eventually produce a full-featured system, in the meantime, many capabilities aren't available. In an ideal world, there would be a comprehensive database of individual song metadata that includes the composer, performer, and subject of each song, as well as each song's genre, date of creation, sales levels, awards, and perhaps a few key words. One could request, for example, the top ten songs for a particular year and style, recent songs about Halloween, all songs that are about a particular city, or all the "covers" of songs written by Bob Dylan. Today, the ability to thematically link musical materials is something that only DJs and other aficionados can really do, but through metadata, everyone could do

it, often better than today's leading experts. It's a great example of how metadata can supplement or replace human expertise with readily accessible chunks of targeted content. But as of yet, these capabilities have not been seriously developed.

3. **Incomplete aggregation.** Another reason the music industry's initial offerings are so weak is that they do a poor job of providing meaningful aggregation. For example, the current version of MusicNet features artists on labels owned by Warner Brothers and Bertelsmann, as Pressplay does for Universal and Sony. The obvious problem with this approach is that virtually no consumer pays any attention to who the recording company is, so that no one really knows which artists such company offerings include. To see how silly this approach really is, imagine a retail CD store that only sold artists that were part of the Universal stable, or imagine for example, if Tower Records organized its CDs by Sony, Universal, Warner Brothers, and so on. Since the demise of Napster, many of the new free services also lack the desired catalog size. The music industry must decide whether to build a comprehensive service for itself or cede the field to others such as Listen.com.

Of course, none of these three points directly addresses the fundamental question of whether free online music should be or can be prevented. However, were the music industry to develop aggressively priced services such as those described above, this might be less of a problem, especially as future Digital Rights Management technology evolves and at least makes it possible to protect new music offerings. From an IT industry perspective, perhaps the best thing would be for the music industry to either acquire, partner with, or compete with someone like Gracenote (now part of the Escient family of companies). It could then aggressively develop and/or support services that allow music listeners to search for music as if there were a single industry-wide database. This would finally give music fans a chance to buy what they really want, without the many complexities, instabilities, shortcomings, and illegalities of the file-swapping alternatives. This would provide a more accurate test of the fee versus free issue.

Unfortunately, as things stand now, the music industry's relatively unattractive offerings leave it with no choice but to aggressively try to stamp out its free service rivals. The industry has also felt the need to adopt the controversial and unpopular stance of lobbying for copyright protection on new forms of computers and audio equipment. There's even been interest in the idea of deliberately flooding the free services with various phony files and other tactics designed to frustrate or identify copyright violators. If the music industry heads further in these directions, things could get very nasty indeed. Some observers, such as Stanford law professor Lawrence Lessig, have suggested that the government step in to break the impasse, perhaps by imposing some sort of mandatory music licensing system. Unless a solution is found soon, this option may well gain support.

In many IT businesses, these sorts of deliberate delays, defenses, and missed opportunities would likely prove fatal. But since the recording companies legally control most of the key music industry content, they feel they have an extra layer of security. Perhaps they do. On the other hand, it's more likely that today's and tomorrow's free services will prove unstoppable, and therefore the music industry would be wise to compete via value-added services. But whichever way the future turns, music remains a great example of what happens when customers can't or won't provide the leadership needed to fully exploit a new technology. It's also a sign of the times when music and metadata could have such a profound influence over the very future of the IT industry.

While this example might seem too small to have much effect on the overall IT industry, it is important to realize that the range of similar content applications is very great indeed. There is almost limitless potential to use reengineered content to build new classes of expert systems across many consumer and entertainment fields, including sports, movies, theater, poetry, art, education, law, health care, taxation, politics, history, customer service, and statistics. Taken together, there is the potential to create a whole new wave of powerful and long-term information assets. Perhaps more importantly, such systems can open up major new frontiers of IT usage, greatly expanding the Web's overall utility and appeal. This is why structured metadata will become such an important industry force.

If these new services can be supported by advertising, great, but if not, they will have a much better chance of being sellable on the Web than the standard news and information available today. Much of the content on the Web today is available from so many sources that it is essentially oversupplied, and therefore likely to remain free for the foreseeable future. In contrast, at least some consumers have shown that they will pay for unique forms of content such as news archives, sports events, *The Wall Street Journal*, online training, legal searches, investment information, and other specific areas.

Looking forward, an emerging new generation of value-added services, coupled with the winnowing away of many of the free content dot-coms, could provide a viable path forward for today's troubled online content industry. But this can happen only if customers put the necessary systems in place. Since most consumers still have a strong aversion to paying for online content, truly compelling offerings will be required. Thus far, this hasn't really happened.

Example #2–Establishing Effective Online Advertising

As most readers know, problems in the online advertising business were also a major cause of the dot-com collapse. The limitations of banner ads and the inability of the advertising community to satisfactorily measure the results of online advertising led many major advertisers to avoid the sector, leaving providers of free Web content all but stranded. Given the inherent capabilities of this new media and the hundreds of millions of everyday Web users, this was certainly not an inevitable development. For the first time, advertisers actually had the means to reach people as they used computers in their work; how could things ever have gone so badly?

Indeed, nowhere among all of the dot-com troubles is there such a clear example of an industry getting into deep trouble because it simply failed to provide the necessary leadership. Consider that, to much fanfare, the banner ad first became an industry standard format way back in 1996. However, by 1998 or so, the limitations of these ads had become pretty clear to the advertising industry. It was all too easy for Web users to ignore banners—which were always in the same place—and therefore click-through rates were abysmally low. Since the advertising industry had promoted click-throughs as the unique benefit of Internet advertising, when consumers didn't click, the industry branded banners as a failure.

Despite being in the terrible position of trying to sell banner ads that didn't appear to work, the online industry didn't respond. It wasn't until

August 2001 that the Interactive Advertising Bureau (IAB), which represents the major companies that sell online advertising, released voluntary guidelines for a whole new range of more compelling ad unit formats. As shown in table 7-1, these specifications enabled the use of large rectangles that could be placed anywhere on the screen, skyscrapers that run in long vertical columns, pop-up and under windows and transitional ads (also known as interstitials) that appear over or between the delivery of one Web page and another. Along with the more pervasive use of Macromedia's Flash technology, Web advertisers suddenly had a much more formidable tool kit. Although these new techniques haven't provided a quick fix to the industry's problems, the online advertising market has stabilized and confidence seems to be slowly returning.

This begs the question of why it took so long for the advertising industry to respond. Much of the delay was due to a cultural reluctance to deploy more intrusive methods. While advertisers on radio and television have always felt free to periodically grab 100 percent of the consumer's time, on the Web such tactics were considered outrageous. Much of this was due to the "Internet should be free" mind-set that often seemed to deny that Web-based companies were actually businesses

TABLE 7 - 1

Online Advertising Format Standards

It took the online advertising industry more than five years to agree upon and endorse new and more compelling ad formats. In the future, new formats will likely follow much more quickly.

1996	2001	200X?
Banners	Banners	Banners
	Rectangles	Rectangles
	Skyscrapers	Skyscrapers
	Pop-up/under windows	Pop-ups/unders
	Transitionals	Transitionals
		Superstitials
		Streaming audio/video
		3D

trying to make a profit. This belief, of course, had its roots in the Internet's public sector and university origins.

Additionally, the large volumes of venture capital that poured into the dot-com content business made it all but impossible for any one company to break with this pattern. It would have been very difficult for a single firm to aggressively market new and more intrusive formats. Even worse, the scorn from consumers would have been severe, with many Web users turning to other content sources. Clearly, a more collective response was needed. Unfortunately, the online advertising industry had to suffer greatly before it started to take the steps it needed to survive. The recent work of the IAB in improving ad measurement techniques and developing uniform contract terms and conditions is also a good example of an industry coming together to jointly address problems that no single member could. It's just too bad these changes took so long.

Other sacred cows are also falling. For example, most search engine companies now give their advertisers much more prominent placement than would have been considered acceptable during the Internet boom years. Similarly, companies such as Yahoo! are revisiting many of their free services to see where revenues might be gained. Additionally, companies are having success with more personalized advertising such as targeted e-mail campaigns and content-intensive vehicles such as Webcasts. Through the use of Flash as well as streaming audio and video, the impact of tomorrow's multimedia ads will be much more compelling than today's. This will be especially true once consumers have access to high-bandwidth Internet services. Finally, there have even been several important tests of the idea of online advertisers paying their agencies based entirely upon business results.

If nothing else, the current financial pressure in the advertising industry is resulting in a great deal of experimentation, which will eventually help determine what works and what doesn't. Of course, some might say that this trend has already gone too far, and that the Web is becoming littered with ever more intrusive ads (witness the rise of AdSubtract and other ad-blocking software). Clearly, some truly objectionable tactics have emerged, including windows that can't be closed, have disabled back buttons, or continue to spawn new windows faster than you can close them. Many of these strategies quickly backfire and fall out of use.

However, as of today, things still need to move in a more intrusive direction. The advertising business has always been defined by the need to find a balance between the money needed to fund various forms of content and the amount of intrusion consumers will tolerate. Presented with the choice of viewing ads, paying for content, or not seeing that content at all, many consumers would opt for the advertising model. Remember it's advertising that makes it possible for us to see spectacles such as the Olympics for free. In the end, it's all about finding and establishing acceptable new norms.

Given how important advertising is to the very future of the Internet, the cooperation and leadership of the advertising industry has emerged as one of the industry's critical success factors. According to industry estimates, the Web now accounts for some 8 percent of the time people spend with various media, yet Web advertising is just 2 percent of total media advertising. Clearly, in a healthy market, these two numbers should converge. The Internet has far too many inherent capabilities and advantages for these gaps to remain acceptable. Should online advertising reach its potential, the implications for new Web content offerings and overall consumer usage would be very great indeed.

Fortunately, after years of inaction, the advertising industry does seem to have finally begun the process of recovery. Once again, the cooperation of a customer-driven IT segment is having vast implications for the evolution of the Internet itself. Eventually, this sector will thrive and help revitalize the Internet marketplace, but undoing both the excesses and cultural norms of the dot-com past has taken much more time than necessary.

Example #3—Market Exchanges as a Cooperative System Challenge

As with online content, Internet market exchanges also suffered greatly from the effects of premature dis-integration. The vast majority of such exchanges were set up as independent entities, with no real influence over the participants they depended upon. With hindsight, it was a predictable formula for disaster and very representative of the extent to which so many people underestimated the difficulty in moving to a purely horizontal model. Among the high-profile failures were Chemdex,

Aerospan, and PaperX. As with the Internet advertising business, the large numbers of B2B failures has tended to give the sector a bad name.

To put this issue in perspective, a little statistical data can be helpful. In the fourth quarter of 2001, the consulting firm of Booz-Allen & Hamilton, Inc. released the results of its study of the global B2B exchange environment. The company identified an amazing 2,233 active e-marketplaces around the world and received survey responses from 1,802 firms. No doubt, many of these marketplaces have very low revenues, and some have since gone out of business. Nevertheless, this was a remarkably large and seemingly representative sample, which was certainly among the best in the industry. The research showed that some 92 percent of the identified exchanges were independent, pure-play endeavors, while just 5 percent were consortia-owned, with the remaining 3 percent privately managed. Since it is now the consensus view that consortia and private systems tend to be much more viable strategies, these numbers show just how off base the initial highly horizontal approach has proven.

Although there have been some successes, pure-play companies have had a tough time funding the required infrastructure and obtaining the necessary commitments, cooperation, standards, and fees from their members. They have also found it difficult to get their target customers to make the necessary changes in business processes and internal system integration. Additionally, their close relationships with IT suppliers such as Ariba and CommerceOne reflected the once-widespread belief that IT companies would take the lead, a view that is now largely discredited. Not surprisingly, both of these once-high-flying software companies have scaled back their ambitions and are now largely focused on specific applications, especially procurement, now sometimes referred to as spend-management. Whether they will remain viable separate companies or be absorbed by larger software industry players is still an open question. It's another good example of the competition between specialized and more integrated IT forces.

In contrast, both the consortia and private-exchange approaches are very much in line with the models for cooperative systems outlined in chapter 4. Both are examples of the type of strong company and/or industry leadership that so many IT industry platforms have previously required. For example, single-vendor exchanges such as those managed by Dell and Wal-Mart (and at one time Enron) are quite similar to what American Airlines did with its SABRE system or what the Bank of America did in the early days of Visa. Eventually, both of these efforts evolved into broader industrywide platforms. As in the past, these private systems are the simplest way of establishing the initial operational standards and rules. However, this model doesn't scale very well. Just imagine the inefficiencies if every large business chose to pursue the private-exchange option.

Consequently, the supplier-controlled consortium-based exchanges—such as Covisint (General Motors, Ford, DaimlerChrysler, and eight other major automakers), Aeroxchange (thirteen U.S. and non-U.S. airlines), and many others—will likely prove to be the dominant model in many, although certainly not all, sectors. These systems have tended to resemble the early days of MasterCard or the initial ATM networks, where a small group of major players took the lead in developing a new technological approach that was eventually controlled by a broader base of participating companies. Conceptually, this transition from an independent to a consortium-based model is shown in figure 7-1.

In this model, the key issue is whether the members can avoid the rivalries and conflicts that have slowed, for example, the minicomputer and music industries in the past. In general, the jury is still out, and the consortia approach has yet to prove that it can move forward effectively. The decision of BMW and Volkswagen not to be part of Covisint (at least not yet) is a good example of the inevitable competitive tensions. Even with sincere cooperation, building these systems is not easy,

FIGURE 7-1

Changing Business Exchange Models

Over the last few years, the standard model for a B2B exchange has been turned upside down, with customer-controlled consortia taking over from the original pure-play, independent exchange operator model.

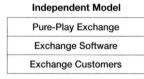

Independent Model

Pure-Play Exchange
Exchange Software
Exchange Customers

1997–2000

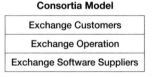

Consortia Model

Exchange Customers
Exchange Operation
Exchange Software Suppliers

2001–

especially when dealing with complex goods and services. Many participants have seriously underestimated the difficulties in scaling online exchanges and dealing with the necessary customization and internal business process integration.

However, the fact that many exchanges are off to what might seem to be a relatively slow start should not be surprising and is probably irrelevant. By any reasonable standard, today's systems are still quite new, and therefore having a few glitches along the way should be viewed as consistent with the way most important new computer platforms have emerged. Overall, the historical evidence says that eventually industries should be able to set up shared platforms that benefit their members on a more or less equitable basis. The incentives to do this simply outweigh the likely costs and concerns. If the established players exhibit sufficient leadership, there is little reason why most B2B exchanges should be disruptive to their participants; history shows quite the opposite.

Not surprisingly, in the post dot-com period, the focus of the industry has shifted to applications that can have an immediate payback. According to the same Booz-Allen study, catalog buying and auctions remain by far the most common and important applications. However, as the theory of simple systems suggests, these basic purchasing, invoicing, and auctioning applications should be more than sufficient to drive widely used systems, even if they only automate the acquisition of basic commodity goods. Today, considerably less than 10 percent of B2B purchasing takes place online. Similarly, although Covisint alone now handles over a billion dollars in auction sales per year, the overall B2B auction and electronic procurement markets have barely been scratched. Clearly, these simple applications could drive a great deal of new IT activity.

Eventually, however, online payments and other basic forms of transaction processing will become routine. The history of established stock market and commodity exchanges suggests that to prosper, industry participants will have to focus on new sources of value in areas such as new types of market information, futures pricing, various forms of hedging, improved inventory management, supply-chain integration, enhanced collaboration, surplus liquidation, specialized expertise, and a wide range of consulting services. Of particular recent interest are the so-called e-logistics systems, whereby, for example, companies can share their trucks, which often leave the warehouse full, but come back empty. Over time, these new types of value will greatly exceed the importance of reduced transaction costs. And while IT suppliers will help in many of these areas, it's pretty clear that customers are taking control over this important new class of e-commerce systems.

Example # 4—Breaking New Ground in Health Care

Ever since the commercialization of the Internet, e-commerce enthusiasts have predicted that information technology would play an important role in controlling health care costs in the United States. According to the U.S. government's Centers for Medicare and Medicaid Services, health care costs in 2000 increased by 6.9 percent and reached a staggering $1.3 trillion, which is the equivalent of some 14 percent of U.S. GDP, a share that is expected to rise even higher over the next few years.

Thus far, however, the Internet's impact upon the health care and insurance industries has been surprisingly modest. Indeed, over the last few years the health care debate has mostly focused on the pros and cons of managed care and various forms of government coverage, such as prescription drugs. Technology hasn't been a big part of the discussion. While there is a great deal of useful health care information on the Web, the Internet has played little role in either the doctor/patient relationship or in the health insurance processing system. For example, many medical offices still rely on paper-based records, an expensive and dangerously error-prone process. Similarly, few doctors or hospitals use e-mail to communicate with patients or transfer records.

However, over the last few years, there have been important early signs that the so-called defined-contribution (DC) health care model might change this situation. The basic principle of a defined-contribution system is simple. Consumers are either given by their employer or otherwise acquire an annual defined amount to spend on health care, which they then have an incentive to use carefully. For example, in one such system, a company provides each employee with $2,000 each year, which the employee can spend pretty much as he or she wishes. If annual health care expenditures exceed $2,000, the next $1,000 comes from the employee. After that, the employer pays for all other costs. Additionally, any money not spent in a given year can be rolled over into the next. Details, of course, vary and there are now many versions of DC plans, which make up a continuum of consumer empowerment options.

As shown in figure 7-2, DC programs are designed to give consumers a strong incentive to manage and control their own health care costs, a motivation that is almost entirely lacking in most programs today. Equally important, these plans push at least some specific health care decisions down to the individual consumer, who then can decide whether to buy brand name or generic drugs, or opt for certain tests and procedures. The main analogy is with personal finance. As many DC supporters argue, if 55 million Americans can manage their 401(k) retirement plans, why shouldn't they be able to manage their health care choices? While there are still many serious bureaucratic barriers, venture capitalists have responded, with large sums being poured into DC health care companies such as Definity Health, Vivius, Healthmarket, and others. However, thus far the DC market is still very small, with perhaps one hundred thousand early users.

By almost all accounts, employers are very interested in such plans, which could help them move further away from having to make de facto decisions about the health care of their employees. This is something

FIGURE 7 - 2

Alternative Private Sector Health Care Models

By giving consumers an incentive to spend their money wisely and having clear lines of decision making, defined contribution health care systems could improve the efficiency of health care services and trigger the beginnings of a health care industry value chain. This would be a major change from today's confusing health care market structure.

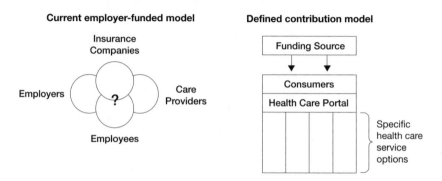

that medium and large U.S. companies have been doing since the 1930s, when Henry Kaiser first started approaching doctors about providing health care to his construction company employees. (Kaiser went on to be one of the key builders of the Hoover and Shasta dams.) Kaiser's efforts led to the founding of the California-based Kaiser Permanente Network, the nation's first major HMO. However, while there certainly have been many good things about the concept of employer-sponsored health care, in retrospect this one factor has led directly to some of the United States' biggest and most intractable health care concerns.

For example, because the health care system is skewed toward the employees of large and medium-size corporations, it's the self-employed, the unemployed, and those who work for small businesses who find health care coverage expensive, and therefore often don't have it. Similarly, employees who wish to change jobs have to worry about losing their current coverage, a significant restriction on labor mobility. Additionally, the involvement of employers further complicates the industry bureaucracy, resulting in complex decision-making, paperwork, and privacy concerns. One can easily argue that these shortcomings simply are not worth the declining advantages of employer involvement, which seems to be a particularly outdated model as more people work for themselves, change jobs, and move in and out of the labor force.

Many employees are also attracted to DC plans, since under most versions, many of the restrictions of the managed care world are eliminated, making it much easier for employees to choose their own doctors, or opt for various alternative health care services—such as acupuncture, chiropractors, and other employee-specific preferences. Consumers also like the idea of keeping their employers as far away from their health care situation as possible. While some critics have worried that, if left on their own, consumers would inevitably opt against needed care in order to save money, the evidence here is still unclear. In the end, there is a philosophical question as to how much individuals can be trusted to take care of themselves. Inevitably, this will bring the DC debate into the political arena.

However, from a pure IT perspective, the potential importance of such a change is difficult to overestimate. Should consumers be put in charge of their own health care decisions, the use of the Internet would almost certainly skyrocket, even more than it has for individual investors.

Employees would have a strong incentive to shop around and carefully tailor plans to meet their particular needs. As part of their effort to improve services and reduce their own costs, health care providers would also have a much stronger incentive to use modern technology. It's the sort of application that could cause both providers and consumers to be much more active online. We might even be allowed to keep and see our own medical records. (Doesn't it seem odd that we automatically get as much detail as we want on our various financial dealings, even over the Internet, but we often have to explicitly ask for copies of our own medical records?)

Unfortunately, the inertia and outright resistance will be significant. Few employers will be comfortable being the first to experiment with this model, especially if tax laws are not updated to better support the DC option. Additionally, as employees make diverse health care choices, short-term costs could actually rise as the efficiencies of volume purchasing are reduced. There is also likely to be fierce resistance from those with a vested interest in the existing system, especially employee benefits administrators, hospitals, and the insurance companies themselves. Last, but certainly not least, strong political resistance is likely to come from many Democrats, who, particularly in light of recent business scandals, often distrust deregulating important systems such as health care, pensions, utilities, and social security. Taken together, rapid progress appears unlikely, and it could easily be several years before any major shift begins.

However, it seems clear that unless the health care industry finds a way to give consumers meaningful cost-control incentives, medical spending in the United States will continue to grow faster than the economy as a whole. It is important to keep in mind that, unlike the other examples in this chapter, interest in DC systems is mostly a U.S. issue. Most of the rest of the developed world decided long ago to use largely nationalized single-payer systems, and thus they face a very different set of health care challenges. Among major developed nations, only the United States continues to strive for a primarily market-based solution. Those who believe that market principles can work within the health care industry should give DC plans a closer look. The idea is certainly in keeping with the individual empowerment philosophy often promoted by the Bush administration.

From this work's perspective, defined contribution health care is an excellent example of an area that could unlock a great deal of IT potential, but only if a deeply entrenched industry shifts in a major new direction. It is also perhaps the best single example of an area over which traditional IT suppliers have virtually no influence. However, should the health care industry make these types of changes, someday there might be a hundred million or more online health care consumers in the United States alone, making this perhaps the most important of all IT applications. It's a compelling possibility, but one where employers, employees, insurance companies, hospitals, politicians, and the American Medical Association will make nearly all of the key decisions. The IT industry will typically not be a major part of the debate.

Example #5—The Emergence of Internet Payment Systems

As we saw in chapter 4, IT and automated payment systems have been closely intertwined for more than thirty years, with computers playing a central role in the rise of credit-card services, point-of-sale systems, and ATMs. Given the capabilities of the Internet, it's only natural that new payment methods would emerge once again. After all, the Internet offers huge potential improvements in speed, reach, and transaction costs, especially when the payments between individuals or companies are only occasional or even one-time events.

During the Internet's brief history, three main types of payment concepts have emerged. First, through services such as PayPal, the Internet can be used to transfer money from one individual to another, just as we send e-mail today. Second, many companies now allow their customers to use the Internet to pay their bills online. Third, and most ambitiously, promoters of so-called microtransactions (also known as micropayments) envision a whole new infrastructure where very small payments, theoretically even less than one cent, can be efficiently made over the Internet, and used for new applications such as paying for small amounts of content. Such systems are still mostly in an experimental stage.

In this section, we will look at each of these three concepts from our perspective of identifying the types of leadership needed to establish these potentially important new platforms. Each example will highlight a different market launch aspect. The story of PayPal will show the on-going competition between integrated and horizontal market forces. Online bill-paying services are a good example of the need to entice consumers to do things over the Internet, while micropayments are perhaps the best example of an advanced system that can only be built through extensive customer cooperation.

The Challenge of Money Transfer Systems

Money transfer systems have, like e-mail and telephones, very strong network effects, in that the more people who use them, the more useful they become. History says that in these situations, the initial market launch model is especially important. This has certainly been the case with PayPal, the current market leader. In order to solve the familiar chicken/egg problem, PayPal cleverly leveraged three existing resources—the ubiquity of Internet e-mail, the capabilities of the credit-card industry, and, especially, the success of eBay, whose customers needed a fast, simple, and inexpensive way of paying each other. It then added an important fourth, dot-com–style ingredient, an initial $10 credit just for signing up. The strategy has worked well, and the company claims to have some 13 million customers; it clearly has a dominant market share.

As in other markets with strong network effects, once PayPal became the most popular eBay payment mechanism, its success had a significant element of lock-in, which has allowed the company to withstand some serious security and quality-of-service problems. On the other hand, since more than half of PayPal's revenues come from eBay transactions, its position has always been inherently vulnerable, much as independent exchanges and telecom start-ups were far too dependent upon players much stronger than themselves.

This vulnerability first became clear in 1999 when eBay acquired a majority share in a PayPal competitor called Billpoint. However, for a variety of reasons, consumers generally stayed with PayPal. In July of 2002, eBay essentially admitted defeat, but then used its financial might to acquire PayPal in an all stock transaction valued at some $1.4 billion. There are two important messages from this story:

1. Historically, the financial services industry has been able to co-opt new payment mechanisms such as credit cards and ATMs. If the eBay/PayPal combination can hold its dominant position, this will be an important structural change.

2. The fact that PayPal is no longer an independent company might well be an early indication that many future Web Services innovators will be absorbed by larger industry players.

Overall, the story of Internet payments is a great example of both the competition between the new and the old, and between vertical and horizontal forces. In this case, score one for the new world and one for the forces of vertical integration.

The Potential of Online Bill-Paying

Paying bills over the Internet might seem like a pretty mundane application. However, because the annual volumes of consumer and small business bills are so huge and because virtually every household is affected, the rate of acceptance of bill-paying services could say a great deal about the overall growth and vitality of consumer e-commerce. Additionally, once a pervasive bill-paying infrastructure is established, value-added services based on payment information would certainly emerge. For example, since bills will be increasingly presented via e-mail, consumers could be made aware of other payment options, personalized tips, bonus points, or other programs, and consumers could certainly benefit from having access to their historical spending records.

Perhaps more important, moving most bill payments to the Internet would inevitably result in a sharp decline (perhaps eventually as much as 50 percent) in first-class postal mail volumes. A drop of this magnitude would almost certainly force significant postal rate increases on the remaining mail, further tilting the field for other electronic services. In the end, postal and electronic systems compete with each other, and rises in postal mail costs are generally good for the IT business. Although much of what the U.S. Postal Service does is amazing, because of its vast infrastructure, eight hundred thousand employees, labor rigidity, and semi-privatized status, it's very vulnerable to any significant drop in revenue. This is why an aggressive push toward online bill-paying could mean a great deal in terms of the overall pace of IT industry change.

Additionally, the online bill-paying business is a great case study in the factors that can drive the rate of a new service's acceptance. Consider that the idea of paying bills electronically, either via telephone or computer, is now some two decades old. (I actually did research on this business in the early 1980s.) Yet today, less than 15 percent of people in the United States regularly use any kind of automated bill-paying service, and well under 5 percent of total bills are paid electronically. While many have forecasted strong growth ahead, people have been predicting this for many years. The bill-paying business continues to face a difficult chicken/egg problem. For example, unless there are more consumers using online bill-paying, the incentives for companies to develop the service are insufficient. Conversely, unless more companies aggressively promote their bill-paying services, consumers' motivation can easily fall short.

The good news is that the fundamental value proposition still seems solid. From the consumer's point of view, paying bills online can cut bill-paying time from perhaps an hour or two per month to as little as a few minutes. For companies, the savings should be even more compelling. Online bill-paying proponents cite figures showing that bills paid by paper checks typically cost about $1.50 to process, while electronic bills cost only about 25 cents. Cost savings in B2B environments are even greater, and clearly these differentials can only widen over time. From a bank's perspective, online bill-paying provides an important means to improve customer loyalty, and offers a platform for regular communication and new service offerings. It seems as if everyone should win, which is why many observers believe that the widespread use of online bill-paying and the demise of the paper check are still only a matter of time.

Consequently, the key issue is whether such services will continue to grow slowly, or whether the market will suddenly catch fire. This seems entirely up to the bill senders and the banking industry, which need to provide the necessary incentives and promotion. The most obvious of these is real consumer cost savings. Whereas some bill-paying services actually charge consumers a monthly fee, it's the opposite scenario that is desirable. For example, if consumers received a permanent discount on whatever bills they pay online, they would respond much more enthusiastically. Charging an explicit premium for paper bills would likely be even more effective, although certainly not without controversy. In 2002, AT&T began offering some of its customers a gift certificate with Amazon.com as an incentive to use its online billing option.

The market for online bill paying services should prove to be highly competitive. Unlike money transfer systems, bill-paying services are not characterized by strong network effects. Whether you do or do not use a bill-paying service doesn't make my use of such services any more or less attractive. As we have seen in other areas, low network effects typically mean that no single supplier will be able to gain an overwhelming market share. This certainly seems to be the case with online bill-paying. Today, companies such as Checkfree, PayMyBills.com, and Paytrust all have significant business, as do many individual banks that directly serve their customers. Large companies, such as AT&T, also have an interest in directly offering online bill-paying services. All signs suggest that bill-paying will remain a competitive market. It remains to be seen whether it will be delivered as a third-party Web Service or be integrated as part of a larger company offering. As with the other major applications discussed in this section, there is generally little that IT suppliers can do to influence or accelerate the growth of the online bill-paying business.

The Struggles of Micropayments

In contrast to the early success of online money transfers and the slow but fairly steady acceptance of online bill-paying, micropayments have thus far failed in solving their initial chicken/egg challenge. This is particularly noteworthy in that micropayments are arguably the best example of a system that, if it is to exist at all, really needs to be developed on a cooperative basis. With the possible exception of AOL, no one company could hope to establish such a system on its own.

The firms with the strongest incentive to lead here should have been the content companies. However, as described previously, the "Internet should be free" mentality made it impossible for most Web sites to sell subscriptions to their content. Looking back, it's possible that a micro-transaction system might have succeeded, if, for example, a number of the leading Web content companies—such as *The New York Times, The*

Washington Post, CNN, Slate, Yahoo!, MSN, AOL, CNET, and Salon—had all embraced such an idea. However, if any one of these companies tried to implement micropayments on its own, it would almost surely have failed. The irony is that the very cooperation that would have been needed to initially establish a microtransaction system might very likely have been deemed a form of illegal collusion or price fixing.

Given these realities and the daunting technical challenges involved, it's not surprising that the concept of microtransactions has seemed to fade away, especially in the United Sates. However, in Europe there is considerably more interest. For example, BT Retail (part of the former British Telecom, now known as BT Group plc) is experimenting with its "click and buy" service based on micropayment concepts and models that have had some initial success in Germany. Perhaps even more promising, European firms—such as Vodafone in the United Kingdom and Sonera in Finland—are also now developing micropayment systems for mobile phones, for which consumers are accustomed to paying monthly usage-based bills. Indeed, wireless micropayments could very well succeed even if micropayments never catch on for the wired Web itself.

For example, there has already been some experimentation with the idea of using mobile phones as an electronic wallet that could automatically make payments to, for instance, vending machines or fast food restaurants. However, the appeal of these early systems has yet to be proven. More likely, consumers will relate to the idea of playing games on their wireless screen phones or receiving specialized news, music, information, or other content services. In these applications, small payments can easily be added to a subscriber's monthly bill without a lot of complex transaction processing infrastructure. If this model catches on, the incentive to provide improved wireless value-added services could easily fall into place. The recent interest in video phones and the possible integration of cell phones and video cameras also suggests intriguing possibilities.

Outside of the wireless space, it might take a two-step process for serious interest in microtransactions to return, especially in the United States. First, leading content providers would have to successfully establish a base of premium content that consumers would be willing to pay for. Right now, it looks like most of these efforts will focus on selling monthly or annual subscriptions in areas such as sports, music, and business/investment information, and the early evidence suggests that these renewed efforts have a reasonable chance of at least some success. Should the subscription business reach critical mass, it's easy to imagine that service providers would then try to supplement their revenues via some sort of individual pay-as-you-go system.

If these dynamics could be combined with an effective Digital Rights Management system, content providers would then be in a position to begin selling access to a single song, image, article, or sports event. Once such a system is established, it is then only a relatively small step to extend this capability to a much broader range of Web-based content than most subscription packages are likely to include. Consequently, the idea remains an important and possibly compelling long-term cooperative system vision, but one that will depend almost entirely upon the dynamics within the fee-based content business.

Conclusions

Enhanced metadata-driven content, online advertising, robust cooperative exchanges, consumer-empowered health care, and pervasive new payment platforms are just five applications out of the vast range of current and future Internet usage. However, taken together, these examples alone could make a huge impact in expanding the range and extent of Internet usage. Many types of content need to be reengineered for the Internet. This enhanced content needs to be supported by either advertising or fees. Market exchanges must first reach critical mass and then start to offer new value-added services. Information technology could play a much more positive role in the health care industry, and the Internet will evolve to support a variety of efficient and very low-cost online payment capabilities. Each of these can be viewed as important industry milestones.

More important, much of the future of these five areas will be almost entirely determined by the efforts of customers, and will often require extensive industry cooperation. Customers generally have to rethink and then reengineer their content for themselves. Online advertisers need to find proven methods for reaching their target customers. Competitors have to come together to build effective exchanges. The health care industry would have to change radically to enable consumer-driven defined contribution plans to enter the mainstream. To become viable, microtransactions would need the support of either a set of key content players or an integrated service and content giant such as AOL, BT, or a major cell phone company.

These five examples should make it clear that customer leadership is now required to create major new generations of IT industry capability. But what can we say about the nature of this leadership and how it resembles and differs from what IT suppliers have provided in the past? Right now, it would seem that the most significant difference is the relative absence of start-ups, and therefore the relatively reduced role of entrepreneurs. Whether we are looking at the music industry, business exchanges, advertising, or bill-paying, most of the key decisions are being made by existing corporations and industries, and therefore do not tend to be associated with particular individuals. This is a very significant cultural change compared to the IT industry, which, as we have seen, has tended to create highly visible and influential figures.

All of this is just another way of saying that considerable innovation and leadership has to come from existing players, often without strong pressure from new market entrants. As we have seen in the music and advertising businesses, amassing this leadership can be difficult, and certainly doesn't happen automatically. In other areas, such as business exchanges, the initial signs of cooperation appear to be positive, but it's still very early in the game. Similarly, it's far too early to see if the health care and political establishments can manage the many wrenching changes that a shift to a defined-contribution system would require. This could easily take years. To go back to one of this work's major themes, the speed of these industry changes and the ability to establish new technology-based platforms will tell us a great deal about the vitality of the IT industry value chain. Within the business world, it's still a very mixed picture.

CHAPTER EIGHT

The Emerging e-Learning Value Chain

IN NO OTHER SECTOR do all of the past and present forces of the IT industry come together as completely and compellingly as they do in the e-learning business. Virtually every major theory and pattern described in this book is significantly represented. The e-learning market has been characterized by a long and difficult market development process, important new platform standards, the creation of significant new value, strong start-up competition, clashes between vertical and horizontal supplier structures, innovative Web Services, Semantic Web applications, disruptive technologies, ontologies, societywide systems, and the need for long-term commitment. Online learning is also a major example of IT customers—in this case "pure play" learning companies, universities, and publishers, creating IT-based value for other customers, with the role of technology suppliers generally of secondary importance.

For all of these reasons, the e-learning business is perhaps the best example of the competition, interaction, and blurring between the IT supplier and IT customer worlds. This is especially so since, perhaps more than any other major dot-com segment, e-learning is an area in which the horizontal, venture-backed models spawned during the Internet bubble still have a good chance to succeed. By understanding why and how this has occurred, we can gain important insights into the online learning industry's current and future dynamics, and its impact on the university and publishing industries. From this perspective, we will also see that the e-learning industry is perhaps the best example of Internet-induced disruption on a potentially large scale.

The stakes are very high. According to the U.S. Department of Education, the U.S. education market alone represents more than $700 billion per year, or nearly 8 percent of GDP, and by just about all accounts education spending should continue to grow at least as fast as the economy as a whole. While over half of this spending comes from the K–12 sector, business and university learning in the United States—which will be the primary focus of this chapter—represent roughly a $300-billion opportunity.

Clearly, e-learning is only a tiny fraction of this total today, and therefore, despite the considerable challenges ahead, the potential for growth is almost unlimited. Indeed, while we hear phrases such as *human capital* and *lifelong learning* so often as to render them nearly lifeless, this doesn't make them any less true. In this chapter, we will see that it is the Internet itself that makes the need for continual individual learning and corporate knowledge transfer so essential.

A History of Challenges

Despite this generally positive outlook, it is important not to lose sight of the fact that using technology for educational purposes has never been easy.[1] Over the last half century, virtually every new technology has been touted as a major educational breakthrough. This was certainly the case for television, cable television, satellite transmission, VCRs, PCs, and CD-ROMs. All of these technologies did eventually grow into large and important industries, but few would argue that they have significantly transformed K–12, university, or business education. This failure is certainly not for lack of trying. There has always been a large community of talented people committed to using technology to improve societal learning. But the often lackluster results warrant at least some initial skepticism regarding the near-term prospects for the e-learning business.

It is worth stepping back to understand why using technology to improve education has consistently been so difficult. Clearly, all of the technologies listed above have been major new sources of both information and entertainment, and all have proven popular with consumers. Each has also enabled significant new learning capabilities, especially in low-cost, stand-alone environments. However, none of these technologies has come close to matching, let alone replacing, the value of a committed and qualified teacher. Additionally, people generally learn best by doing, and educators have found it difficult to use new media to create an "actionable" learning experience. Too often, new technologies have been used in a passive manner.

Computers, in particular, have presented serious learning challenges, almost regardless of the target market. For example, extensively using computers in K–12 education would require massive investments in systems, software, networks, training, and maintenance, with costs far out of proportion to any proven benefits. In contrast, business education has traditionally put a major emphasis on company morale and team-building, goals not well-suited to media-centric individual learning experiences. Finally, before the arrival of the Internet, few universities even attempted to make significant use of technology-based education, which seemed to run counter to their entire professor-centric learning tradition. In short, technology has mostly remained on the educational periphery.

Given this history, one can't help but ask why anyone should believe that the impact of the Internet on these sectors will be significantly different. Indeed, those who make the case that the Internet will be more successful simply because it is more powerful might well find themselves in a position that's difficult to defend. In retrospect, many previous technologies have also been quite capable, especially when compared to what was available before them. For example, in terms of educational capability, the leap from videotapes to PCs was, at least arguably, even greater than the leap from, for example, CD-ROMs to the Internet. Indeed, at least at this stage in the Internet's evolution, the differences between the courses available over the Internet versus those designed for CD-ROMs often don't seem all that significant.

Only a little more than a decade ago, people predicted great things for CD-ROM–based education, and a new industry began to grow around this idea. Like the Internet, a CD-ROM can provide high-quality, multimedia courseware that, given sufficient production volumes, can be delivered at very low per-unit costs. As with the Internet, CD-ROMs can be used in a self-paced manner, at any time, and on virtually any PC. However, the potential of CD-ROM–based learning was never realized. And once suppliers began to appreciate the importance of the Internet, investments in CD-ROM courseware vanished almost overnight. In the end, the industry was abandoned before it ever really took off.

Compared to CD-ROMs, the Internet does offer important new capabilities in terms of two-way communication, real-time updates, individual tracking, "blended" human interaction, custom in-house content, and various hyperlinks. Perhaps more important, the Internet enables access to an almost infinite range of offerings in a way that a collection of CD-ROMs never really could. Eventually, these advantages should help enable people to learn in a real-time and ad hoc manner so that learning can be more tightly integrated with actual job requirements. Nevertheless, as important as these advantages are, it's not clear why they should prove decisive in the marketplace.

Why Internet-Based Learning Is Different

The real reason that e-learning is likely to eventually be a big business success where its predecessors have not has little to do with its new technical capabilities. In other words, one doesn't want to have to make the case for e-learning based solely on how much better than CD-ROMs the Internet really is. Looking back over the patterns in this book, it's clear that the ability to increase customer demand has often been the key to establishing an important new market. In this section, we will see why the arrival of both the Internet and electronic commerce has had the unintentional effect of greatly increasing the actual need for learning, especially in the business world. It is this huge new source of additional demand that will ultimately make Internet-based learning so much more successful than previous technology-based learning efforts.

Consider that virtually every job in a typical corporate environment —marketing, sales, customer support, administration, finance, strategy, distribution, production—has been significantly affected by the Internet and therefore requires frequent job training. People need to understand how the Internet has affected their industry, their company, and the specific aspects of their jobs. For example, in recent years many corporate marketing people have had to learn about concepts such as Web site visits, hits, stickiness, click-through rates, personalization, and privacy. Most of these topics simply didn't exist a decade ago. Additionally, these same employees must also be trained to use and understand new and often highly complex internal company marketing systems such as those that track and report on Web site activity, or those that solicit and collect customer feedback.

Customer service is another excellent example. This is an area where employee educational backgrounds are often relatively modest, but where the supporting technologies—such as databases, e-mail, Web usage, and expert system-based problem-solving—continue to become ever more powerful and complex. The need to train customer service employees will likely increase again as companies experiment with both instant messaging and integrated voice/Web applications. Sales, finance, distribution channels, and business partnering are also major areas where employees need to be fluent in Internet issues and usage. While some of this learning can be done through internal training and knowledge-management efforts, in most cases external training is also required.

This need for ongoing learning was simply not part of most previous technologies. While VCRs and CD-ROMs were both useful business learning tools, they did very little to increase the overall need for business learning. In contrast, PCs did somewhat increase the need for knowledge in that workers had to learn how to use a PC as well as core applications such as word processing, database, and spreadsheet programs. In many areas, employees also had to learn specific job-related PC applications. Not surprisingly, a large PC-training industry rapidly emerged. However, the needs of the PC industry were not nearly as broad nor as ongoing as those created by the Internet and e-business, which affect not just individual skills but the entire way that most companies operate. This also helps explain why the PC training boom proved relatively short-lived.

As it turns out, not only is the Internet the cause of much of this new demand, it is also by far the best way to fulfill it. It is only natural that businesses would try to use their existing network infrastructure as the starting point for any enterprisewide learning initiatives as well as any similar efforts to train partners and customers. From this perspective, it follows that the fates of the e-business and e-learning industries will likely be closely linked. E-business can't progress unless there is effective employee and ecosystem learning to support it, and e-learning won't succeed unless e-business continues to expand and evolve. Consequently, both are dependent upon the broader value-chain dynamics described in this book, and thus, not surprisingly, both have suffered through the post-dot-com period. However, since in the long term, the expansion of e-business appears a virtual certainty, it seems logical that the same can be said of e-learning. Only together can the two fulfill their inherent potential.

Training, Learning, and the Initial Market Launch

While there has always been an academic debate about whether students and employees are better off being trained in specific skills or presented with a broader conceptual understanding, this has always been somewhat of a false choice, since both types of training are clearly needed. However, improving employee skills has been particularly important to the growth of the e-learning business since the origins of many of today's e-learning leaders can be traced back to very specific technical training. Perhaps more significant, these origins in the skill-based world help explain why the e-learning business has been able to avoid the "content should be free" attitude that still pervades much of the Internet. They also help explain why the e-learning business is evolving quite differently than the other major segments discussed in part 2, and why technology companies themselves are positioned to play a significant role in the e-learning industry.

As we have seen many times, the structure of the initial market launch often has profound long-term consequences. This is certainly the case with online learning, for which computer professionals were the primary initial market. In fact, the use of online networks to deliver technical support to computer professionals substantially predates the commercial use of the Internet. In the 1980s and early 1990s, CompuServe was particularly successful in this regard. Many IT suppliers as well as independent topic-specific IT user groups maintained bulletin boards and other services to keep technical professionals aware of new products, services, and issues.

In retrospect, of course, it makes perfect sense that computer professionals would be the early adopters of online learning. After all, they typically had the necessary equipment and were, by definition, comfortable with computers. Additionally, computer technology itself is both complex and ever-changing and as such, IT professionals need regular training in order to maintain their skills. Finally, IT suppliers have a strong interest in training the technical community in their products, as both a form of marketing and customer service. Overall, it would be hard to imagine a more ideal starting point.

As unsurprising as all of this may seem, the consequences of the e-learning industry's origins are hard to exaggerate. It led directly to the following:

1. The initial e-learning customer funding often came from employers and professionals, not mass-market consumers, eliminating the "free content" tendencies in other Web sectors. Unlike other forms of online content, there has never been much doubt that people would be expected to pay for most job-related training programs.

2. Since the IT industry was already large, so was the associated training market; this enabled the e-learning business to reach an initial critical mass relatively quickly. It also provided a clear target market for the venture-capital investments needed to build the required e-learning tools and infrastructure.

3. Since IT markets continually change, so must IT training. This created the need for regularly updated content. It also provided a clear industry road map, since the technology training market closely followed the mainstream markets for advanced IT products and services. In other words, unlike most other Internet content markets, technology training was from its earliest beginnings part of a healthy and coherent industry value chain.

4. Since business schools, universities, and publishers didn't really provide training in specific IT skills, the market was left wide open for new entrants. Just about all of today's U.S. e-learning leaders were once start-up companies that began in the 1980s or 1990s.

5. Since IT professionals were becoming more involved in broader business issues, there was a natural link to the provision of non-IT general business training. This combination of "hard" technology skills and "soft" business education provided the initial model for an all-around employee learning program. This was a critical bridge to the wider, non-IT skills e-learning opportunity.

Taken together, these five points show why the e-learning business has gotten off to a fundamentally healthier start than most other Internet content businesses. There was a real source of significant customer funding, a proven need and business model, a clear sense of direction, and a natural path toward future opportunities.

The point is not just to promote the prospects for the e-learning business; the industry certainly has a number of serious challenges, including convincing many customers that e-learning really is worth investing in, especially during a recession. However, it does seem that this business is one of the few major Internet areas in which start-up companies have maintained a strong early leadership position, to the great potential risk of the established business education industry. The following section will argue that, unlike most of the areas discussed in this work, the Internet has a chance to be as disruptive to the learning industry as PCs were to the minicomputer business.

Is This a Classic Case of Disruption?

While it is still very early in the game, thus far, the answer to this question is at least a qualified yes. The emergence of a new and dynamic e-learning industry value chain, evolving independently of the traditional educational and publishing establishment, does seem to repeat the disruptive patterns described in chapter 2. In fact, the closer one looks at the situation, the stronger the resemblance becomes. Consider the following:

1. Because of the significant new demand for learning created by the Internet, online education, like previous disruptive technologies, has great long-term potential. On-demand, customized learning accessible to all employees and students from anywhere on the globe clearly represents both a big market and a compelling long-term vision.

2. As with minicomputers and PCs, the initial use of the Internet for e-learning has been mostly focused on new applications and new customers, for example IT professionals, not well-served by the existing educational establishment.

3. As with previous disruptive technologies, the initial efforts of the e-learning business to enter soft skill areas have not been considered to be of as high a quality as those of established business schools. In fact, they have often been dismissed in much the same way minicomputer vendors once poked fun at PCs.

4. Even as significant e-learning sales took off, their impact upon the established business education industry has been minimal, often nonexistent, since most of the use was by an entirely new group of customers, typically IT professionals or mid-level office employees.

Although the future of any IT-oriented business is always subject to change depending upon the actions of the players involved, it's not that hard to imagine the possible path from here. Since the corporate learning market is potentially so much larger than the business school market, scale economies and marginal costs advantages will increasingly accrue to the e-learning industry. Additionally, as with other disruptive technologies, e-learning products and services will improve dramatically over time, eventually matching or exceeding many of the capabilities of earlier modalities. Signs of this improvement are already emerging, as e-learning companies start to attract well-known experts to enhance their courseware.

Of course, even in such a scenario, the established players, like their mainframe predecessors, can still prosper in their high-end world, where teachers and group experiences clearly have distinct value. But if this is all that occurs, the bulk of the learning marketplace will have moved elsewhere. There is simply no way that the vast amount of required business learning can be delivered through the traditional face-to-face model. E-learning is where the high-volume market will have to be. Perhaps even more important, in any market with very low marginal costs, the sectors with the highest market volumes will almost always have a significant competitive edge. Fortunately for any would-be future e-learning industry leaders, these volumes are still a long way from being achieved. The competition is still very much in its early stages, and many of today's e-learning companies are financially vulnerable.

The Clash of Value Chains

As we have seen in previous IT eras, the impact of a new technology is only partially due to the power of the technology itself. Ultimately, it is the response of the established industry that determines how the overall supplier structure will evolve. History shows that the quality of this response often varies and is usually a combination of individual management skills and the degree to which the new technology fits an established firm's business situation. We have already seen how companies such as Microsoft and AOL responded effectively to the emergence of the Internet, just as Digital Equipment misplayed both the PC and Unix marketplaces, while Hewlett-Packard did not. None of these responses were inevitable, and only in hindsight have their consequences become clear.

While one cannot predict how today's e-learning players will respond to today's realities, it seems safe to say that the marketplace once again faces a number of possible paths, with great fortunes depending on the actions taken over the next few years. If anything, the e-learning business is even more difficult to predict than the previous waves of technology development, since four very different sets of players—pure-play e-learning suppliers, software companies, publishers, and universities—are increasingly finding themselves both cooperating and competing. On the other hand, this was also generally true during the PC era, when three very different types of companies—start-ups, established IT companies, and large consumer electronics firms—were all viable entrants. In that case, the market eventually became a nearly equal mix of all three, with start-ups (Dell and Apple), established computer companies (IBM and HP), and consumer electronics giants (Sony and Toshiba) all playing important PC industry roles.

The e-learning business is still in this type of early formative period. And while the start-ups seem to have won the first round, this is like saying that Apple, Commodore, and Radio Shack won the early rounds of the PC industry. The real competition is only just beginning, and as we have seen many times over the years, the initial market leaders often fail to maintain their positions. Only in segments with very high customer lock-in and very strong network effects is the "first mover" advantage typically decisive. No one has this sort of controlling position in the e-learning business today, and thus the market is still wide open to competition. To get a sense of the diversity of possibilities, let's look at the position of the four main sets of players. We will see that each has a very different set of strengths and weaknesses, a reality that should make for a volatile process of market evolution.

The Pure-Play Position

As we have seen, start-up companies have taken the early e-learning lead, and they now have considerable momentum and strength. Chief among their assets is the emergence of a fully functioning horizontal e-learning industry value chain, with focused companies now providing advanced content, software, and services. Given that the Internet learning industry is less than a decade old, this is a significant accomplishment. It's the closest thing to the PC industry model that the Internet industry has produced, and has resulted in an open and innovative market well-suited for new Web-based services. The main components of today's pure-play e-learning value chain are shown in figure 8-1.

The downside of this layered structure is that there is no clear global market leader, and therefore the e-learning business is often somewhat confusing for the customer. In the absence of a dominant player, many customers will postpone their purchase decisions rather than risk making the wrong supplier selection. This is especially so because like most horizontal value chains, the e-learning industry is dependent upon standards for the required interoperability. But without a clear market leader, these standards such as the SCORM (Shared Content Object Reference Model) are much more de jure than de facto, and often not easily tested.

These concerns are particularly relevant to the acquisitions of Learning Management Systems (LMS). These are the software systems that enable an enterprise to deploy and monitor individual employee learning programs, and for many companies the adoption of an LMS marks the start of a serious enterprise commitment to e-learning. However, because LMSs are characterized by relatively high costs, complex deployment issues, and long-term lock-in, LMS buying decisions are not made lightly. From a

FIGURE 8 - 1

E-Learning Industry Value Chain

Unlike most other customer-driven sectors, the early years of the e-learning industry have been characterized by a healthy, start-up–driven, horizontal value chain, resembling that of the PC industry.

Services and Consulting	Accenture, IBM, DigitalThink
Content and Courseware	SkillSoft,[1] NetG[2]
Communications Services	Webex, Centra
Content Authoring Tools	Macromedia and many others
Learning Management Systems	Saba, Docent

1. Recently merged with SmartForce
2. Owned by Thomson

155

supplier perspective, the LMS business may well be one of the last great enterprisewide horizontal software markets, in the lucrative tradition of ERP, HRM, CRM, and other now widely used systems. Additionally, LMSs often enable significant account control, and thus the winner in this segment could well be the long-term e-learning industry leader.

While some e-learning industry consolidation is likely to partially alleviate the lack of leadership, the problem is pretty much implicit in any horizontal value chain without a single dominant player. Imagine how chaotic the PC industry could have become without the leadership of first IBM and then Microsoft and Intel. The lack of a strong market leader is also an important reason the established players are likely to have considerable time to respond. Most of today's specialty e-learning players are still very small, with revenues in the hundreds of millions of dollars or less. This makes acquisitions relatively inexpensive and therefore much more likely.

It's also fair to say that the start-up e-learning companies generally still lack access to the best and latest business e-learning content. Indeed, most of the courses of the pure-play e-learning companies are prepared by business writers and instructional designers who take popular business books, journals, textbooks, and other sources and distill them into their main messages. In other words, expert content is not licensed from their original sources and therefore there are typically no royalty payments, which is one reason that e-learning content companies enjoy very high gross margins. However, this approach also means that developing courses can take considerable time, making it difficult to keep up with new and changing topics.

Additionally, it doesn't seem too harsh or unfair to suggest that another downside of this approach is that some of the urgency, vitality, nuance, and controversy of business writing and thinking is lost in this process of creating general-purpose courses. Indeed, perhaps the most common complaints about many business e-learning courses today are that they are too basic, too dull, and from an international perspective, too U.S. and English language oriented. Since limited bandwidth is still an important issue for a significant number of customers, most courses take little advantage of the Web's multimedia capability. Thus they often look like little more than a series of static PowerPoint-like screens, hardly the most absorbing way to learn.

Nevertheless, the e-learning companies understandably believe that they have both the right business model and the right value-chain position. Even in a difficult economic environment, e-learning's relatively low costs per employee can show hard savings versus previous training and learning approaches. Such tangible savings are important because many of the benefits of e-learning are inherently soft and long-term, and therefore are a natural area to cut when times get tough. In the short term, employee learning investments can almost always be curtailed, and in 2001–2002, this has clearly occurred.

But from a long-term perspective, today's e-learning suppliers are confident that they can overcome any content, language, and related pedagogical shortcomings. This is another way this market closely resembles previous disruptive technologies. While it might be easy to dismiss many of the initial offerings as primitive, it's also easy to see how these offerings can be greatly improved over time. It's the classic Silicon Valley approach of investing in an emerging industry value chain and then watching it grow in capability over time. That's why it's so important for the existing university and publishing worlds to effectively respond.

The Opportunities for Software Companies

As noted above, e-learning offerings are basically a mix of software and content. Clearly, course authoring tools, LMSs, and the various forms of online collaboration are the sorts of products that software companies have long developed and brought to market. On the other hand, software companies have generally fared poorly in their efforts to pursue content markets, a reality that even Microsoft has had to acknowledge. Nevertheless, because of the strong component of IT training in many e-learning applications, as well as the great potential of the e-learning business, it would hardly be surprising to see some of the major software companies become much more aggressive in this area. The key strengths of these companies would include:

1. Many actual customers who are potential buyers of enterprise e-learning services

2. Significant sales and field service organizations to support complex customer implementation requirements

3. Strong brand recognition, albeit not necessarily in learning applications

4. Significant financial resources to develop markets and/or make acquisitions

In the long run, it's likely that software companies will be better off sticking with software and leaving the content to others. Thus, the market for LMSs and their related tools looks particularly attractive, since whoever leads in this area will likely have a strong long-term e-learning position. However, given the market's still immature stage, software companies have the opportunity to play a much broader role, perhaps in conjunction with any of the other three sets of players. Of all of the industry-specific markets discussed in this work, e-learning is the one that today's leading IT suppliers are most likely to participate and succeed in.

The Publishers' Perspective

From the perspective of the world's major business book publishers, the Web has been a tough market to participate in. In many ways, the problems all started with the rise of Amazon.com. The ability to sell books via the Web created the opportunity for all sorts of new publishing industry value creation—recommendations, reviews, reader feedback, sales rankings, affinity marketing, expanded title availability, more efficient distribution and inventory management, chapter samples, tables of contents, and so on. Unfortunately for the traditional book publishers, just about all of this new value has been provided by Amazon. As shown in figure 8-2, the publishers' position within the book industry value chain has actually shrunk at a time when the overall chain has been lengthening. This is almost never good news.

In terms of e-learning, book publishers face a similar set of challenges. Chief among these is they tend to have no real relationship with the end-user customer, and thus their brand recognition is often very low. In this regard, their position is analogous to the major recording companies in that their principal role is in understanding market needs, identifying, developing, and promoting individual talent, and then taking the necessary business risks. All of these roles are still important, but have proven difficult to transport onto the Web. Additionally, just as music industry services from just one or two recording companies are inherently and transparently incomplete, the catalogs of

FIGURE 8 - 2

Online Content Value Chain—A Book Publisher's Perspective

From a publishing industry value-chain perspective, the biggest effect of the emergence of Amazon.com was that it became the principal source of new value creation, limiting traditional book publishers to the left side of the spectrum.

individual book publishers are typically much more like a collection of distinct offerings than a unified and coherent product line.

However, publishers have several important assets that the pure-play e-learning companies typically lack. The most import of these is a deep understanding of student needs in particular subjects, and long-established expertise in what constitutes quality learning content. Additionally, major publishing companies have vast quantities of expert content, which they will continue to try to leverage. For example, as the producers of most of the world's textbooks, publishers should be in the best position to develop the online equivalents of the standard university text. As we will see later in this chapter, there are immense possibilities and challenges in this area that will involve the development of robust, topic-specific, and metadata-driven databases. The potential for real value creation is virtually unlimited.

Finally, today's multibillion dollar global publishing conglomerates such as Pearson and McGraw-Hill have financial resources that the pure-play companies typically can't match. They also have a long history of using acquisitions to move into new areas and expand their current offerings. Once again, there are a number ways that they could become major e-learning players should they choose to do so, especially if the stock valuations of the pure-play companies remain low or sink even farther. As long as venture funding remains scarce and stock prices remain sluggish, cash counts for a lot and the major publishers generally have it.

The University Situation

The major universities and business schools constitute a fourth distinct set of players and capabilities. Here the center of gravity revolves around students and teachers. In this sense, traditional universities can be seen as being under the most direct challenge, since e-learning is a potential alternative to the face-to-face student/teacher model. However, as noted above, there is little evidence that e-learning will replace the in-school experience anytime soon. Instead, e-learning will expand the educational market to reach millions of new customers. It's easy to envision a scenario in which the growth of the e-learning industry leaves the traditional business schools largely intact, even as the classroom accounts for a rapidly declining share of the overall business education market.

Therefore, the more interesting question is to what extent universities will participate in the broader business learning market. As with the other three sets of players, the university community has its own clear set of strengths and weaknesses. The strengths include an unmatched sense of the interrelationships among courses, content, teachers, and students. Additionally, in both the business and nonbusiness worlds, universities have a tremendous base of content and expertise, which in theory they should be able to leverage online. Perhaps most important, the major business schools have by far the strongest brands and the most respected forms of accreditation. In these areas they are the clear envy of the online learning industry. Indeed, it will take a long time, if ever, before any pure-play company can match the cache of the leading universities, which is why partnerships between established universities and pure play e-learning companies are so interesting and delicate. It's a classic case of the need to balance brand protection and brand extension interests.

Yet these considerable strengths are offset by some equally significant weaknesses. The most important of these are structural. The traditional university is a vertically integrated institution. Each school has its own campus, curriculum, professors, customers (students), and in many cases its own e-learning programs. This model has been replicated thousands of times in locations around the world, typically at very high price points. From an Internet perspective, it's hard to imagine a more antithetical initial structure. The Internet and much of the e-learning industry is geographically independent, operates mostly according to various degrees of the horizontal model, and tends to reward high-volume, low-price strategies. Consequently, vertical integration makes it difficult for universities to enter the mainstream business e-learning market without sales, service, and technology partners.

The Case for Cooperation

The major differences in the positions of the four main sets of players are summarized in figure 8-3. From this figure and the arguments made so far, it should be clear that there is significant potential for major partnerships among the four types of players, since the strengths of one segment tend to be the weaknesses of another. Many such partnerships are now being experimented with. The benefits of cooperation become even more obvious when one looks at this situation from the perspective of the customer, who as always wants the best of all worlds. In the world of e-learning, this would include the credentials and professors of the universities, the content and resources of the major publishers, the technology and field support of the software industry, and the focus and low prices of the pure-play e-learning vendors. Delivering this may well require a mix of in person and online options, hence the recent interest in "blended learning."

Equally important, e-learning industry cooperation is the best way to ensure that an advanced new generation of content is actually built. All four sets of players have an interest in providing self-contained, reusable learning objects that are labeled via metadata and searchable via various taxonomies. Similarly, many potential online learning customers don't want to learn via a traditional course format at all; all they really want is real-time access to the actual content itself. They want to retrieve specific chunks of knowledge via the sorts of reliable transactions used in other e-commerce applications, what was referred to as "transactional reading" in chapter 6.

Objects, Chunking, and Ontologies

There is probably no better example of the need to systematically manage content than the e-learning business. With the ever-growing volumes

FIGURE 8 - 3

Strengths of Major e-Learning Players

The positions of the four major e-learning market participants are so different as to almost certainly invite important acquisitions and/or partnerships. In many cases, one group's strengths are another's weaknesses.

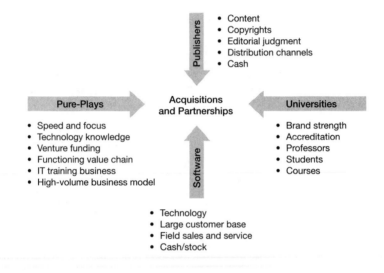

of information in just about every educational field, the need for a more transactional reading style will only grow over time, as readers have to find ways to be more efficient. As noted in chapter 6, the main tools for transactional reading are clear information classification systems, or taxonomies, and the packaging of information into discrete, reusable, and relatively small learning objects. The process of creating these learning objects is often referred to as "chunking." These are the tools and processes required to provide true learning-on-demand, an increasingly important requirement in both business and academic fields. It's where much of the e-learning business is headed.

The range of these new information structures is virtually unlimited. For example, SkillSoft claims to have developed more than ten thousand different business learning objects and another 1,750 job-aids designed to provide a quick description and guide to all sorts of specific business issues and problems. NETg says it has more than eighty-two thousand learning objects spread across its content catalog. To be useful, these collections have to be easy to sift through so that customers can reliably find the information they want. This is where taxonomies and metadata come into play. Fortunately, the creation of these objects is often a natural extension of an e-learning company's course development process. Indeed, the pure-play companies have an advantage here in that their courses have generally been designed quite recently, often with the idea of learning objects, chunking, and metadata tagging clearly in mind.

In contrast, consider the challenge for the print publishing industry. Here, the great majority of content is locked up in books and periodicals. These works were not written with the idea of being broken down into discrete learning objects. Instead they are, as is this book, written to be integrated narratives with frequent self-referencing. Breaking down this content into discrete objects has proved to be a daunting although not impossible task. I spent more than a year working on this issue for an innovative start-up firm called MeansBusiness. During this experience, it became clear that reusable learning objects could be extracted from business trade books and journals, but that doing so required a great deal of human editorial judgment. (Like many content-oriented dot-coms, MeansBusiness attracted a lot of intellectual interest, but not nearly enough revenue. As of this writing, the company's future remains uncertain.)

Another possible path forward for the publishing industry is in the traditional textbook area. It seems obvious that properly structured on-line content should have capabilities far superior to those of a printed textbook or its CD-ROM equivalent. I often think back to my college days. It would have been great to have powerful online databases dedicated to, for example, the works of Shakespeare, Freud, Keynes, or the ancient Greek philosophers. Such systems could have the complete works of an author searchable by subject or keywords with hyperlinks to supporting reference sources in each subject area. For example, imagine a single Web transaction that could instantly search the works of Plato, Aristotle, and others for their views regarding particular philosophical, social, or political topics.

Clearly, today's academic publishers could build powerful subject-specific databases in these and countless other areas. There are currently two main barriers. As in the case of online music, publishers have serious concerns regarding copyrights and their ability to prevent unauthorized usage. Additionally, there is already a great deal of useful and free Web information on most major academic subjects, which makes it difficult to establish for-fee services. However, in reviewing many of these free sites, it's clear that there are often serious limitations to how much capability a free service is likely to offer. For example, while many free Web sites provide interesting material about Shakespeare, there aren't many that match the editorial standards of a high quality textbook, and thus one often has to do a great deal of browsing to find specific information.

Between copyright concerns, the large amount of free information, and the inherent challenges of selling any Web-based content, it's easy to why these markets are taking time to develop. Ironically, many of the free academically-oriented services on the Web today have been built by universities and their students, who in the pre-Web world have always been publishers' best customers. This interplay and competition between content customers and suppliers will be an important theme of chapter 9.

Overall, the failure to develop a new generation of semantic learning applications continues to hold back the growth of the e-learning business. Virtually every significant educational topic can and should be reengineered into a database of discrete learning objects easily located via taxonomies and metadata. However, only through a sustained effort to build clearly superior for-fee offerings can the e-learning industry fulfill its academic promise. This will likely require strong industry leadership of the sort not yet widely evident. Certainly, few businesses have more incentive than the education community to demonstrate advanced content and delivery systems. If the e-learning industry can't take the lead in this area, one has to wonder who will.

CHAPTER NINE

Consumers and Communities

WHILE THE MAINSTREAM business and IT media mostly talk about the B2B and B2C marketplaces (respectively, business-to-business and business-to-consumer), the much less discussed realm of C2C (consumer-to-consumer) activity is in many ways still the heart and soul of the global Internet.

This has actually been true since the Internet's very beginnings. The early use of the Internet by the research community was an excellent example of individuals creating value for other individuals, with little formal organizational involvement. Additionally, as Internet usage spread into the wider university environment, services such as Usenet, Telnet, and FTP (File Transfer Protocol) all emerged to make it easier for specific groups and individuals to rapidly share information. Focused communities and their various online resources were among the first major applications of the Net and became the model for much of its growth. Businesses were not an important part of the picture.

It wasn't long before it became clear that the most powerful of these early applications was electronic mail (e-mail), which more than any other service helped bring the scientific and university communities together. More important, from 1993–1996, e-mail was *the* driving Internet application for both businesses and consumers. It is hard to overstate the significance of this initial pattern. The efforts of the government and research communities bestowed the Internet upon the IT industry. Then students, businesspeople, and consumers began using it for e-mail, requiring relatively little in the way of traditional IT supplier support. In other words, the Internet's single most important application was not created or controlled by the IT supplier community.

E-mail proved to be the strongest market driver because it had all of the necessary market attributes. It was simple, widely appealing, inexpensive (usually free), and was a true industrywide standard. E-mail also benefited from very strong network effects. These effects were actually significantly stronger than those in the telephone industry. While both telephony and e-mail systems become much more useful as more users are added, telephone conversations are almost always between just two individuals. In contrast, e-mail messages can—for better or worse—be sent to an essentially limitless number of people, greatly increasing the potential for value creation.

Given these powerful C2C origins, it is only natural that, in an increasingly customer-centric IT industry, we should look once again to see how the consumer market is evolving. In this chapter we will see, as in the past, how consumers create value for each other is having significant implications for the development of the IT industry. Although much of the discussion over the last few years has been about the role of peer-to-peer (P2P) systems, this is actually a much too narrow and technical focus. As shown in figure 9-1, consumer value-creation efforts now cut across just about everything the Internet is used for, including communication, content, commerce, community, and computing itself. As suggested by powerful examples such as eBay and the open-source movement, these consumer value-creation activities will rival and perhaps even exceed those in the business and e-learning realms.

From a broader perspective, both the history of other major twentieth-century electronic innovations as well as the evolution of the IT industry argue strongly that once a technology becomes universally adopted, its impact increases dramatically. Consequently, there are few more important IT industry questions than when Internet access will become universally deployed in the United States and other developed nations. However, long before this level of consumer acceptance is reached, the early and mid-adopters will have established the dominant IT usage patterns. In this chapter we'll see that while much of the business IT story has been about commitment and perseverance, with consumers the issues are more ones of enthusiasm, preferences, and skills.

FIGURE 9 - 1

Major Realms of Consumer IT Value Creation

The size of each circle represents each area's relative importance. Content and community overlap because sometimes content is created by individuals, but often it stems from a community. While the computer resources area is currently small, the possibilities of P2P make this area a long-term wild card.

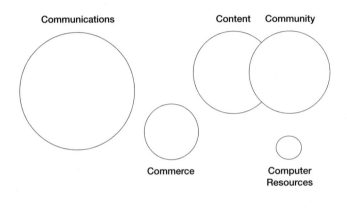

Communications Preferences

The importance of e-mail suggests that how consumers prefer to communicate will say a great deal about the future use of the Internet. One thing is clear: The technological options have been multiplying rapidly. Among the current choices are wired telephones, facsimile, voice mail, mobile telephones, pagers, e-mail, online chat, instant messaging, discussion groups, groupware, video conferencing, Web conferencing, Web cameras, wireless Internet, mobile short message services, and integrated voice/Internet services. And while it is possible that all of these technologies will play a significant role, it seems inevitable that consumer preferences will render some styles of communication more important than others. From an efficiency point of view, we may well have too many options, a situation that could force us all to make some choices.

Table 9-1 divides these technologies into two categories—synchronous and asynchronous. By "synchronous," I mean that there is essentially a real time (or a virtually real time) connection between two or more communicating parties. A telephone conversation is the classic example of synchronous communication technology in that the experience is essentially the same as a live conversation (at least from an audio perspective). In contrast, asynchronous communication typically means that a message is first sent, then stored somewhere, then read and/or acted upon later. Voice mail, e-mail, and postal mail are all important examples of asynchronous communications, which are also referred to as store-and-forward systems.

Synchronous and *asynchronous* are certainly odd and technical-sounding words, but they have powerful real-world implications. Increasingly, the biggest communications choice that most of us will have to make is whether we prefer to communicate in real time or in a store-and-forward manner. The evidence here is rather mixed, but at least from a U.S. point of view, there appears to be an underlying preference for asynchronous systems. Certainly, the heavy use of voice mail and home answering systems in the United States suggests that many of us prefer to screen our calls and respond at our convenience. E-mail enables a similar type of individual discretion and control.

In recent years, these issues have grown in importance as new generations of wireless systems have emerged. Of course, for many years,

TABLE 9 - 1

Major Forms of Consumer Communication

The table reveals that many of the newer communications modes are synchronous in nature and therefore are inherently much more intrusive for the user.

Asynchronous	Synchronous
Postal mail	Face-to-face
Express mail	Wired phones
Telegraph	Mobile phones
Facsimile	Instant messaging
Voice mail	Web conferencing
Pagers/beepers	Video conferencing
E-mail	Webcams
Text messaging	Video IM
Discussion groups	Voice over IP

some people have carried beepers and pagers to ensure that they can be reached instantaneously. However, most of this usage has been for very specific applications—such as doctors, soon-to-be fathers, construction workers, traveling executives, and, more controversially, gamblers and drug dealers. In these cases, real-time usage is more a matter of need than of individual preference. This helps explain why beepers and pagers never became more pervasive mass-market successes. Most people don't really want to use them unless they feel they have to.

Wireless telephones have provided a more recent and meaningful test. Yet despite the very high levels of consumer adoption, even here there is considerable evidence that people prefer to make calls on their cell phones rather than receive them. For example, outside of certain professions, such as sales, it is still relatively rare for U.S. businesspeople to put their cell phone numbers on their business cards. Instead, many of us only give out our mobile numbers to our immediate friends, family, and associates.

That there is a strong cultural element to these patterns seems evident when one looks at cell phone use internationally. As someone who has worked in more than thirty countries, including much of Europe, Asia, and Latin America, it still amazes me how there is often so much public cell phone use and so little use of voice mail. While this may well be due more to historical local telephone monopolies—and their resulting high fees and spotty service—than actual consumer preferences, for whatever reason the pattern is well-entrenched. Even today, many European businesses have little or no voice-mail capability, and in much of Europe, for example, cell phone numbers are often included as part of a business card. At the risk of stereotyping, it still seems true that all one has to do is walk through a few international airports to see that in many countries cell phones are used much more intensively than in the United States.

The reason that these differences in synchronous and asynchronous usage patterns matter is that many of the most important new communications technologies just happen to be synchronous in nature. The most important example is instant messaging (IM). Technically, IM uses the same asynchronous messaging as Internet e-mail, but because instant messages are delivered more quickly, in actual usage it is much more like a synchronous experience. IM services have proved to be very popular, particularly among teenage girls who have flocked to IM with the same sort of energy that teenage boys have brought to computer games. (Since many people have registered multiple names and rarely use their IM accounts, published estimates of as many as 70 million IM users in the United States alone are no doubt highly inflated, but the number of active users is clearly in the tens of millions.)

Today, the big question is how successful IM will be in business environments. Certainly, usage is growing and there are many potentially useful applications, especially in customer service and with highly interactive but dispersed business teams. But business IM usage is still relatively limited, primarily because there are many serious issues regarding security, confidentiality, message logging, encryption, directory services, application integration, quality of service, and other concerns. These are the sorts of problems that often emerge when a technology that was designed for consumers has to be adapted to the enterprise market. Many companies are working hard to address them.

But assuming that technical progress is made, the key question is whether employees really want to allow large groups of people—be they friends, family, clients, coworkers, or bosses—to know when they are at their desks (and implicitly when they are not). Thus far, the evidence is mixed. While there are a number of useful niche applications, it is only logical that extensive employee use of IM could sometimes be distracting and intrusive. For example, one of the reasons many of us often prefer to use voice mail is that we can leave a message without having to engage in the time-consuming courtesies that are an inevitable part of many phone conversations. IM systems can create similar needs for social interaction, which are often not required in, for instance, basic e-mail communication.

These social concerns are likely to increase as technologies become more capable. The best example of this has always been video conferencing. While video communications has suffered in the past from various price and performance shortcomings, the more serious problem might actually be a much more fundamental lack of demand. With today's Internet, low- to mid-grade video conferencing is fairly simple, yet there has been relatively little uptake by businesses and consumers. One reason for this is that many people just aren't very comfortable with being "on camera," other than perhaps with their close friends and family. Given that, like other communications technologies, video conferencing has strong network effects, this cultural resistance could be a serious long-term adoption barrier. The rapid business acceptance of non-video conferencing systems such as Webex and the initial consumer interest in talking to friends via wireless video-capable phones also support this interpretation.

These same concerns will tend to multiply as one moves on to even more advanced communications applications such as Webcams and video-based IM. From a consumer perspective, the former, thus far, has mostly been used for pornography, and the latter, at least initially, may be as well. However, eventually, a variety of business and consumer uses will emerge. Certainly, Web-connected cameras are an increasingly pervasive security and management option. Similarly, video-based IM will find significant business usage in many of the same groups interested in text IM today. The underlying costs of putting cameras and the necessary software on each PC have become relatively modest.

In sum, the key question is whether it will eventually become commonplace for most of us to regularly want to use text and/or video-based IM-style services. From an IT industry perspective, both technologies have the potential to drive the need for high-bandwidth systems and services. However, it is entirely possible that consumers and employees will continue to prefer more asynchronous communication modes, which tend to be much briefer and more text- and voice-oriented, and therefore require significantly less bandwidth. In this one, but particularly important, area, it would appear that there may well be a significant gap in terms of what IT suppliers wish for and what IT consumers really want. From this work's thematic perspective, consumers can create value for other consumers by making themselves available in real time. But it is not clear how many of us will actually be willing to do this on a regular basis.

The Outlook for Consumer-Driven Commerce

Given the enormous amounts of venture capital invested in B2C and B2B marketplaces, it is ironic that the single most important Internet e-commerce success story has been the mostly C2C story of eBay. Although consumers were certainly buying and selling lots of used and specialty items long before the arrival of the Internet, eBay has taken the business to a whole new level of scale and efficiency. Indeed, one could argue that e-mail and eBay are the two most successful Internet applications. That both are primarily C2C in nature must say something important about how the Internet will evolve.

Of course, eBay has expanded significantly and is no longer just an auction service for consumers and small businesses. It now supports medium and large companies, and even government agencies, especially in liquidation sales, and has complemented its auction business with fixed-price services. It has even become an important source of used IT products for enterprise customers. In all of these areas, eBay enjoys extremely strong network effects in that the more people who use the service, the more valuable it becomes. From a financial perspective, the company is in the enviable position of having its customers hold inventory, pay for marketing, and even pick up the shipping charges.

While the company might seem to have a near monopoly position, Amazon's rapid success in the used book market shows that future competition is likely. But the key issue for our purposes is to what extent IT consumers will be creating value for other consumers. Even with eBay's great success, its share of the potential used and specialty goods market is still very small, especially in major categories such as automobiles. This all but guarantees that, although growth in this sector will surely slow, consumers will continue to expand their buying and selling online. Early concerns regarding fraud have, despite a few high-profile cases, generally proved manageable, although Internet-based fraud will probably always be somewhat higher than for commerce in the physical world. The bottom line is that this type of C2C buying and selling will remain an important Internet business.

Harnessing the Energy of a Community

While the phrase *Internet community* is now often derogatorily associated with the more Utopian phase of the Internet industry, such groups are still a very powerful IT industry force. There is no better example of the ability of communities to create substantial new value than the so-called open-source movement. While the work of this community may not matter directly to most consumers, its current and future importance to the IT industry is difficult to overestimate.

A decade ago, who would have thought that the volunteer efforts of the world's programmers could build an operating system competitive with what Microsoft's vast army of highly paid talent could develop? At the root of this issue is a fascinating intellectual debate. Should software be developed via a grand top-down design, or should it emerge incrementally by the bottom-up actions of its users? Indeed, even today it is still far from clear which model will prove more powerful, the structured "cathedral" approach of a Microsoft, the sharing and peer review of the open source "bazaar," or some sort of hybrid process.[1]

But intellectual interests aside, the efforts of the Linux open-source community are basically the only thing that have prevented Microsoft from all but monopolizing the computer server operating system market in much the same way it has monopolized the desktop business. This is particularly true at the low end of the server market. At the high end, Unix-based systems from Sun and IBM continue to sell well, but these systems account for a declining share of overall server usage. (In contrast, in the microprocessor business, only Advanced Micro Devices [AMD] and its founder Jerry Sanders have prevented Intel from having virtually unlimited monopoly power; but at least AMD is an actual company, not a loose collection of microprocessor volunteers.)

For this, as well as the success of Apache in the Web server software market, the Perl programming language, and many other key Internet software standards and components, the entire world owes the open-source movement a huge debt of gratitude. And while it may be too much to ask, Linux is also the only likely challenge to Microsoft's desktop monopoly as well. Progress on this front is far from certain. But if Linux on the desktop ever became a serious alternative to Microsoft Windows, the efforts of volunteers would have accomplished what IBM, Apple, and all the lawyers of the U.S. Department of Justice could not: the diminishment of Microsoft's still overwhelming industry influence. It would be an even more extraordinary business story than what's happened in the server marketplace.

For our purposes, the accomplishments of the open-source movement are an example of just how powerful Internet-based communities can be, even when developing highly complex products such as computer operating systems. Clearly, not all of these efforts will succeed. Open-source projects need to maintain the right balance between sufficient but not overwhelming community input, and the long-run commercial pressures of open-source business competition have yet to fully play out. Only time will tell whether the open-source model can be sustained over several decades, the way commercial operating systems clearly can. However, given the previous successes, it's only logical to ask how replicable this movement really is, and to what extent community-based activity will help develop additional IT industry platforms.

Customer Created Content—Software and Tools

The issue of consumer-created value is best examined by separating these efforts into two broad camps: software and related tools such as metadata, and actual content such as information and entertainment. These two types of activity do have many things in common. For example, both software and content have effectively zero marginal costs and have many of the same copyright and national language concerns. However, from a market perspective, these similarities are outweighed by one great difference, market concentration. For example, no matter how much time I spend writing, I only use one word processing package. In contrast, if you like music, you might easily have hundreds of CDs. This is why software markets are usually very concentrated, while content markets tend to be much more fragmented. It's also one of the main reasons that software companies often find it difficult to succeed in content businesses.

In looking at the software side of things, the most obvious parallel to the open-source movement is the various types of community-developed metadata. We have already described how Gracenote managed to enlist the support of music listeners to build its database of individual song information. Another excellent example is the Dublin Core Metadata Initiative (DCMI), which since 1995 has focused on developing general information metadata. Volunteer participants tend to come from the library, museum, university, publishing, digital information management, and knowledge-management communities. DCMI now has seventeen working groups, which closely cooperate with other associations such as the European Committee for Standardization (CEN), the Internet Engineering Task Force (IETF), the W3C, the IEEE, and many others.

Similarly, the Open Directory Project, also known as dmoz, has been an important part of the growth of the Web search-engine business. Founded by Netscape (now part of AOL), thousands of volunteers have identified and classified Web sites to help the major search engines find them. In the spirit of open source, all information has always been free, as long as modest usage terms are adhered to. Similar volunteer classification efforts remain an important resource, especially in highly specialized fields such as the sciences. These projects strongly suggest that, where there is a proven need, volunteers and other communities will continue to play an important role in setting information standards, and creating new types of value. Overall, it's a very impressive track record.

Community Content

While metadata and software are very important in certain fields, content is a much more widespread form of consumer value creation. And thus, for our purposes, the key question is to what extent either individual consumers and/or communities will create important new content value. Curiously, it appears that we may be about to repeat an important IT industry pattern. In chapter 2, we saw how the failure of the minicomputer industry to agree upon a standard version of the Unix operating system and the subsequent dominance of Microsoft played a central role in the motivation for the Linux development effort. Similarly, the future of many forms of community-created content will also likely depend on what happens in the broader content industry. If commercial interests don't provide the content—and prices— that the market wants, the need for community-created content will increase correspondingly.

In other words, successful Web communities are all about filling actual market needs. This means that, even though commercial companies and Internet communities typically see themselves as coming from completely different worlds, their fates are really closely intertwined. In many cases, both are serving a common audience and competing for a common block of consumer time. Consequently, since the outlook for both for-fee and advertising-based content remains uncertain, it follows that the future of community content is equally unclear. The example of Linux showed how community content can emerge to compete with private-sector products. Conversely, in other cases—such as with many

Internet protocols and standards—community-created products have essentially replaced the need for what would otherwise have been private-sector efforts. The process can work in either direction.

In this sense, community-created content should be viewed as a potentially effective long-term check on the power of the content industry. This could prove especially important since, as we will see in chapter 10, corporate interests are now trying—not necessarily successfully—to draw an increasingly hard line on copyright and even fair-use practices. By this logic, one can conclude that community-based content has the potential to be important in any market where there is now significant commercial and/or copyright activity, especially in areas such as specialized news, information, commentary, analysis, entertainment, expertise, and advice.

This competition between commercial and community content is summarized in figure 9-2. The diagram provides a perspective by which to view today's main classes of community-created content, including "blogs," user groups, information, expertise, affinity systems, and access to particular files, all of which are dependent upon what happens in the larger content industry. This idea is expanded upon below:

- **Blogs.** Short for Weblogs. Over the last few years, the concept of "blogs" has attracted a great deal of media attention and has emerged

FIGURE 9 - 2

Community versus Commercial Content Competition

The boundaries between commercial and community content will be fluid, as the two activities both complement and compete with one another.

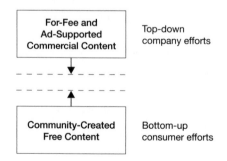

as an intriguing new class of C2C content. Blogs are essentially a form of link-intensive self-publishing and, arguably, a new style of writing. They can take many forms, including diaries, public rants, specialized commentary, and links to related materials. Thanks to tools from companies such as Blogger, it is now relatively easy for anyone to publish his or her own blog, or respond to the blogs of others without knowledge of HTML.

Consequently, there are now some five hundred thousand "bloggers" on the Web, some much more active than others. However, the long-term importance of these efforts seems dependent upon larger content industry trends. While there will always be interest in the real-life stories of real people, the large-scale and systematic creation of major new sources of value is unlikely unless current commercial content is withdrawn or only available for a fee. Perhaps this explains why some popular bloggers ask for "donations," and why many commercial Web sites (and many celebrities) now offer their own blogs.

- **Information/expertise.** Again, much depends on what happens in the professional content market. If the expertise of scholars, historians, journalists, doctors, scientists, mechanics, lawyers, financial advisors, collectors, and others is made available for free or perhaps is just very inexpensive, the need for consumer-created content in these areas won't be so great. Of course, no matter how much expert content is available, consumers will always add their own comments on top of it. But, as discussed in chapters 6 and 7, the big question is whether the world's vast array of information, knowledge, and expertise will be made systematically available through increasingly powerful semantic databases, and if so, at what price. To the extent that consumers are satisfied with commercial offerings, the need for community content will be diminished. But since over the next few years, significant amounts of free commercial content may well be withdrawn from the Web, this could create the need for increased community efforts.

- **File sharing.** The issues regarding online music have been covered extensively in chapters 3 and 7. Clearly, Napster, Gnutella, and other systems have proven that directories—be they centralized or decentralized—can make it possible to find and share particular files on particular individuals' PCs.

Clearly, everything that can be said about online music can also be said about other copyrighted materials such as films, e-books, photos, video, and images; all of which have similar copyright concerns. However, in terms of legal, noncopyrighted materials, the list of file-sharing possibilities is much more modest—pornography, recipes, and term papers, along with self-published music, videos, or writings are really all that come to mind, and it's not clear that any of these have the potential of the major forms of copyrighted material. This suggests that if commercial interests provide the copyrighted services that people want, the need for P2P file sharing might not be all that great. This will be even more true if it turns out that, as many have claimed, Gnutella-based systems won't scale very well.

- **Ratings/affinities.** The aggregated ratings of actual customers have become an important e-commerce influence in areas such as books, travel, restaurants, and music. The most prominent example is Amazon where a five-star system makes it easy to see what others think about just about every book on offer, certainly any that have sold reasonably well. Such rating systems are, of course, notoriously easy to abuse. For example, many books on Amazon have received favorable reviews that were essentially planted by various friends and supporters. Conversely, it's equally easy to unfairly criticize the work of another. Nevertheless, in aggregate, these customer reviews are often more useful than the self-promoting information provided by publishers. Similarly, while consumers certainly appreciate professional reviews, these often don't exist or are not easily and freely available. For these reasons, consumer ratings are another good example of the competition between commercial and community content.

- **Games.** Although online games are easy to dismiss as something for idle teenagers, the reality is that many online game sites are drawing large and loyal audiences. And while most of these games are really just B2C applications, the increasingly popular multiplayer option adds a significant C2C dimension, as game players can now compete and interact with one another. Through both instant messaging and Internet-based voice transmission, these interactions can now be as extensive as any other form of Internet communication. Eventually, 3-D technology will enable all sorts of more exotic and realistic environments.

However, the big potential for online games cannot be realized without extensive broadband deployment. Both Sony, with its PlayStation 2, and Microsoft, with its Xbox, are now experimenting with broadband game offerings. It's easy to imagine highly energized communities centered around various online competitions; it's already happening in South Korea. In the long run, this will almost certainly be an area where customers create real value for each other.

Resource Sharing

Last, but not least, is the whole area of leveraging the immense computing power and storage capacities distributed among the hundreds of millions of PCs now in use around the world. Here the question is to what extent people can effectively take advantage of the capabilities of a highly distributed resource. This topic generally comes under the heading of P2P systems. While definitions of what is or isn't a pure P2P system vary, for our purposes a P2P system is any system or application in which an individual can easily take advantage of another individual's computer resources—be they processing power, storage, printers, software, or digital files.

Since the potential for file-swapping services was covered earlier, in this section we will focus only on the types of value being created in the distributed processing power and storage areas. Both are examples of computer resources that are often greatly underutilized, and in the case of processing power, any unused computing cycles are, like an unfilled airline seat, essentially lost forever. In some cases, the envisioned systems are not really C2C applications at all; they are more like C2B or what could be called E2B (employee-to-business) systems. However, although the use of these types of resource sharing systems is likely to be appropriate for only a relatively narrow range of activities, in these areas they offer the potential for dramatic price and performance improvements. Let's briefly look at both the processing and storage options.

Processing power. Here, the best known example is clearly SETI@ home (the letters are drawn from the Search for ExtraTerrestrial Intelligence). Launched in 1998, the SETI system essentially divides vast amounts of satellite data into relatively small files or "work units." These work units are then sent over the Internet to participating client computers along with the necessary application software. The SETI client software works much like a screen saver, processing the received data whenever the computer is not otherwise busy. Once each client computer has finished its processing, it sends the results back to the SETI servers. Consumers have eagerly volunteered their machines' services, and well over 100 million work units have been processed by more than 2 million participants around the world. After some initial launch struggles, SETI believes that this process delivers more processing power than a supercomputer, but at less than 1 percent of the cost.

There is now significant use of this distributed computing approach in genetics, pharmaceuticals, physics, economic and financial modeling, and other computationally intensive disciplines. Some of these systems exist inside a single company or across a college campus; others are opened up to a much wider range of machines. These computing "grids" can make possible applications that otherwise would not be feasible, and it's entirely possible that this approach will eventually lead to dramatic breakthroughs in a number of fields. It's an exciting area of development, and one that has captured the attention of a number of leading computer suppliers, including IBM and Intel.

Information storage. While less glamorous than searching for life in outer space, the immense storage capacity of the world's PCs is also a powerful potential resource, which could be especially useful in making video available over the Internet. Whereas with music, Internet file sharing was largely a tool to make music more accessible, video file sharing requires very large storage capacities, for which distributed P2P systems could be useful. For example, while it may not be economical for any commercial entity to make available all of the episodes of a television comedy such as *Gilligan's Island,* there are almost certainly many individuals who would be willing to host an episode or two, especially as storage costs continue to plummet. Should copyright owners ever allow it, video could be the real driving force of P2P activity.

Conclusions

The success of e-mail, eBay, and the open-source movement strongly suggests that the consumer arena will continue to be a major source of new platform development, rivaling those developed by IT suppliers, businesses, and the education industry. The most likely areas of influence will be in individual communications, buying and selling, software and content development, and potentially video-sharing. How available we agree to make ourselves, how well consumer-created software and content compete with commercial offerings and how copyright law evolves will likely determine how much value this portion of the industry value chain will create. Overall, it's hard to avoid the sense that, once again, something big will happen in the consumer domain.

Yet as important as all of this is, perhaps the most fundamental source of consumer value will reside in the IT skills that all of us do or do not acquire. While the Web has made IT applications such as e-mail and basic Web surfing relatively simple, in many other areas additional training is badly needed. For example, what percent of the citizenry is really comfortable handling digital images, installing cameras or scanners, using MP3 files, running a Web-based conference, participating in a threaded discussion, or creating their own blogs? Part of this is simply a matter of generational change and experience, but enthusiasm and motivation are also important factors. Like driving a car, there has to be a motive to learn the necessary skills.

In this sense, the key question regarding consumer computing is how much time and effort people will give to their information technology-based activities and skills. In chapter 8, we saw how a great deal of education and training will be required for many employees to effectively do their jobs. This training will tend to naturally occur, since it is clearly in an employee's interest to improve his or her job-related skills. But the use of computers at home is another matter altogether. Here, the question is much more one of preference and enthusiasm. Today, there are very few consumer uses of technology that one could say are really necessary. Therefore, much of the market depends on how IT usage compares to other ways that people can spend their time.

As noted in chapter 1, in this regard, PCs haven't fared particularly well for most of their history, and even today, many consumers clearly prefer television, and probably even telephones and radio, to what the Internet has to offer. Through the use of online music, video, advanced semantic systems, online learning, chat, and enhanced telephony these attitudes could change. Let's hope so. Ultimately, the skills and enthusiasm of consumers will say as much about the future of the IT industry as anything that businesses or IT suppliers can do.

CHAPTER TEN

Government As a Source of IT Industry Value

ONE OF THE WORST predictions of the Internet boom years was the widely circulated idea that somehow the Internet would render obsolete many of the traditional roles of government. In its extreme forms, people talked about how the world's "artificial" national boundaries would quickly give way to the Internet's truly borderless reality. We were also told that much of our economic and social activity would become "emergent" and "self-governing" in nature, with little need for the fixed rules and hierarchies of the past. Additionally, the strong economy of the 1990s greatly increased many people's (especially U.S. citizens') faith in the private sector, further feeding what has been called a spirit of cyber-libertarianism.

Of course, this view was always a bit ironic, since the government itself was responsible for many of the activities that eventually led to the very creation of the Internet. As discussed in chapter 2, IT industry history strongly suggests that left to its own competitive instincts, the computer industry would never have developed a platform based entirely upon open standards not under the control of any one supplier, or even any group of suppliers. In this sense, the public sector created something that the private sector probably could not. And despite all the IT industry damage that has occurred since the Internet bubble burst, it would still be hard to argue that the Internet was not a major net positive for the IT business—although we can never really know how things would have otherwise evolved.

But irony aside, many of the arguments of the cyber-libertarian crowd have always been manifestly false. The reality is that the Internet has greatly increased the role of government in the IT industry. Indeed, this chapter will show that in a broad range of areas, government activity is an important IT industry facilitator, arbitrator, regulator, legislator, and occasionally a developer. And while public policy is always easy to criticize, many of these roles—especially as they relate to spectrum allocation, copyrights, privacy, security, taxation, and antitrust—remain extraordinarily complex and difficult. Yet increasingly, government decisions are directly affecting the IT industry's overall structure, dynamics, and ability to perform. This makes the public sector an essential value-chain component, as illustrated in figure 10-1.

Public-sector developments can also be particularly difficult to predict. Obviously, government IT policy ultimately stems from our elected officials, but these officials are usually elected for reasons that have nothing to do with IT policy. For example, who can say with any confidence whether Democrats or Republicans will have the edge over the next decade? And while not all IT issues should be seen in terms of the traditional debate between the left and the right, many can be. Clearly, the uncertainties of electoral politics are not just an IT industry concern. Every industry lobbies for a supportive legal and regulatory climate. However, as we will see in this chapter, the range of current and emerging public policy issues affecting the IT business is considerably wider and more rapidly changing than those faced by most other sectors.

Government Influence on the IT Industry Value Chain

Virtually every sector of the IT industry is significantly affected by numerous forms of government activity, which is why public policy has become a critical IT industry value-chain component.

Simplified IT industry value chain	Typical areas of public sector involvement
Customer Activity	Information, transactions, voting, licenses
Professional Services	Education, visas, anti-fraud, privacy, decency
Network Services	Regulation, spectrum allocation, antitrust, taxation
Software	Copyrights, standards, encryption, antitrust
Hardware	Patents, R&D, universal service, global trade

To get a sense of the effects of these issues, this chapter presents an overview and assessment of today's most important areas of government and IT industry interaction. The focus will be on IT-specific topics, rather than equally important cross-industry business concerns such as tort reform, financial reporting requirements, labor rules, tax laws, health and safety regulations, and unnecessary market barriers. And while the topics that follow don't constitute the entire public sector IT agenda, they should be sufficient to provide a sense of the many critical and often truly difficult policy issues that need to be addressed. These issues have been grouped into five main categories

- The development of specific enabling technologies

- The moderation and oversight of industry forces

- The delivery of government information and services

- The protection of the individual consumer

- The welfare of society as a whole

Some readers might question whether these activities should really be viewed as evidence of a customer-centric IT industry. After all, many of these topics are not directly related to the buying and use of IT products and services. However, this chapter will show why this broad range of government activity really is a part of the same general pattern in that public-sector actions, like those of customers, are shaping the IT industry's dynamics and potential. Perhaps the best way to summarize the situation is to say that rising customer and government influence must, by definition, reduce the relative value-chain influence of IT suppliers. This is why assessing the government's value-chain contribution is every bit as important as assessing that of businesses, educational establishments, and consumers.

To compare and accumulate the evaluations that follow, I have employed a relatively simple, three-part rating scheme:

- First, the overall importance of each issue will be ranked on a 1–5 scale, with 5 being very important, and 1 being not important.

- Second, the overall importance of each issue will be described as rising, falling, or staying the same over the next five years.

- Third, how well the government has been performing in each area will also be ranked on a 1–5 scale, with 5 indicating excellent performance, and 1 indicating poor performance.

By assessing the current and likely public-sector performance in each of these five main areas of government and IT industry interaction, we can better understand how this part of the IT value chain is performing. Overall, this analysis will show that, despite not having any clear overall IT strategy and despite several problematic areas, the total public sector contribution has been significant, even as many important challenges remain ongoing and/or unresolved. Additionally, although most of our focus is on the situation in the United States, the general set of public sector issues is quite similar throughout the developed world.

Key Internet-Related Public Policy Issues– Enabling Technologies

Spectrum Allocation

U.S. wireless systems continue to lag behind much of the developed world, a fact often used to support criticism of our current spectrum management approach. But the odd thing is that this approach is criticized from two very different directions. While many see the success of the European GSM standard as evidence of the need for more government coordination, others say the problem is far too much public-sector meddling. Consequently, the spectrum allocation scenario in the United States is still one of extended gridlock, as the telecom industry, the Department of Defense, television broadcasters, and others seek wide swaths of valuable frequencies. The FCC has found it difficult to keep everyone happy and thus has put off many key decisions.

So much remains uncertain that all we can say for sure is that the available spectrum is vast, but it is not infinite, and therefore given the conflicting interests of suppliers, some would-be market participants won't get all of the spectrum they want. Thus, unless there is an unexpected philosophical revolution, spectrum allocation decisions will continue to be made mostly in the political arena, and will remain subject to some of the most intense levels of industry lobbying. This certainly isn't just a U.S. problem. Most other developed nations are also struggling with this issue, with many suppliers grossly overbidding for wireless licenses, especially in Europe. But at least from a U.S. perspective, it seems pretty clear that unless spectrum allocation issues are resolved soon, there will be an adverse impact upon the IT business. *Current Importance:* 5; *Direction:* Rising; *Government Performance:* 2.

Industry Standards

As the single largest buyer of information processing goods and services, the federal government has a long history of directly influencing major IT industry standards. For example, federal government support played a key role in the acceptance of COBOL as the dominant business computer programming language of the 1970s. The federal government was also the biggest supporter of the Data Encryption Standard (DES), initially developed by IBM, which eventually became the main encryption technology of the 1980s. In the 1960s and 1970s, U.S. government efforts led to the establishment of the Global Positioning System (GPS), which eventually became a critical component of both the wireless and Internet infrastructures.

In recent years, public sector research influence has lagged, as government IT usage has fallen behind that of the private sector, although the Department of Defense has played an important role in developing the SCORM standard for the e-learning industry. However, given today's heightened security concerns, there is a good chance for renewed government leadership. Individual authentication, database linkages, secure communications, Radio Frequency Identification (RFID), smart cards, and various biometric technologies are among the areas where the federal government can significantly contribute to the standards-setting process. It's also possible that should independent groups such as the Internet Corporation for Assigned Names and Numbers (ICANN) continue to struggle, governments might have to get more deeply involved in establishing standards for IP addresses, domain name management, and related issues. If nothing else, the ICANN story shows that private sector solutions are not always easy to attain. *Current Importance:* 3; *Direction:* Rising; *Government Performance:* 3.

Security

Today, the list of technology-related IT security concerns seems virtually endless. It includes all forms of surveillance, encryption, privacy, database usage, hackers, virus protection, denial of service attacks, information warfare, infrastructure resiliency, disaster recovery, sensors, facial recognition, iris scanning, fingerprinting, global positioning, automated flight control, shipping standards, and more. But the broader concerns are perhaps even more important. Our heightened sense of vulnerability has put some of the most basic assumptions regarding the evolution of the global economy at significant risk.

For example, if every step in a company's operations has to be completely backed up and regularly double-checked, concepts such as highly interdependent global supply chains, just-in-time inventories, and mobile workforces could lose much of their appeal. More specifically, a great deal of international trade now depends on the efficient use of cargo containers, which just happen to be among the most difficult of security challenges. Since the emergence of the Internet, many people have talked about an increasingly friction-free economy. However, it's now entirely too easy to imagine future scenarios where all manner of new frictions are introduced. Additionally, while private sector spending on security will increase significantly for both security personnel and technology, government security efforts will continue to be our front line of defense, especially in the critical areas of national borders, harbors, transport systems, and air spaces. In other areas, close public and private cooperation will be required, such as with the recently formed Critical Infrastructure Protection Board. Clearly, no issue will more directly shape the business and social climate of at least the next few years, with implications for a wide array of public and private sector technology issues. *Current Importance:* 5; *Direction:* Rising; *Government Performance:* 3.

Individual Authentication

The ability to positively know that someone is who he or she claims to be is also an important potential source of new value creation. While the debate over the need for a national identification system brings out extreme views from both ends of the political spectrum, much of the anti-ID rhetoric seems overblown. After all, our social security numbers already serve as de facto national ID numbers, and like driver's licenses are used for all sorts of purposes beyond those initially envisioned. The only difference is that both of these systems have often been loosely administered and thus easily abused. But since my driver's license already includes both my picture and social security number, why should I object to it being based on technology that can't be easily changed or forged? Someday, embedded individual identification technology might make it easier to find people who are lost or buried under debris. Many people might then wear or carry it by choice.

Although there are a number of diverse national ID proposals, getting all fifty states to support a shared set of driver's license specifications seems to make the most practical sense (although getting all fifty states to agree upon anything is never easy). A reliable ID card would likely prove useful in a number of new IT applications. There might even be a link to the issue of online authentication, a market dominated by private-sector companies such as Verisign. In contrast, so-called trusted-traveler cards that rely on complex database profiles are likely to be much more controversial and probably less effective. Right now, both ideas are in the experimental stage at best, but if a standard does emerge it would have many long-lasting consequences. If nothing else, the technology choice—be it magnetic stripe, semiconductor smart card, bar code, or whatever—would have many long-term ramifications. *Current Importance:* 4; *Direction:* Rising; *Government Performance:* 2.

Research and Development

We have already discussed two of the U.S. government's major historical contributions, the Internet and the GPS. In addition, the Defense Department in particular has played an important R&D role in areas such as programming languages, wireless communications, encryption, flat panel displays, semiconductors, satellites, supercomputers, and robotics. However, the capabilities of the private sector have increasingly matched or exceeded those of the public sector, and thus the relative importance of the government as a source of IT R&D has declined. It's now just one of several significant players.

The big question going forward is whether the combined efforts of the public, private sector, and university communities will prove sufficient. Ensuring adequate R&D levels is a particularly important issue in sectors that have moved to a highly horizontal structure. Almost by definition, new areas of research don't necessarily fit into the needs of existing horizontal markets. This is why in the past vertically integrated giants such as IBM and AT&T could justify advanced laboratories that could pursue a wide range of technologies that would hopefully find specific applications later. Today, while Microsoft and Intel do a great deal of research within their specific domains, other areas of IT industry R&D are often undernourished, particularly in long-term basic research. Increasingly, universities have taken the lead in this area. However, the big post-September 11 boost in military spending will also likely lead to increased high-tech R&D investments in areas such as satellite control, nanotechnology, life sciences, night vision, guidance systems, robotics, and other areas. *Current Importance:* 3; *Direction:* Same; *Government Performance:* 4.

Key Internet-Related Public Policy Issues— Moderating Industry Forces

Telecom Regulation

As long as local telephone companies maintain near-monopoly positions, government interest in overseeing local telephone rates and business practices will likely continue. While many have criticized the federal government's handling of this issue, most of the complaints have been unfair. Over the last twenty years, government policy has helped transform the telecom landscape from one controlled by a monopolistic AT&T into a truly competitive business. Strong, often brutal, competition now exists in long distance services, telecom and datacom equipment, wireless services, and Internet access. Only in the so-called local loop are there strong monopoly players, and because of broadband cable, telephone-based DSL, high-speed wireless, and various satellite possibilities, even these areas should eventually become much more competitive. Overall, despite a number of questionable steps, this is a pretty successful record.

Nevertheless, deep philosophical issues remain ahead. The most important of these is whether the local telephone and cable television businesses should be treated equally or continue to be subject to differing regulatory processes. Similarly, the federal government will have to decide if and when local phone and cable television markets should be substantially deregulated, and whether "open access" policies should be imposed. At stake is how tomorrow's high-bandwidth infrastructure will be built and operated, and who gets to say how this infrastructure will be used. There are few more critical public policy decisions. From a longer-term perspective, government policy regarding television, cable television, radio, and newspaper cross-ownership could also have significant IT industry impact. *Current Importance:* 4; *Direction:* Same; *Government Performance:* 4.

Antitrust Enforcement

While this is always a controversial topic, the overall government record in this area has been positive, and has often helped the IT industry cope with its strong single-supplier tendencies. Certainly, the government-imposed breakup of AT&T in 1982 greatly benefited the IT industry, unleashing rapid telecom innovation and growth. Similarly, while opinions regarding the three antitrust cases against IBM vary widely, the terms of the Consent Decree of 1956 and the antitrust pressure that in 1969 encouraged IBM to "unbundle" its products and services were also very important and beneficial IT industry changes.

As of this writing, the Microsoft antitrust case is dragging on, with the outcome still uncertain. Many industry participants were understandably unhappy with the settlement reached with the Bush administration, which is why the states that have continued to fight have received significant public support. However, although many of us had hoped for a breakup of Microsoft or at least much stronger restrictions on the company's ability to bundle its software products, these were always a bit of a long shot. Thus modifying Microsoft's business practices, contract language, and software interface policies is probably all that can reasonably be expected. Perhaps the best way to frame the issue is to ask whether the IT industry would be better off if there were no government check on Microsoft's power at all. I very much doubt this.

Ironically, once the Microsoft case is behind us, the strong single-supplier leadership that has been the traditional focus of IT industry antitrust enforcement will probably be replaced by concerns over collusion and other issues regarding supplier cooperation. Increasingly, the antitrust cases of the future are likely to be more like those brought against Visa and MasterCard than against IBM and Microsoft. However, the overall issue of antitrust appears to be a permanent aspect of IT industry competition. *Current Importance:* 4; *Direction:* Same; *Government Performance:* 4.

Copyright Law

Over the last few decades, U.S. copyright and patent law has steadily drifted away from its original Constitutional purpose. The primary goal of these laws is not to protect the interests of artists, writers, and other creators. The main goal is to promote societal progress. According to Article 1, Section 8 of the U.S. Constitution (emphasis added): "The Congress shall have Power to . . . promote the *Progress* of Science and useful Arts, by securing for *limited* Times to Authors and Inventors the exclusive Right to their respective Writings and Discoveries. . . ." In other words, copyrights and patents were initially envisioned as a means to an end. However, largely because of heavy corporate lobbying and perhaps the implicit bias in the widely-used term *intellectual property rights,* we have been steadily turning copyright law into just another form of individual property protection. Consequently, copyright holders have been gaining almost unlimited rights to control the use of their work for ever-lengthening periods of time. The current life-of-the-author-plus-seventy-years standard is now totally out of line with the idea of using copyright protection to provide meaningful creative incentives.

However, the ability to enforce these rights online has thus far proven limited, and if anything there are more copyright violations today than ever. The key question going forward is which way this balance will shift. One scenario says that content will not be able to be protected unless strong laws are imposed on both hardware manufacturers and the Web sites that deliver content. Others argue just the opposite, saying that future Digital Rights Management technology will soon become so powerful that copyright owners will have an almost unlimited ability to control the use of their work, and therefore laws will be needed to ensure the "fair use" rights of consumers. It would be hard to imagine two more different perspectives. The sad thing is that business interests have much more political clout in this area than consumers. This is a worrisome reality, as recently evidenced by broadcaster efforts to collect what many consider to be prohibitively high royalties from the emerging Internet radio industry. *Current Importance:* 5; *Direction:* Rising; *Government Performance:* 2.

Patent Law

Today, the biggest areas of patent concerns are outside of the IT industry, particularly in cases involving life-saving drugs, genetic innovations, cloning, and other life sciences frontiers. In these areas, policy makers are being asked to make fundamental decisions, ultimately involving life and death. While nothing in the IT industry can match the magnitude of these concerns, the IT business has always had a strong interest in U.S. patent law. Indeed, the most famous and important patent of all time was awarded to Alexander Graham Bell, which despite many challenges, became the foundation of what eventually became AT&T and the U.S. telephone system.

Given this legacy, it's hardly surprising that the issue of Internet patents would be both controversial and important. Indeed, whether the government maintains strict or liberal definitions as to what Internet innovations are patentable will have long-lasting technology industry repercussions in the United States and around the world. Although this issue has quieted down somewhat from the Amazon one-click controversy of the late 1990s, it was never fully resolved and therefore is likely to eventually resurface. Personally, I would like to see the entire field of software-based business processes become subject to copyright and not patent law. This would allow others to take advantage of a new idea, but not the actual software code behind it.

Unfortunately, there is little chance of this happening anytime soon. Powerful business, legal, and patent office interests continue to push for strong patent protection. If anything, the U.S. government is still granting patents too quickly, and with not enough comment from those affected. The fear is that only in hindsight will we realize that major mistakes have been made, and that patents are retarding innovation, not facilitating it. From an Internet perspective, the biggest patent battles may well lie ahead, especially if important future enhancements to the Web itself come under patent consideration. For example, it remains to be seen whether standards bodies such as the W3C can keep privately owned patents from becoming key parts of the Internet's future architecture. If they can, it would be an important achievement. *Current Importance:* 4; *Direction:* Rising; *Government Performance:* 2.

Tax Policy

Thus far, federal law has prevented state and local sales taxes from being applied to most transactions over the Internet. In terms of both simplicity and actual online prices, this policy has given a significant boost to the e-commerce business. However, this special status is unlikely to last forever, especially as e-commerce sales grow. Pro-Internet and anti-tax forces have thus far been very effective in protecting the Internet's special status, but now that the dot-com industry has lost much of its public support, this task will likely become increasingly difficult. For example, in 2001, Congress extended the Internet tax moratorium for just two years instead of the five that proponents had sought.

This decision is actually hard to argue with. In the end, if you're buying a book in Dayton, OH, common sense says that the taxes you pay should be the same regardless of whether you buy the book online or at a traditional store. Otherwise, one side or the other is receiving a special government-induced advantage. This basic line of reasoning should eventually allow those who favor a consistent tax environment to prevail, especially if state governments can work together to develop a system that is relatively easy to implement. In this work, they will generally have the strong support of traditional retail industry. However, given the very different interests of each state, reaching agreement won't be easy, and thus the long-term Internet taxation outlook is still quite uncertain, not only in the United States, but also internationally as discussed below. *Current Importance:* 3; *Direction:* Rising; *Government Performance:* 4.

International Cooperation

Many of the issues discussed in this section have a strong international dimension, especially copyrights, patents, privacy, taxation, antitrust, standards, and establishing jurisdictions. International disputes are particularly frequent between the United States and the European

Union (EU), which often seems to adopt stricter standards and policies than does the more wide-open U.S. market. There have already been significant differences regarding Internet taxation, privacy, and antitrust policies. Additionally, because the European market is so large, most multinational companies will tend to conform to any reasonable European requirement. And since conforming to two different sets of rules in the United States and Europe can be difficult, it is often the stricter policies that prevail. This suggests that the rules of international trade could be increasingly written in Brussels.

This situation would not be so inherently problematic were it not for the very different positions of the U.S. and European IT industries. Outside of the wireless area, U.S. firms are so dominant in Internet-related markets that it is almost impossible for U.S. and European policy makers to see these issues similarly, especially given the many broader cultural and political differences that already exist and have deepened during the Bush administration. Certainly, few tears will be shed in Europe for any IT policies that adversely affect U.S. suppliers. Looking forward, it's possible that these issues will spill over into more customer-centric IT domains. For example, the EU's ability to block the proposed merger of two U.S. companies, General Electric and Honeywell, suggests that future cooperative ventures may have more antitrust problems in Europe than in the United States. *Current Importance:* 4; *Direction:* Rising; *Government Performance:* 3.

Key Internet-Related Public Policy Issues— Government Services

Government Information

While there is a great deal of government information available online, the near-term outlook here is not particularly encouraging. Even during the IT-oriented Clinton administration, little progress was made in knocking down bureaucratic fiefdoms and delivering advanced public-sector services. The Bush administration generally has few such inclinations and has not put much emphasis on the government's use of IT, other than in the security applications. Shifting government priorities, rising security budgets, and high levels of inertia seem likely to prevent major innovations and changes over the next few years, making ambitious projects such as a national digital library unlikely. Many potentially advanced online government services will likely have to wait for more peaceful times.

In theory, virtually all of chapter 6's discussion regarding the need to semantically reengineer content for the Web is applicable to government information. However, most government information—be it federal, state, or local—is controlled by its particular agency. Perhaps this partially explains why, although usage is growing, the majority of U.S. citizens have never visited a government Web site. In a November 2001 report, the Progressive Policy Institute (PPI)—a centrist Democrat nonprofit research group (which I have worked with a few times over the years)—outlined a number of steps by which federal and state agencies could make their information much more useful to the general public.[1] One of the key recommendations was that government information should be available by topic as opposed to just specific agency function.

For example, a Web site might pull together all of the government's information regarding nutrition, charter schools, or farming, or be aimed at particular constituencies such as seniors, students, people with disabilities, or children. However, although the potential here is real enough, so is the lack of cooperative culture and the general sense of bureaucratic inertia. Clearly, the incentives to change are often much fewer than in the private sector. Thus far at least, the Bush administration has not made any of these issues a priority. Al Gore might well have, at least in a peacetime environment. It's a good example of how essentially unpredictable changes in administrations can lead to very different IT policies. *Current Importance:* 2; *Direction:* Rising; *Government Performance:* 3.

Online Transactions

While improved information access would certainly be nice, the biggest opportunities to increase citizen use of government services come under the broad topic of transaction processing. According to the same PPI study, among the government services that people most want online are renewing driver's and other licenses such as hunting and fishing, voter registration and voting, getting park information and making reservations, ordering copies of birth, death, and marriage certificates, and filing taxes. The direct deposit of benefits, tax refunds, and other disbursements is another potentially major area of value-added service.

While many state governments are in various stages of development in these areas, the overall usage is still quite low. As with bill-paying and other business applications, it is in the government's long-term interest to encourage people to do many of these activities online, since the costs will often be considerably less. However, in many ways, today's public sector situation represents the worst of both worlds, as in-person services are still required, and many online offerings are not used enough to efficiently amortize costs. It's not clear what, if anything, will be done to help many online citizen-government transactions achieve critical mass.

From this perspective, the government's challenge is actually considerably more difficult than in the private sector. If new transaction services are only made available online, government officials can be sure that they will be criticized for catering only to the "digital haves." This is the opposite of the way things work in the private sector, where it is taken for granted that new applications will be targeted at potential early adopters, with the mass market hopefully following later. Unfortunately, especially among many Democrats, this basic market mechanism is often deemed to be fundamentally unfair.

This is just another reason public services are unlikely to take the lead in driving increased levels of societal usage. It is also why it is increasingly likely that other nations will move faster in many of these areas. A recent study by Accenture argued that both Canada and Singapore already match the United States in the overall use of Web-based government services, with several other nations not far behind.[2] In many ways, the United States' layered system of town, county, state, and federal government is simply not well-suited for many advanced IT-based applications, especially voting. *Current Importance:* 3; *Direction:* Rising; *Government Performance:* 2.

Voting and Registration

Online voting is perhaps the best example of a powerful new government IT application platform. It is also a daunting technological challenge. Indeed, it would be hard to imagine a more difficult transaction processing task. Any online voting system must be completely reliable, easily verifiable, and thoroughly secure in terms of both preventing fraud and protecting the privacy of each individual voter. Additionally, the whole system might only be used every other year or so and even then just for a few separate days.

However, successfully implemented, online voting could mean a great deal to voters and even our democracy itself. Surveys show that online registration and actual voting could greatly increase today's relatively low rates of voter participation. It's also likely that if such a system could be put into place, it would be used for other purposes, particularly referenda and other forms of participatory democracy. Similarly, the technologies required for such a system, especially those related to authentication—would likely find wider government and commercial use. Unfortunately, given the United States' complex mix of local, state, and federal election laws, it is almost certain to lag in this area. Smaller but technologically advanced nations such as the Scandinavian countries, Singapore, or the Netherlands are likely to be among the early online voting leaders. *Current Importance:* 4; *Direction:* Rising; *Government Performance:* 2.

Key Internet-Related Public Policy Issues— Consumer Protection

Individual Privacy

Surveys suggest that many U.S. citizens would be willing to trade off some privacy if it would meaningfully increase public security. Once taboo subjects such as explicit racial, ethnic, and psycho-graphic profiling are now being seriously debated, and the government is considering much more direct linkages between its many national databases, which for better or worse, are a potentially huge area of new value creation. Many people have argued that explicit forms of racial profiling might well have prevented at least some of the September 11 attacks. Clearly, the use of technology is central to any such debate.

During the Internet bubble, the big privacy issue was the use of "cookies" and related customer profiling. This issue has receded somewhat, largely because the advertisers themselves are having doubts about the effectiveness of costly and detailed customer profiling, and thus are scaling back some of these efforts. Nevertheless, Congress is considering legislation that would establish rules for the way businesses collect information online and rights for consumers to see this data and sue for any misuse. Businesses continue to push for self-regulation, or, if this strategy fails, they seek to be treated no differently than many offline businesses. Republicans tend to support this business perspective, while Democrats take a more consumer approach, but the bigger privacy differences are ultimately likely to be between the United States and Europe, which is considering much stricter privacy legislation. *Current Importance:* 4; *Direction:* Rising; *Government Performance:* 3.

Minimizing Fraud and Abuse

The Internet is still rife with all manner of fraudulent activity and consumer complaints are rising, especially in areas such as investments, health care, and auctions. However, both the Federal Trade Commission and leading private companies such as eBay have made a serious effort to identify and punish online crime. While the prevalence of Internet scams will probably always be higher than the rate of fraud in the physical world, thus far, it has not been a major e-commerce barrier.

More broadly and more seriously, public confidence in private markets has clearly been shaken by the collapse of so many once highly touted dot-coms, the conflicts of interest for Wall Street analysts and the major accounting firms, and the high-profile bankruptcies of Enron, WorldCom, Global Crossing, and others. If the public comes to the conclusion that private markets are fundamentally corrupt or unfair, the consequences could be severe. These issues will be addressed more deeply at the end of this chapter and again in chapter 11. *Current Importance:* 4; *Direction:* Rising; *Government Performance:* 4.

Pornography

In the early years of the Internet industry, it often seemed that the only high-tech issue that politicians could agree on was the need to pass laws designed to protect children from online pornography. Unfortunately, they have found it difficult to do this in a way that the courts find constitutional. Although this once-heated issue has cooled considerably since the late 1990s, there is now more pornography on the Web than ever, much of it promoted by very explicit forms of spam. Recent legal debates have focused on whether public libraries should have the right to put filtering software on their Internet-connected computers, and to what extent local communities can establish their own Internet pornography standards. The digital simulation of child pornography is also an active issue, one that has made its way to the Supreme Court.

Looking ahead, further controversies appear likely. Pornography has been one of the earliest major applications of just about every new media—including printed books and magazines, VCRs, cable television, CD-ROMs, 900 numbers, and now the Internet. Already, new technologies, particularly video-based chat and the widespread use of Web cams, are triggering a wave of X-rated high-bandwidth innovation. There is also the possibility that the emergence of new domain names, such as the oft-suggested XXX, might spur the government to take another look at the pornography issue. Widely different cultural attitudes toward pornography make this a particularly tough issue internationally. *Current Importance:* 2; *Direction:* Falling; *Government Performance:* 3.

Gambling

In most states, the reigning political philosophy seems to be that gambling is a bad idea except when run by state governments themselves, or as part of some sort of Native American reservation deal. There is now so much hypocrisy and vested interests built into this issue that a sensible national policy seems unlikely. Although online gambling on the Internet is both extensive and growing (mostly on Web sites outside of the United States), these systems are unlikely to attract mass-market use because of the high degree of fraud and total lack of consumer protection in what is essentially an illegal activity. Additionally, in today's heightened security environment, illegal international financial transactions are being taken much more seriously. On the other hand, in both the United Kingdom and Australia, certain forms of online gambling are legal, and a number of international companies are lobbying to get the United States to change its laws. In the short term, this remains highly unlikely.

The one thing we do know is that if online Las Vegas-style gambling on sports and other events was ever made completely legal, gambling volumes would almost certainly boom. (It's already an important, but controversial use of PayPal.) However, since this remains unlikely, a more probable step is that some states will take their lottery operations online. From a broader perspective, the ability to effectively discourage illegal gambling at offshore casinos will be a good indicator of how borderless the Internet eventually becomes. *Current Importance: 2; Direction:* Same; *Government Performance: 2.*

Key Internet-Related Public Policy Issues— Improving Social Welfare

K–12 Education

Since state and local governments manage most of the nation's K–12 schools, these same governments will ultimately determine to what extent computers and the Internet will be part of our basic grade-school education. During the Clinton administration, the need to have computers and the Internet in the classroom was given a great deal of emphasis. Al Gore, in particular, was instrumental in pushing through the so-called E-Rate program that still provides several billion dollars per year in subsidies to increase Internet access in our public schools and libraries. Such programs were seen as an important symbol of the government's commitment to both technological progress and equal opportunity. Additionally, many leaders of the IT supplier community also took up this cause, partly out of their sincere belief in the power of technology and perhaps partly for the clear and valuable PR.

However, while much good work has been done, there is increasing evidence that the use of computers has relatively little to do with receiving an effective K–12 education. Classroom sizes, teacher training, the school environment, regular testing, and involved parents are all now recognized as more important factors. These diminished expectations have become part of the general public deflation regarding the near-term possibilities of IT. Today, you don't hear very much about the need for computers in the schools, and it's not clear if or when the issue will seriously resurface. It's an important aspect of the post-bubble phase. *Current Importance: 3; Direction:* Falling; *Government Performance: 3.*

Labor-Force Skills

By far the most important issue here is the government's controversial H1-B Visa program, under which hundreds of thousands of foreign nationals have been allowed to temporarily work and reside in the United States. Since the program began in 1990, its supporters have argued that the United States doesn't produce nearly enough programmers and computer scientists, and therefore skilled immigrants are necessary if the economy is to fulfill its potential, and the country is to keep its IT lead. Opponents see the HI-B program as a way to suppress high-tech wages, and as a disincentive for U.S. citizens to acquire advanced software and engineering skills. Others have even called the program immoral, in that visa recipients often come from relatively poor countries, especially India and Pakistan, which, it is argued, need all of the human capital they can get back home. However, most H1-B source country governments generally disagree with this position.

In the United States, the balance of the argument often seems to shift depending on the cycles of the economy. During the boom years, the program had strong support. But once large layoffs began to sweep through the IT industry, the idea of importing IT talent lost much of its logic. Additionally, the H1-B program is now under much tighter security scrutiny, since clearly computer professionals could create substantial havoc if they so choose.

Other than the H1-B issue, public sector efforts to enhance the nation's IT skills are relatively inconsequential. In the 1960s and 1970s, the federal government, especially the military, was an important source of IT training. But largely because of noncompetitive salaries, the federal IT work force has aged to the point of becoming a serious staffing problem, and thus is no longer a source of broader IT industry supply. *Current Importance:* 5; *Direction:* Falling; *Government Performance:* 4.

Universal Service

During the Internet boom there was much talk about a coming "digital divide" between those with and those without Internet access and skills. As described in chapter 1, public-sector help was instrumental in bringing electricity, telephone service, and highways to remote parts of the nation. Since universal access greatly expands the overall potential of a technology and its impact upon society, many have argued that the government should be committed to ensuring universal Internet access. As with computers in the classroom, this was an idea heavily associated with the Clinton administration.

Certainly Internet usage is, like many forms of consumer spending, significantly influenced by income. However, the fact that many people who could easily afford Internet service still haven't acquired it tends to diminish the urgency of the universal service argument, and thus far the idea of subsidizing consumer access to the Internet has been resisted. Similarly, people once worried that the concept of a digital divide would become particularly acute with high-bandwidth Internet services, especially in rural areas and the inner city. But while this once seemed plausible, the rapid emergence of Wifi high-bandwidth wireless technology may well resolve the issue, especially since high-bandwidth services have yet to prove anywhere near compelling enough as to warrant concerns about lack of access. *Current Importance:* 3; *Direction:* Same; *Government Performance:* 3.

Preparing Tomorrow's Workforce

More broadly, the three topics in this section—K–12 education, laborforce skills, and universal service all share a common source of concern, the technical know-how of U.S. society. From this perspective, the issues of universal service and computers in schools are at least arguably less about education than about vocation. In other words, the reasons that students should be exposed to computers are similar to those used to justify teaching shop, home economics, or driver's education. They help prepare us for the adult world that lies ahead. This suggests that the main issue is not whether computers are in every classroom, but rather making sure that each student learns how to effectively use computers, a much more manageable challenge. If society could be confident that every student would receive this type of training before leaving high school, much of the universal service debate would likely fade away.

Conclusions

The five groupings of public-sector activities presented in this chapter provide a convenient way of summarizing the overall scope of government activities affecting the IT industry, especially as they relate to our larger purpose of viewing government initiatives in terms of their ability to advance or retard IT industry progress. A summary of this chapter's key findings is provided in table 10-1. Assuming one agrees with this table's ratings, it's hard to avoid the conclusion that while there are a number of clearly negative forces such as copyrights and patents and many areas that could be improved, the overall contribution of government to the IT industry is still a significant net positive. This continues a long tradition that goes back through the early years of the computing and telecommunications industries.

Additionally, the evidence shows that government is now a more influential part of the IT industry's value chain than ever before. And since political strategies and decisions will likely vary greatly around the world, this introduces an important competitive dynamic. From this perspective, the key question is not whether the U.S. public sector is perfect, but rather how well it compares to other nations. Just as each nation is largely responsible for overseeing the development of its own telecom infrastructure, it is also responsible for its own policy decisions across the many areas discussed in this chapter. Clearly, some countries will make different and more effective decisions than others, with major implications for domestic IT usage. In many public policy areas, countries with smaller populations and stronger central governments might well have some significant advantages.

However, when compared to global economic rivals such as Europe, Japan, and China, the U.S. public sector position appears strong. The EU still faces immense decision-making and implementation challenges across its many diverse members; Japan is still consumed with its overall economic problems; while China lags far behind in the sophistication of its Internet industry. Although there will be many international challenges, this bodes well for the future competitiveness of the U.S. IT industry.

Consequently, the main public-sector risks remain at home. During the heady growth of the economy and the IT industry in the second

TABLE 10 - 1

Rating the Government Contribution by Factor

The first column ranks the importance of each issue using a 1–5 scale, with 5 meaning very important and 1 not important. The second column indicates whether the overall importance of government activity in each area is rising, falling, or staying the same. The third column rates the recent performance of federal, state, and local governments; it also uses a 1–5 scale, with 5 being excellent and 1 poor.

	Current Importance	Direction	Government Rating
Enabling Technologies			
Spectrum Allocation	5	Rising	2
Industry Standards	3	Rising	3
Security Technologies	5	Rising	4
Individual Authentication	4	Rising	2
Research and Development	3	Same	4
Business Oversight			
Regulatory Policy	4	Same	4
Antitrust Enforcement	4	Same	4
Patent Law	4	Rising	2
Copyright Law	5	Rising	2
Taxation Policies	3	Rising	4
International Cooperation	4	Rising	3
Delivering Services			
Government Information	2	Rising	3
Online Transactions	3	Rising	2
Voting and Registration	4	Rising	2
Protecting the Consumer			
Individual Privacy	4	Rising	3
Fraud and Abuse	4	Same	4
Pornography	2	Falling	3
Gambling	2	Same	2
Improving Social Welfare			
K–12 Education	3	Falling	3
Labor Force Skills	5	Falling	4
Universal Service	3	Same	3

half of the 1990s, it often seemed that the IT industry could easily get its way on Capitol Hill. Important examples have been the moratorium on Internet sales taxes and the Y2K liability protection, which was pushed through Congress in 1999. (The latter, of course, proved to be completely unnecessary.) Overall, Congress and the general public was clearly attracted to and influenced by the IT industry's ideas, status, and money, and therefore a pro-IT policy environment prevailed.

Today, however, the situation is entirely different, and the IT industry is viewed much more warily. The spectacular dot-com bust, the scandals with Wall Street analysts, Enron, Arthur Andersen, World-Com, Adelphia, and Global Crossing, the excessive levels of executive pay and dubious sweetheart loan deals, and the tawdry behavior of many parties in the Microsoft antitrust trial, have all combined to create a significant "trust gap," with deep concerns about the quality of U.S. corporate governance, especially in the IT sector.

And it is here that the government is providing one of its most important services of all—the restoration of public trust. In the aftermath of just about every boom and bust cycle, there are both clear cases of wrongdoing and a natural search for scapegoats. Government action can often be helpful in both improving the existing rules and making sure the public reaction does not spin out of control. Both Congress and the Bush administration deserve great credit for quickly making it clear that top executives are responsible for the accuracy of their company's financial results and that fraud will be criminally punished. An IT industry that once spurned public sector involvement is now grateful that the federal government has intervened to minimize the damage.

III

Summary and Conclusions

CHAPTER ELEVEN

Implications for IT Suppliers and Customers

ONE REASON THIS BOOK started off by reviewing the history of twentieth-century technological adoption is that, in many respects, it's still hard to ignore the parallels between today's IT industry and the situation of the late 1920s. The emergence of radio, motion pictures, telephones, automobiles, airplanes, and all sorts of electric appliances helped drive a huge bubble of societal optimism and financial excess. Who could have known that we would first have to suffer through a vast depression and a terrifying war before the technology promises of that era were fulfilled? But even through the toughest of times, industry participants understood that these marvelous new inventions were not like tulip bulbs; their importance was not going to go away. And of course, neither is the Internet.

This begs the question of whether many of the grand late-1990s claims regarding the Internet were also wrong more in timing than in substance. Overall, the evidence suggests that this is the case. Looking back, the Internet's core initial promises of globally connected communities, increasingly seamless e-commerce, and information at your fingertips should all eventually be realized. Sure, there have been many silly predictions regarding the irrelevance of government and need for all information and software to be free. But these were similar to the Utopian promises of the 1920s, such as the once widespread belief that the emergence of a new technocratic elite would soon lead to a more just and rational society, devoid of the ethnic and religious biases of the past. Sadly, the twentieth century proved otherwise.

Thus, gauging the general pace of transition away from the pre-Internet world is still the key IT market forecasting issue, and hopefully this book has shed some light on the many factors involved. As a means of summarizing our key themes, below are ten key questions that I think will tell us whether or not the IT industry is on track to live up to its potential. Not surprisingly, all of these will be customer/application issues, but in each case, I have also identified the particular industry or industries most likely to make progress in each area. As the structure of part 2 suggested, these ten topics cut across business, education, consumer, and government realms.

1. Are medium and large businesses doing the bulk of their purchasing, invoicing, and payments online? Have the major implementation and security issues been overcome, and has the industry come to define and adopt the necessary standards? Are new value-added services being built on top of these basic transactional systems? *Key industry leaders:* manufacturing and retail.

2. Are consumers paying most of their bills online? Do they have any cost incentives to do so? Have the volumes of first-class mail dropped so much as to put a significant dent in U.S. postal system revenues? Is the future of the Post Office an important topic on Capitol Hill? Are the same sorts of changes occurring in the paper check industry? *Key industry leaders:* financial services and utilities.

3. Are there proven markets for various forms of online content, and have providers found a way to use technology to build the most attractive services they can, or are they still holding back because of financial and/or copyright concerns? Do these new online systems go far beyond the capabilities of offline alternatives? Are there coherent markets for free, for-fee, and advertising-supported services? *Key industry leaders:* media and publishing.

4. Are consumers directly managing their health care choices and spending? Has a set of online services emerged that are roughly equivalent to the way many of us manage our personal investments today? Are most health care and insurance claims being processed entirely electronically? *Key industry leaders:* health care and insurance.

5. Are 80 percent or more of consumers online? Do they have the communications bandwidth and skills needed to manage music, images, video, and home-based networks? Are consumers willing to make themselves available in real time through instant messaging and other forms of synchronous communication? *Key leader:* consumers.

6. Has a whole new generation of powerful semantic databases emerged to make expertise more accessible in specific areas such as academic subjects, music, sports, medicine, and law? Is access to relevant knowledge increasingly viewed as a simple matter of transaction processing? *Key industry leader:* education.

7. Are most globally marketed products tagged with standard RFID or similar wireless labels? Is this technology being widely used in supply-chain, e-commerce, and security applications? *Key industry leaders:* retail and distribution.

8. Is there a new generation of government services, particularly in high-profile areas such as information databases, individual identification, voter registration, referenda, polling, campaigning, and even voting itself? *Key industry leader:* government.

9. Does just about every major industry have a shared set of industry metadata that is implemented in custom and packaged software, Web Services, and cooperative marketplaces? Is there a standard set of metadata that is used consistently between these industries? *Key industry leader:* businesses of all sorts.

10. Is the economy noticeably moving toward a more specialized horizontal structure, with companies increasingly becoming a composite of the services provided by others? Is there a new generation of major ASP/Web Services companies emerging, or have established industries created new entities that are focused on Internet-driven change? *Key industry leader:* just about every sector.

These are the types of questions that will determine how this particular phase of the IT industry will eventually be judged. The emphasis will be on how well the economy adjusts to the potential of the Internet and whether major institutions such as government and education facilitate

FIGURE 11 - 1

Industry Opportunity Matrix

This figure shows the relevance of many of this book's themes to specific industry sectors. The lead industry in each area is highlighted. Overall, the distribution of leadership is notable.

	Web Services	Shared taxonomy	Semantic applications	Bill payments	Content chunking	Industry exchange	Advertising focus	Industry restructuring	100% usage	Total
Retail	X	[X]	X	X		X	X		X	7
Manufacturing	X	X	X	X		[X]	X			6
Finance	X	X	X	[X]			X		X	6
Insurance	X	X	X	X			X		X	6
Health care	X	X	X	X	X	X	X	[X]	X	9
Distribution	X	X	X	X		X				5
Transportation/utilities	X	X	X	X		X				5
Publishing/media	X	X	[X]	X	[X]		X		X	7
Education	X	X	X	X	X			X	X	7
Government	X	X	X	X	X			X	X	7
Consumers	X			X					[X]	3
Total	11	10	10	11	4	5	6	3	8	

or retard this change. In the end, these ten specific challenges seem to stem from four broader themes:

1. **Simple technology.** Most of these applications are well within the scope of today's technology. Other than perhaps RFID and online voting, these systems could be implemented today if sufficient effort were made. But while these uses might be simple, if these goals are met, the consequences will be profound, and much of the Internet's promise would be on its way to being fulfilled.

2. **Critical mass.** Each of these applications tends to have very strong critical mass effects, meaning that once a certain threshold of activity is reached, the rest of the market could follow quickly. Critical mass is shifting from a supplier to a customer issue.

3. **Low capital spending.** Many of these applications don't require a great deal of investment in new hardware and telecommunications capacity. While certainly software and other investments are required, application implementation and proliferation will account for the bulk of the costs. In other words, the costs will mostly be borne by customers, and will not necessarily flow to suppliers.

4. **Distributed leadership.** Virtually every major industry is the lead sector in at least one of the application areas mentioned, demonstrating that customer leadership is now spread across a wide range of sectors. This is a big change from the traditional supplier pattern of a few dominant general-purpose companies. This view is expanded upon in figure 11-1, which summarizes how the key topics discussed in this book tend to be most relevant to particular industries. The overall diversity is noteworthy.

In short, these ten questions present goals that the IT industry can and should be able to achieve in the United States and other technologically advanced nations. Consequently, customers clearly have the ability to take IT usage to the next level should they choose to do so. In contrast, it would be hard to come up with many supplier initiatives that are of similar overall importance. Looking ahead, this list can also be used as a simple yardstick by which to measure the coming era. If major progress is made in these areas over the next few years, it's likely that the IT industry will not only have grown and prospered, it will also be much more of a social and economic force than it is today. On the other hand, should most of these goals not be reached by the end of this decade, it would be fair to say that the IT business has stagnated to a significant extent.

Some of the new market entities that might be required to realize these goals are summarized in figure 11-2, which shows that sometimes new companies will take the lead, but equally often the lead players will be spawned by the existing industry itself; an important change from the traditional IT industry pattern, and another good example of the importance of distributed leadership.

Of course, in much of the developing world, progress will take longer. While we often hear about the idea of nations leapfrogging one another technologically, there is little historical evidence to support this. The local software and business experience required for advanced IT systems tends to make radical shifts in technical evolution rare. Contrary to what is often said, leapfrogging is not simply a matter of moving to more modern infrastructures such as high-bandwidth networks and/or wireless systems. This is a classic supply-side view, and

FIGURE 11 - 2

Examples of Internet-Based Cooperative Entities

In terms of establishing important cooperative ventures, some industries are much further along than others. Sometimes the lead organization is an actual company, other times it is a nonprofit association. Each of these examples has been covered in detail in previous chapters.

		Current Status
Airlines	Orbitz	Emerging
Automakers	Covisint	Established
Retailers	UCC/RosettaNet	Merged in August 2002
Finance	Micropayments	Experimental
Consumers	Open Source	Powerful
Advertisers	Interactive Advertising Bureau	Growing influence
Music Industry	Unified database	Speculative
Health Care	Defined Contribution	Slow emergence
E-Learning	Blended Services	Tentative steps
Government	Inter-agency services	Little current activity

thus only tells the smaller half of the story. As noted earlier, networks alone can't guarantee a new generation of advanced services; these must come from specific industry sectors, which need time to develop the required skills and motivation.

The Effect on IT Suppliers

The main reason that it is important to explicitly recognize these broad industry patterns is that we now have a pretty good sense as to how changes of this nature tend to play out. For example, we have already seen what happened when mainframes, minicomputers, and PCs ceased to be the industry's center of gravity. The results in each of these eras has led to the oft-repeated observation that while the impact of major IT industry changes are usually overestimated in the short run, in the long run they tend to be underestimated. In other words, we should never lose track of the fact that changes in IT industry dynamics have often led to radically different industry landscapes.

Historically, these changes have focused on the competition between various generations of suppliers. Perhaps the best recent example is that of Compaq and Dell, where a seemingly minor shift from selling PCs directly instead of through dealers completely reshaped the PC industry hierarchy, and left Compaq (now part of Hewlett-Packard) a shadow of its former self. However, during the shift to a customer-led industry, supply-side changes will be less between one vendor and another, and more about changes in the IT supplier climate itself. The following areas seem to be especially worth monitoring.

Growth Dependency

Just because a market is no longer the IT industry's center of gravity does not mean that it is destined to decline. The historical evidence actually provides mixed messages. Certainly, the greatest years of the PC industry came after the Internet emerged to give more people an incentive to own a PC. On the other hand, PCs largely eliminated the need for traditional minicomputers. But then again, they soon created tremendous new demand for minicomputer-like LAN servers. There's no obvious answer.

Looking ahead, it seems safe to say that although customers are now the center of IT innovation, opportunities for suppliers are not diminishing. As long as the IT industry continues to fulfill its potential, suppliers can flourish. In this sense, the future financial performance and stock valuations of the IT supplier community are increasingly tied to the actions of their customers, whose efforts should eventually lead to another major cycle of industry growth. The real train-wreck scenario would be if customer leadership does not emerge and IT suppliers feel pressured into exploiting whatever lock-in they have to get the revenues they need. Should there be growing tensions between the supplier and customer communities, a negative industry spiral is certainly possible, but still appears unlikely.

Consolidating Sectors

Once an area ceases to be the focal point of IT industry innovation, a process of consolidation typically sets in, even if the market continues to grow. Supplier consolidation is often needed to eliminate weaker competitors, firm up market prices, and improve industry profitability. We have seen this in the past with mainframe and minicomputer systems, where just a few companies—IBM, Sun, HP/Compaq, and increasingly, Dell—now dominate the U.S. market for computer servers. During 2002, the same pattern has been occurring with PCs, witness the merger between HP and Compaq and the financial problems at Gateway. Hitachi's taking over of IBM's disk drive business reflects similar forces at work.

Looking ahead, we should expect that many of today's computer hardware, software, datacom equipment, and telecom services markets will go through further consolidation, often via mergers and acquisitions. That such mergers generally have a poor track record doesn't make them any less necessary or likely. Often, as in the 1986 merger of Burroughs and Sperry to form Unisys and the 1998 acquisition of Digital by Compaq, mergers may have been the least worst option. Overall, the IT industry will continue to follow its long-established pattern whereby the consolidation of mature sectors is more than offset by the emergence of new players and markets (such as Web Services and industry generated start-ups), with the net effect being that the total IT industry becomes considerably more fragmented over time.

Increased Commoditization

This almost goes without saying. Clearly, processor cycles, disk storage, semiconductor memory, and communications bandwidth are all moving toward commodity status, if they are not there already. This is partly the result of increased competition, where with the exception of software just about every product has multiple sources of supply. However, even if, for example, a company such as Advanced Micro Devices eventually failed to continue to offer a real alternative to Intel, the reality is that additional hardware and telecom capacity is steadily moving toward diminishing returns in most market segments.

These diminishing returns are ironic since the increases in computing power are greater now than ever. Consider that in the past, the shift from a 1-megabit memory chip to a 4-megabit chip was considered a very big deal, even though the net difference was just three megabits. Looking ahead just a few years, it's easy to imagine people taking a ho-hum view of the movement from a 1 billion-bit to a 4 billion-bit chip, even though the net difference will be 3 billion, not 3 million bits. In this sense, the capacity of the upcoming generations of hardware will dwarf their predecessors to an unprecedented degree, even as the percentage rate of improvement tends to slow. That these great increases are having diminishing effects is symptomatic of a shift in industry orientation. It will take entirely new areas such as the life sciences, and video and speech processing to consume the computing power soon to be available.

Services Leadership

It is no coincidence that companies such as IBM, EDS, and Accenture have seen their services business grow substantially in recent years. Professional services companies are fundamentally in the best position to directly help customers create value for one another, especially as applications and technologies become ever-more complex. While there will always be a big difference between outside contractors and actual company employees, the bounds between a company and its services firm are more fluid than ever. Indeed, although the idea is not new, the concept of tying a services company's compensation to its customer's business results should finally start to come into its own, as IT performance becomes more externally oriented and therefore much more objectively measurable. IT industry profitability should also migrate to the services sector.

The biggest question today is how well these services firms can deliver. If customers lose faith in their external providers, the pace of overall industry expansion would slow. In today's downbeat market, there has already been a significant amount of customer concern regarding services companies that over-promise and under-deliver. On the other hand, should services firms come to aggressively facilitate customer and industry-specific change, they could become a substantial driver of IT industry growth. The post-Enron separation of the auditing and IT services businesses will ultimately be good for the services business, as the market becomes more open to competition and as conflicts of interests are reduced.

Vertical Market Opportunities

While industry-specific or "vertical" markets have always been a focus of many IT suppliers, their importance will increase significantly in a customer-driven marketplace. Major IT suppliers, especially IT services companies, need to take a holistic view of the problems and possibilities in particular industries. They then need to encourage and facilitate the necessary industry change. This will often require close relationships with major non-IT industry trade groups, standards bodies, and other associations. The examples provided in chapter 4 show that many business benefits tend to accrue to vendors that play key roles in the establishment of new technology-based platforms. IBM has benefited from this pattern in the airline and point-of-sale businesses, and it and other major product and services firms are well-positioned to participate in any future industry-specific cooperative systems. IBM, in particular, is investing significant marketing and development resources in trying to motivate industry sectors to take on advanced IT-driven change. For smaller companies, vertically focused software has always been a viable strategy, but it is now becoming much more of a growth market. Overall, IT marketing will increasingly reflect a vertical market focus.

The Migration of Talent

One of the surest signs of change is the migration of individual talent to areas of higher opportunity and status. This was certainly the case through the mainframe, minicomputer, PC, and dot-com eras, and should occur once again in today's customer-driven industry. The implications of this shift away from suppliers and toward customers will be examined in more detail later in this chapter. But from a supplier perspective, suffice it to say that the days of the CEOs of leading IT vendors being granted near rock-star status are probably coming to an end. Already, dominant IT industry spokespeople such as Bill Gates, Larry Ellison, and Scott McNealy are finding it increasingly difficult to speak to the issues that are really driving the IT industry, and few new spokespersons have emerged. The power of the major IT company brands, while still strong, has substantially decreased, as has the ease of recruiting individual talent. Overall, the supplier side of the business will not be the talent magnet it has been in the past.

Copyright Compromise

Copyrights will be another important area of adjustment. Increasingly, the software industry has been taking a tough copyright stance, insisting that just about all forms of unauthorized software copying or modification are illegal. Yet the IT industry has often dismissed the similar concerns of other businesses. For example, IT industry leaders have been quick to point out the exaggerated fears of the entertainment industry regarding audiotape, VCRs, and CDs. But somewhat hypocritically, the software industry has been reluctant to apply this same logic to its own products. For example, anyone who makes unauthorized copies of software programs is now subject to increasingly stiff criminal prosecution, whereas at least the entertainment industry has mostly used less threatening civil laws to prosecute its copyright violators.

Ultimately, software and content will likely be subject to similar copyright protection. Consequently, the software industry must embrace the same concept of fair use that it asks the content industry to accept. If the software industry can demand complete control, why shouldn't the content industry? But if both industries insist upon complete control, it's the software industry that will be most adversely affected since it is dependent upon a healthy online content industry. However, any efforts to force hardware suppliers to build copy protection capabilities directly into each hardware device should be viewed with great suspicion and generally resisted.

A New Model for Start-Ups

Throughout the minicomputer, PC, and dot-com eras, the role of venture capital increased dramatically to become one of the IT industry's single most important market drivers, and an extraordinary new source of wealth and fame. Start-up companies were usually the fastest and most effective way to bring new technology to the market, especially when the new technology was disruptive to an established industry. However, as we saw throughout part 2, in today's customer-driven environment, the need for start-ups is much less certain. Indeed, the experience with previous customer-driven markets suggests that new market entities will often be the result of market change, not the cause. Certainly, this is what the stories of Visa, Cirrus, Nasdaq, and others would suggest. This is a major shift in industry orientation.

Consequently, although the venture-capital industry will continue to be very active, especially in emerging areas such as wireless, fiber optics, biotech, and robotics, it will often find it difficult to directly participate in many areas of industry-specific customer innovation. While there will be exceptions in, for example, the e-learning and health care businesses, in general the venture community is being marginalized by current industry dynamics, particularly when compared to its lofty position during the dot-com era. In the end, the need for external cash investments will not be a major issue in many areas of potential customer innovation. Already we have seen venture-capital firms reducing the size of their funds. Many are also laying off staff and having trouble justifying their asset-management fees. Because it's easy to see this downsizing as simply a reaction to the excesses of the dot-com boom, the larger, more secular change has yet to be fully appreciated.

Challenged United States' Leadership

There are many reasons why U.S. firms dominate so many high-tech sectors, including an entrepreneurial culture, a big domestic market, a supportive venture-capital industry, gadget-loving consumers, strong university research, a demanding and R&D-oriented military, and the English language itself. All of these are likely to remain important industry factors. However, many of the key dynamics of a customer-driven industry fall outside of these proven success formulae. The rising emphasis upon information standards, industry cooperation, and consumer skills means that leadership in IT usage is once again open to competition. And while the U.S. position in these areas is also very strong, there have already been signs in areas as diverse as public-sector applications, content payments, online banking, and wireless systems that U.S. leadership can't be taken for granted.

For example, should other nations treat the issue of online copyrights more effectively, the evolution of high-bandwidth services might vary significantly around the world. Similarly, as noted in chapter 9, consumers in different countries may well have different preferences regarding new technologies, especially the various forms of synchronous communications. Japan, in particular, seems much more willing to embrace various forms of video phone technology. Although there is good reason for a strong sense of overall optimism, the current level of overwhelming U.S. dominance will be difficult to maintain. In a customer-led industry, even small countries can emerge as important innovators. Overall, we should expect IT industry leadership to be much more evenly distributed around the developed world.

Reduced Political Influence

The reputation of the IT industry has been badly tarnished over the last few years. Whatever one feels about the government's antitrust case versus Microsoft, few would disagree that the initial testimony of Bill Gates (and other senior Microsoft officials) was often dreadful, and sometimes simply not credible. (Judge Thomas Penfield Jackson wasn't a whole lot better.) The IT industry's credibility took a second big blow when, after months of dire Y2K warnings, virtually nothing happened, completely eliminating the need for the liability protection legislation the IT industry had used every ounce of its strength to push through a reluctant Congress. These lapses were followed, of course, by the dot-com collapse itself, making all those once haughty claims of a "new economy" more than a bit embarrassing.

More recently, the post-bubble scandals involving Enron, World-Com, Global Crossing, and other former high-tech leaders have called into question the very ethics and trustworthiness of the IT community. Questionable accounting, dubious "concurrent transactions," and huge executive payoffs have all further damaged the industry's reputation. Sadly, the IT business is now often grouped with lawyers, consultants, and Wall Street analysts as publicly recognized symbols of greed and questionable ethics. While not all of these criticisms have been totally fair, many have been, and the fall from the heady days of 1994–1999 is rather spectacular.

These sorts of industry black marks would have serious repercussions at any time, but they are particularly important now, since the shift toward a customer-driven industry means that the influence of IT suppliers was likely to decline anyway. Up until the dot-com bubble burst, the IT industry actively sought various special favors from the government in areas such as liability limitations, taxation policy, telecom regulation, spectrum allocation, international development, privacy self-regulation, stock options, copyright law, R&D credits, and antitrust intervention. Because the IT sector was viewed so positively, the industry often got its way.

However, many of these issues are still in the hands of Congress, the FCC, the DoJ, and other government and international agencies. It now looks increasingly likely that future public-sector decisions might be considerably less favorable. Indeed, I would expect that in at least one of the areas listed in the preceding paragraph, the IT industry will suffer a significant policy defeat, as there seems to be a widespread desire within Congress to punish the IT business for its recent excesses. On the bright side, however, these same anti-business sentiments might cause Congress to reconsider today's excessively pro-business copyright and patent laws.

From a longer-term perspective, the key issue is how quickly the IT business can win back the confidence of the public. If it does, the politicians will follow. Fortunately, as long as U.S. firms remain highly competitive around the world, technology is still likely to receive much of the credit, and therefore maintain an underlying floor of good will. Should the U.S. economy lose its competitive edge, perceptions of IT could slip much further, but this seems unlikely.

Supplier Wrap-Up

Taken together, these supplier repercussions show how a major shift in industry orientation can systematically ripple through just about every important business dimension. Eventually, these changes will result in a substantially altered supplier environment. And while the opportunities for IT vendors will be very great indeed, it is also clear that some of these changes may well require difficult cultural adjustments. The leaders of the major IT companies have come to have very high expectations in terms of their positions, influence, and wealth, and will likely struggle with the concept of not being as in control of their own destiny as they would like. This has certainly been the case during the whole discussion regarding high-bandwidth telecommunications, where the IT industry has too often adopted a complaining tone regarding the slower-than-expected rollout of these services.

While all of this may seem to present a somewhat pessimistic picture, I see it more as a return to the standards that just about every other industry faces. During the 1990s, the IT industry enjoyed a position of special prominence, much as the automobile and oil industries enjoyed in their boom years. But as the source of economic dynamism shifts to more customer-centric areas, it's only natural that some of this prominence will be lost. However, just as the car and oil businesses have continued to grow in an increasingly information-oriented society, so will IT suppliers grow in an increasingly customer-driven IT business. There's almost certainly at least one more major cycle of double-digit IT industry growth to be enjoyed, once progress has been made on the many customer fronts described in this book.

Are Customers Ready to Lead?

One of the predictable consequences of any significant industry shift is that, while the previous center of gravity must cope with various *effects* of change, the new center can focus more directly upon actual new *opportunities*. As the ten customer-driven applications provided earlier in this chapter suggest, just about every major industry now has a chance to transform itself through the use of IT. It's certainly not hard to imagine how much more technologically advanced our economy would be if significant progress in these simple areas is made. As IT supporters and as citizens, an expectation of meaningful progress in these areas is not unreasonable.

In previous eras, one could be fairly certain that if there were important new technological opportunities, there would also be companies to pursue them. Looking back, IT suppliers have, despite many ups and downs, done a pretty good job envisioning the potential of information technology, and then doing whatever is necessary to make this vision a reality. Commitment, enthusiasm, and perseverance have all been essential parts of the IT industry story.

However, as we have seen, during this particular shift, the enthusiastic response of IT customers is considerably less certain. In an environment characterized by potentially devastating terrorism and the real possibility of a renewed war, long-term business issues, especially risky technology ones, are not most companies' top priority. Should the security and/or economic situation worsen, today's IT investment caution will likely continue or even increase. Sadly, the odds of this are still disturbingly high. Like many, I have been amazed by how quickly and strongly the United States appears to have recovered from what happened on September 11. We can only hope this continues.

However, since these types of global events cannot be predicted or controlled, in a book such as this, we have to assume and hope that the overall environment will be relatively neutral and that natural economic forces will resume. So let's presume, as the economists do, that all other things are equal. What then can we say about the overall issue of customer readiness? In order to discuss this issue, I have broken it down into four main customer components: vision, motivation, resources, and authority. In other words, do most customers have an ambitious sense of where technology can take them? Are they sufficiently motivated to overcome the difficult business, cultural, and implementation challenges ahead? Are the skills and management talent needed to effectively address these issues generally available? And finally, are the lines of company authority and decision making sufficient to empower significant action?

These questions by themselves point to how different customer dynamics are likely to be from those on the supplier side of the business. For example, if one were to make a list of the four key components of supplier readiness, only vision would likely be included. Instead of company motivation, resources, and authority, we would be using related words such as competition, funding, and execution. The fact that these key supplier and customer concerns reflect different orientations is strong evidence of how much things are changing. Customer-driven IT and supplier-driven IT clearly have very different strengths and weaknesses, which is hardly surprising given their very different roots.

More broadly, the whole issue of customer readiness is greatly complicated by the many players involved. Figure 11-3 depicts the major influences upon today's IT decision making, which includes IT professionals, top executives, IT savvy business people, customers, partners, industry associations, actual end users, and IT services companies.

FIGURE 11 - 3

We're All Technologists Now

Virtually every part of the modern enterprise now has a significant information tech-nology component, and thus virtually all of us affect the IT industry value chain to some extent. The overlap between IS professionals and IT suppliers depicts the idea that professional service employees often function essentially as customer staff extensions.

The figure is designed to show that no one person is clearly in charge. This creates complexities that simply don't exist in the supplier-driven world. As the figure suggests, from a value-creation perspective, we are all technologists now (at least some of the time), with just about every consumer and employee capable of making a significant IT contribution. But whereas IT supplier decision making typically stems from a clear management hierarchy, the customer IT decision making process is much more diffuse. Ultimately, however, CEOs, CIOs, and especially business unit leaders are the three main players. Let's look at vision, motivation, skills, and authority from each of these perspectives. Beyond the primary advice to "just do it," what can we say about the challenges that lie ahead?

Developing Company Vision

The first question is whose vision are we talking about, that of the CEO, the CIO, or various business unit leaders? The fact that this question needs to be asked at all is clear evidence of how different things are from the supplier domain, where strong CEOs, often the company founders, are usually in charge. In IT customer environments, there will be relatively few domineering leaders who almost single-handedly transform IT usage in their companies and industries, as Tom Watson Sr., Bill Gates, Michael Dell, and Steve Case have in their days. As we saw in part 1, strong leaders such as Dee Hock with Visa and Bob Crandall with the SABRE system have played an important role, but the more dominant pattern is one of cooperation, not individual action. Interestingly, neither Crandall nor Hock were the CEOs of their respective firms at the time of their biggest IT impact.

But make no mistake, the level of vision and courage required matches or even exceeds that of the supply-side of the business. Just imagine the commitment and salesmanship that would be required to, for example, get the entire music industry to develop a consistent set of metadata, and then aggregate their crown jewels into a single Web-based service. Do all the major players have to be on board? How will day-to-day decisions get made? How will the costs and revenues be divided? What's the antitrust situation? Clearly, the required level of risk, trust, and cooperation greatly exceeds that typically associated with developing a new hardware device or software program. It's one thing to risk your own time and often someone else's money on a new IT product or service; it's quite another to get entrenched competitors to significantly change the way they operate. Many of the examples presented in part 2 require this type of risk and change.

These issues are particularly challenging when one factors in the actual leadership situation. Certainly, many CEOs and business unit leaders are not particularly comfortable with large and complex technology projects. This just hasn't been a part of their business background and experience. Similarly, most CIOs and other technology professionals have, by and large, not been responsible for major business decisions. Yet there is little doubt that the decision to build many of these systems will be made at the executive level and that the CIO will be the prime person responsible for carrying it out. That the players involved might not be ideally prepared for these challenges is one reason that start-up companies have often moved first in emerging Internet areas. However, as we have seen, the highly horizontal model has its own major limitations in many customer-centric marketplaces.

Consequently, the vision and courage needed to make major IT-oriented change will not happen automatically. This is especially the case in the current environment, in which confidence in the viability of many forms of e-business has been significantly shaken. This has greatly magnified the inherent uncertainties and risks associated with most ambitious IT initiatives. In order to keep the issue of vision alive within an organization, it is often necessary to make a special effort to:

1. **Lengthen time horizons.** Customers must recognize that simply following the dictates of near-term, hard-dollar ROI is not a viable long-term strategy. To survive, just about every business must eventually make significant changes and accept significant uncertainty and risk. The recent emphasis on viewing IT applications as a portfolio spanning a wide range of likely risks and rewards is a positive step in this direction.

2. **Think cooperatively.** Try to imagine the various forms of cooperation, standards, and intelligent applications that could make your industry more successful, and then ask yourself what your organization is doing to help. Remember that industry-created entities such as Visa, Cirrus, Covisint, and Orbitz are likely to be an increasingly important long-term trend.

3. **Anticipate horizontal change.** Customers should expect that the boundaries between IT suppliers and IT customers will blur, and that Web Services will be on the forefront of this change. Industry leaders should try to determine what sort of horizontal structures would make most sense for their specific industries. Are there important common problems that a specialized provider might be able to more effectively address? Would your company support or resist this type of dynamic? Is your IT organization even open to the idea of this type of application or business process dis-integration?

4. **Focus on new information assets.** It's no secret that physical business assets don't have quite the stability and cache that they used to. As shown in industries such as publishing, entertainment, software, and pharmaceuticals, increasingly it's companies with intellectual assets that have the greatest long-term staying power. And while such assets are clearly harder to develop in some industries than others, many of the systems described in this book, especially those related to Semantic Applications, can become important new industry resources.

Finding the Necessary Motivation

As we saw throughout part 2, many of the envisioned customer-driven systems will require a great deal of effort and change. Thus, there is perhaps no bigger question than where the necessary motivation will come from. Again, on the supplier side this has never really been a problem. Entrepreneurs have been strongly motivated by the wealth and status that a successful new business can produce. Often they've also been driven by their desire to contribute to society by doing something new, different, or better. In fact, in many cases, the money and status were really just wonderful secondary benefits. Nevertheless, large and tangible rewards have always been an essential part of the supply-side story. If anything, the supplier-side of the business has tended to be overmotivated, often resulting in overcrowded and overhyped marketplaces. This was certainly the case during the dot-com boom.

The e-learning business described in chapter 8 provides a good example of how this entrepreneurial dynamic can work in customer-driven sectors as well. Because the e-learning industry has both a viable set of venture capital-backed companies and an increasingly capable horizontal value chain, there will be a pressing need for established universities and publishers to respond. If they don't, they will likely miss out on a major new market opportunity, and possibly see their existing businesses put at risk as well. This is the familiar IT industry dynamic. However, of all of the areas discussed in part 2, e-learning, Internet payment services, and music (if you count the mostly illegal free services) were really the only ones where there is a strong start-up push. In other areas, the collapse of the dot-com industry has greatly reduced or even eliminated this type of pressure, and thus, as with vision, much of the motivation has to come from within. Unfortunately, this is much more problematic.

Let's take the example of an industry such as health care insurance, trying to develop a common industry taxonomy and associated transaction standards. What exactly is the motivation for this? Almost by definition, there won't necessarily be any major competitive advantage, since all participants will in theory have access to the same shared results. Even worse, in the short term, such efforts have clear additional costs, while the benefits will only accrue over time. Industrywide terminology can become the basis for increasingly intelligent applications, and thus is an important long-term asset, but like most market standards, the initial development process is complex and implementation can often take several years. Perhaps this is why many previous standardization efforts such as EDI began life well below the executive radar screen; the near-term ROI just wasn't very attractive.

Consequently, even more than vision, customer motivation will likely remain a serious IT industry market barrier. Often it will be relatively easy to put off complex standards or other cooperative efforts for another time when "the resources become available." Certainly, the past experience with bar codes, EDI, ATMs, and other systems suggests that cross-industry standards can take a decade or more to become widely deployed unless they are mandated or otherwise imposed by a dominant player or government agency. It's hard work that just doesn't happen automatically. In order to address the motivation issue, I would focus on the following four issues:

1. **Don't join the reactionary forces.** Endlessly reciting the failures of the dot-com era will de-motivate staffs and make it more difficult to pursue new long-term opportunities. Always keep in mind that those who dismiss the long-term power of the Net will generally find themselves on the wrong side of history.

2. **Instill a sense of urgency.** Companies find ways to create a sense of deadlines and pressure. Otherwise, many cross-industry efforts will drift and perhaps never come to fruition. Currently, the main source of urgency is likely to be key customers and partners that require various standards as part of doing business. A compelling example of at least one industry being radically transformed would also help.

3. **Revisit rewards.** Given the downward pressure that will likely be put on the salaries of IT professionals over the next year or two, it's a good time to focus more on stock options and the creation of new shareholder value. Historically, the use of options for technology staffs in IT customer organizations has been far less than in IT supplier companies. While options have recently lost much of their luster, this will likely (and hopefully) pass, and the options gap between IT customers and suppliers should be narrowed substantially over the next five years.

4. **Expect powerful indirect effects.** While products such as ATMs and credit cards didn't have immediate competitive impact, over time they have radically reshaped the banking industry. Many of the systems discussed in this book will eventually eliminate weaker players, while laying the foundation for a new range of value-added services.

Overall, I would argue that a potential "motivation gap" on the part of IT customers is the single biggest risk facing today's IT industry. This is why so much of this work has stressed themes such as confidence, faith, and commitment. Since many of the hard-dollar incentives enjoyed on the supply side of the business will be lacking, these "soft" motivators will have to suffice in many customer environments. This is what makes the current period so uncertain. It's also why business unit leaders are likely to be the key driver of IT industry change. They are the ones most likely to benefit from successful customer-driven IT initiatives.

Managing IT Resources

The ability to effectively manage IT resources remains an important competitive differentiator. Because IT is now an important part of virtually every enterprise activity, the centralization of IT resources into a mostly separate IT department has created a shadow, but ever-expanding cyber organization. This organizational mirroring explains why business integration and alignment have always been such prominent IT management concepts.

The World Wide Web has, of course, greatly magnified this effect. Having a single business Web site that drives a company's key product, sales, marketing, and customer support activities makes many internal company boundaries seem artificial, increasing the need for cross-functional teams. Additionally, the fact that this same Web site is ultimately something that only technology professionals can really build and operate adds a whole new dimension to business organization and decision making. Many companies are now completely dependent upon their IT organization to implement even the most mundane day-to-day business actions and adjustments.

Consequently, the skills and cohesion of a company and its IT activities have never been more important, and certainly cohesive decision making is required for many of the customer-driven platforms this book has described. Almost all of these applications require a strong and detailed view of the key business and technical requirements. And with all due respect to the power of teams, there is really no substitute for having a single project leader with a broad overall understanding. This is especially the case in highly cooperative environments such as exchanges, where the work is much more manageable if each participant has a representative who is sensitive to both business and technical issues. However, finding and retaining such people has always been difficult.

For example, while CIOs now usually report to the CEO and are involved in many executive committee decisions, many CIOs still lack strong business skills, especially in sales, marketing, and customer/partner relations. The great majority of CIOs have technical backgrounds, and most are uncomfortable straying too far from that realm. The idea that in an increasingly information-driven business world, CIOs might be well-positioned to become CEOs has never made much sense. Most CIOs know that they are not suited for the multifaceted

CEO role, and they are quite happy to stay where they are. On the other hand, it is certainly possible that in some cases the role of the CIO and COO can be combined, especially for companies that are largely technology-based. However, more often than not, CIOs believe that some other business leader should decide what a new strategic IT system should do and whether it is worth doing.

Similarly, while many corporations have experimented with the idea of rotating non-IT executives into the CIO function (often as part of their training for eventual CEO candidacy), most companies are uncomfortable with having a nontechnical person in the CIO position for very long. Most CIOs still have to make complex architectural decisions, and the idea of a nontechnical executive managing a large staff of IT professionals for any substantial period of time is inherently problematic. While business unit leaders are becoming more technically savvy, few have the in-depth knowledge and experience with which to confidently manage major IT-based projects.

All of this suggests that the role of the CIO will probably stay pretty much as it is for the foreseeable future. Consequently, there does seem to be a "skill gap" in the number of technically trained people who can manage complex online businesses. As noted earlier, the migration of talent from the IT supplier community into the customer realm would seem to be a logical solution to this problem. This will become especially likely if there is significant consolidation on the supplier side, especially within software companies. In addition, I would focus on three other skills that customers are likely to need:

1. **Standards management.** Customers should think in terms of specific timetables for establishing new information, content, and transaction standards for their firms and their industries. Although companies may not need a dedicated CSO (Chief Standards Officer), someone should be responsible for a developing and articulating a company's position and strategy regarding important industry-specific IT standards, which should be used internally wherever possible. Many IT suppliers have CSO-type leaders in their particular standards areas.

2. **Utilizing hype.** Many of the projects described in this book will require significant time and commitment. Only by constantly stressing a project's benefits can the necessary support and enthusiasm

be maintained. Many CIOs and their IT staffs tend to be somewhat skeptical and anti-hype by nature, especially in today's post-bubble environment. However, creating major new systems typically requires considerable salesmanship, and hype has often been an important part of IT industry progress. This is another reason why business unit leadership is so important and why outside talent might often be helpful.

3. **Testing antitrust**. Many of the systems described in this work will require cooperation between competitors. While this always raises potential issues of collusion, this is not a time for this to be a barrier. Just about every major IT success raises some type of antitrust concern. But although antitrust pressures have occasionally modified business behavior, they have only rarely reversed it. Executives need to have explicit discussions with their competitors about various forms of cooperation. This is the only way that major new entities such as those suggested by figure 11-2 can come into being.

Assigning Authority

Ultimately, perhaps the biggest difference between a supplier- and a customer-driven IT industry is that only in the former is a technologist usually in charge. Certainly in the IT supplier world, many companies were founded by someone who deeply understood the potential of a particular technology. Even those CEOs who are not actually programmers or engineers are usually pretty adept at being able to sound as if they are. Then again, given the success that nontechnologist Lou Gerstner had at IBM, perhaps the need for technical expertise is overrated. Nevertheless, the overall pattern is pretty consistent, especially in smaller companies. By and large, technology companies have been and will almost certainly continue to be run by technology people.

In contrast, nontechnology companies are almost never run by someone with a rich technical background. Historically, sales, finance, and industry-specific knowledge have been valued much more highly. Therefore, most CEOs and business executives have had to learn about technology as they have risen through the ranks, and certainly some have done this much more deeply than others. This problem has become particularly acute in companies that rely heavily on the Web. Whereas many companies might say that marketing runs their Web site, the reality is that the CEO or business unit head is often the only real point of final decision making. It's a role that many executives are still not fully comfortable with.

Consequently, it is hardly surprisingly that executive attitudes toward technology are once again being greatly influenced by the prevailing attitudes and trends of the times. As we have seen, the more confusing a topic is, the more likely decision makers will seek safety in numbers. That's why FUD has always been such an important industry force. As explained in chapter 5, as much as anything else, the simple human tendency to, in the face of confusion, stay close to one's peers can explain much of the IT industry's forty-year history of strong single-vendor leadership and major boom and bust cycles. We can only hope that the idea of building new generations of Semantic Applications and cooperative, industry-specific systems suddenly becomes trendy, and the overall customer herd begins to move in this direction. Maybe this book will help.

A Final Forecast

All of the evidence suggests that once again the path forward for the IT industry will not be quick or easy. While certainly not insurmountable, the challenges of the customer-centric era are different and arguably more difficult than those traditionally faced by suppliers in that they typically involve major business, technical, and cultural change, often without direct competitive pressure. Consequently, many IT customers will have to work hard to amass the vision, motivation, skills, and decision making needed to make meaningful progress. IT suppliers will do their best to enable and promote various new concepts, but the bulk of the work is on the customer side, and will be done at the customer's pace. Right now, it seems as if this pace will be slower than IT suppliers and other industry enthusiasts might hope. Looking back over all of the analysis in this book, it seems impossible to conclude otherwise.

On the other hand, while the pace of change may be slower than desired, the eventual quality of these changes is likely to be worth the wait. If history is any guide, customers will likely prove more adept than IT suppliers in building the sort of cooperative infrastructures needed to move their industries forward. They will also be less likely to try to exploit the standards development process for their own particular purposes, and will probably do a better job managing some of the inevitable antitrust concerns. In other words, it would appear that the market is about to make the following trade-off: For the next few years, the overall pace of change will likely be relatively slow, but the standards squabbles and winner-take-all battles of the supplier-dominated past will tend to recede.

In the long run, this is not a bad bargain. And while it does seem to argue against a rapid or automatic industry recovery, it also suggests that much better times will eventually return. Whenever customers have established important new platforms, the effects on their industry and the role of IT have been profound. Hopefully, this work has convinced you that this pattern is in the process of being repeated. Unless there is some sort of military, terrorist, or other disaster, we can reasonably expect a major new cycle of growth, as a new generation of systems and applications is deployed. Every generation of technology has enjoyed a long period of expansion, and for the Internet that period still lies ahead.

Of course, the key question is how quickly this next phase of IT progress will be put into place. While we're now within reach of fulfilling much of the Internet's initial promise, it's IT customers who need to make the decisive push. As always, industry progress will be defined by the cumulative actions of thousands of individuals in key market sectors. But for the first time, these individuals will be mostly the people who use information technology, not those who sell it.

Afterword

TYPICALLY, in a book such as this, one tries to avoid discussing controversial externalities such as war, politics, and foreign affairs. But, since the prospects for the IT business are currently being adversely affected by international geopolitical developments, a few additional comments seem appropriate.

At the time of this writing, the international situation regarding Iraq remains uncertain. The range of possible outcomes includes: a satisfactory diplomatic resolution, continued international division and tension, a quick military victory, or a difficult and possibly disastrous conflict. Renewed terrorist attacks, be they related to Iraq or not, are also an ever-present risk. No one knows if or when these dangers will recede.

Obviously, these concerns are far more important than the health of the IT industry. Nevertheless, the future course of the international situation will have direct implications for our business. Clearly, either a prolonged war or new terrorist attacks would cause IT customers to become even more cautious, more security oriented, and more focused on the short term, making overall industry progress that much less likely. On the other hand, as we saw after the 1991 Gulf War, effective international leadership can provide a substantial boost to global business confidence. Few things would benefit the world economy more than a stable and improving situation in the Middle East.

Perhaps all we can say is that until we have a better sense of how the international community will deal with these challenges, it will be difficult for the IT industry to break out of its current slump. Only when customers feel secure in their own future can they exhibit the confidence this industry needs to effectively move ahead. For these and other, greater, reasons, we can only hope for a return to more tranquil times.

Works Consulted

The following texts have been particularly useful in preparing this book:

John Brooks, *Telephone: The First Hundred Years* (New York: Harper and Row, 1976).

Clayton M. Christensen, *The Innovator's Dilemma: When New Technologies Cause Great Firms to Fail* (Boston: Harvard Business School Press, 1997).

R. H. Coase, *The Firm, the Market, and the Law* (Chicago, IL: University of Chicago Press, 1988).

Joseph J. Corn, ed. *Imagining Tomorrow: History, Technology and the American Future* (Cambridge, MA: MIT Press, 1987).

James W. Cortada, *Before the Computer: IBM, NCR, Burroughs, & Remington Rand & the Industry They Created, 1865-1956* (Princeton, NJ: Princeton University Press, 1993).

Martin Fransman, *Japan's Computer and Communications Industry: The Evolution of Industrial Giants and Global Competitiveness* (New York: Oxford University Press, 1995).

Andrew F. Inglis, *Behind the Tube: A History of Broadcasting Technology and Business* (Boston: Focal Press, 1990).

John E. Ewoka Jr. and Lawrence J. White, eds. *The Antitrust Revolution: Economics, Competition, and Policy* (New York: Oxford University Press, 1999).

Lawrence Lessig, *The Future of Ideas: The Fate of the Commons in a Connected World* (New York: Random House, 2001).

Charles Mackay, L.L.D., *Extraordinary Popular Delusions and the Madness of Crowds* (New York: Harmony Books, 1980).

David Moschella, *Waves of Power: The Dynamics of Global Technology Leadership* (New York: Amacom, 1997).

Geoffrey A. Moore, *The Gorilla Game* (New York: Harper Collins, 1998).

David E. Nye, *Electrifying America: Social Meanings of a New Technology, 1880–1940* (Cambridge, MA: MIT Press, 1997).

Andy Oram, ed. *Peer-To-Peer: Harnessing the Power of Disruptive Technologies* (Sebastopol, CA: O'Reilly & Associates, 2001).

Carroll W. Pursell Jr., ed. *Technology in America: A History of Individuals and Ideas* (Cambridge, MA: MIT Press, 1981).

Works Consulted

L. Ray Patterson and Stanley W. Lindberg, eds. *The Nature of Copyright: A Law of Users' Rights* (Athens, GA: University of Georgia Press, 1991).

Eric Raymond, *The Cathedral and the Bazaar: Musings of Linux and Open Source by an Accidental Revolutionary* (Sebastopol, CA: O'Reilly & Associates, 2001).

Daniel Reed, *American Eagle: The Ascent of Bob Crandall and American Airlines* (New York: St. Martin's Press, 1993).

U.S. Bureau of the Census, *Historical Statistics of the United States, Colonial Times to 1970* (Washington, DC: U.S. Bureau of the Census, 1975).

Notes

Chapter 1

1. The term "network effect" is used to describe the fact that the value of being part of a computer network tends to increase significantly as more people are added to that network. Thus, once a certain threshold, or "critical mass," of usage is reached, growth often becomes rapid.

2. Carroll W. Pursell Jr., ed. *Technology in America: A History of Individuals and Ideas* (Cambridge, MA: MIT Press, 1981), 124.

3. For an excellent book on these and related developments, see David E. Nye's *Electrifying America: Social Meanings of a New Technology, 1880–1940* (Cambridge, MA: MIT Press, 1997).

4. For more details, see Andrew F. Inglis's comprehensive work, *Behind the Tube: A History of Broadcasting Technology and Business* (Boston: Focal Press, 1990).

5. See Inglis, *Behind the Tube,* 177–185.

6. See John Brooks's outstanding book, *Telephone: The First Hundred Years* (New York: Harper and Row, 1976).

7. For a superb study of the role of the Japanese government in shaping that country's IT industry, see Martin Fransman's book *Japan's Computer and Communications Industry: The Evolution of Industrial Giants and Global Competitiveness* (New York: Oxford University Press, 1995).

Chapter 2

1. *The Gray Sheet,* a newsletter published by International Data Corp. April 1964.

2. An excellent study of the early days of NCR and IBM is provided in James Cortada's *Before the Computer: IBM, NCR, Burroughs, & Remington Rand & the Industry They Created 1865–1956* (Princeton, NJ: Princeton University Press, 1993).

3. This article can be found, among other places, in *The Firm, the Market, and the Law,* a collection of Coase's essays (Chicago, IL: University of Chicago Press, 1988), 33–55.

4. See *The Gorilla Game,* by Geoffrey A. Moore (New York: Harper Collins, 1998).

5. Ethernet inventor Robert Metcalfe famously postulated that while the costs of computer networks tend to rise linearly as new users are added, the value goes up exponentially. This theory has come to be known throughout the IT industry as "Metcalfe's Law."

Chapter 4

1. A good summary of the relevant credit-card antitrust law can be found in *The Antitrust Revolution: Economics, Competition, and Policy,* John E. Ewoka Jr. and Lawrence J. White, eds. (New York: Oxford University Press, 1999), 286–310.

2. Much of this story is derived from Dan Reed's book, *American Eagle: The Ascent of Bob Crandall and American Airlines* (New York: St. Martin's Press, 1993). SABRE has also been covered in numerous newspaper and business journal articles.

3. The best history of copyright law that I am aware of is *The Nature of Copyright: A Law of Users' Rights,* L. Ray Patterson and Stanley W. Lindberg, eds. (Athens, GA: University of Georgia Press, 1991).

Chapter 5

1. McKinsey & Company, *US Productivity Report 1995–2000,* October 2001. This report is available online at <http://www.mckinsey.com/knowledge/mgi/productivity/index.asp> (accessed 22 August 2002).

Chapter 6

1. IBM Web Services Architecture Team, "Web Services Architecture Overview: The next stage of evolution for e-business," <http://www-106.ibm.com/developerworks/webservices/library/w-ovr/> September 2000 (accessed 22 August 2002).

2. The definitions in this section were published in a similar form in a column I wrote for *Computerworld* published 29 April 2002.

Chapter 8

1. The basic analysis in this and the following section was initially developed as part of a white paper that I wrote while at MeansBusiness. The paper was entitled "Integrating Work and Learning," and was produced in October 2000.

Chapter 9

1. The quoted words are borrowed from the title of Eric Raymond's important book *The Cathedral and the Bazaar: Musings on Linux and Open Source by an Accidental Revolutionary* (Sebastopol, CA: O'Reilly and Associates, 2001), describing the philosophy and potential of the open-source movement.

Chapter 10

1. Andrew Leigh and Robert D. Atkinson, "Breaking Down Bureaucratic Barriers, the Next Phase of Digital Government," *PPI Policy Report* 27 November 2001. This report is available on the Progressive Policy Institute's Web site <http://www.ppionline.org/ppi_ci.cfm?contentid=3966&knlgAreaID=140&subsecid=290> (accessed 22 August 2002).

2. Vivienne Jupp, "eGovernment Leadership: Realizing the Vision," Accenture, April 2002. Available from the Accenture Web site, <http://www.accenture.com> (accessed 22 August 2002).

Index

advertising, online, 124, 125–128
affinities/ratings systems, 178
aggregation, incomplete, 123
airline reservation systems, 64, 74–75
Amazon.com, 36, 158, 172, 178, 193
antitrust issues. *See also* monopolies/
near-monopolies
  in airline industry, 75
  enforcement of, 191–192
  IBM, 27
  industrywide cooperation and, 82
  international cooperation, 195
  micropayments, 141
  Microsoft, 27, 206, 221
  National Cash Register (NCR), 26
  Sherman Antitrust Act, 26
  testing of, 233
AOL, 24, 36, 175
asynchronous communications, 167–171.
  See also synchronous communications
ATMs (Automated Teller Machines), 23, 64,
71–73
authority, assignment of, 233–234

bank fund transfer systems, 79–80. *See also*
ATMs (Automated Teller Machines);
credit cards; money transfer systems
bar codes, 64, 65–68
biotechnology, 59–60
blended learning, 161. *See also* e-learning
blogs (Weblogs), 176–177
BMI (Broadcast Music, Inc.), 64, 76
bottom-up metadata, 122–123
budgets for IT resources, 92–94
business attitudes toward IT, 86–91
business exchange models, 129–131,
165–166, 171, 178–179, 210
Business Process Outsourcing (BPO), 107, 108
business resources, 92–95

cell phones, 141, 169. *See also* wireless
communications
chunking, 115, 161–164
commoditization of IT industry, 217
communications, 14, 141, 167–171. *See also*
Internet/Internet industry;
telephones/telecom industry; wireless
communications
community content (Web), 175–177
community energy, 172–174
company vision, development of, 226–228
competition, 24–25
  community versus commercial, 176
  competitive structure of IT industry, 33
  among credit card companies, 70
  international, 86–87
  Internet giants, 37
  SABRE, 73–75
competitive advantage, 73–74
computers, 3–6, 7, 10, 15, 29, 44
  consumer acceptance/adoption of, 15–18
  development of, 29–30
  mainframes, 20–21
  minicomputers, 23, 28, 44
connectivity, 56. *See also* communications
consolidation, 156, 216
consumer-driven commerce, 171–174
consumer IT value creation, 167
consumer protection, 198–201
consumers, 5–6, 7, 192, 209–210. *See also*
customers entries
content assets, 159, 160, 176–177
content chunking, 115, 161–164
content management, 109. *See also* management issues
  content reengineering, 112, 124, 125
  e-learning, 159, 162
  fee-based system of, 142
  market forecasting, 210
  metadata, 120–125
  micropayments, 141
  taxonomies, 114
  taxonomies/metadata, 163
cooperation/cooperative markets
  credit card companies, 72–73
  customer, 54, 227, 233
  e-learning, 161
  exchanges, 128–132
  Internet-based, 214
  launch systems, 80–81
copyright issues, 75–76, 181
  ASCAP, 76–77
  community content, 176
  compromise, 219–220

Index

gorilla firms, 36–38
government/governmental services, 12–15.
    See also public policy issues (Internet-
    related)
    government information, 195–196
    in history of IT industry, 183–185
    industry support, 11, 13, 15, 165
    market forecasting, 211
    rating of contributions by factor, 205
growth, 18. *See also* trends
    customer-led, 95–96
    dependency, 215–216
    drivers of IT industry, 55–56
    evolving attitudes toward IT, 86–88
    future of leadership, 142–143
    usage rates of computers, 10
    Web Services, 106

health care industry, 132–136, 210
herd effects, 27, 85, 234
high bandwidth services, 58–59, 60–61
horizontal limitations of industry, 34–36
horizontal markets, 128–129, 145, 189–190
horizontal structure
    change, 228
    of industry, 29–30
    and integration, 104, 211
horizontal value chain, 28
hype, 54, 81, 232–233

IBM, 26–27
    Consent Decree of 1956, 191
    IBM PC, 5, 21, 30
    IBM S/360 mainframe, 20–21
    standards, 23
    strategic planning, 87
Independent Software Vendors (ISV), 62
individual authentication, 188–189. *See also*
    privacy; security
individual privacy, 198–199
International Data Corp. (IDC), 86
industries, establishing new, 10–15
industry forces, moderating, 190–195
industry leaders, 226
industry opportunity matrix, 213
information, 15, 17–18, 115, 177
    as asset, 228
    government, 195–196
    storage of, 180
initial market launch, 150–151
Innovator's Dilemma, The (Christensen), 24
Instant Messenger (IM), 169–173. *See also*
    Microsoft
    standards, 24
Intel, 21, 173
intellectual property rights, 192
intelligent applications, 110–112

international cooperation, 194–195
    European Article Numbering (EAN)
        International, 68
    W3C, 102, 116, 194
International Standards Organization (ISO),
    116
Internet/Internet industry. *See also* dot-com
    bubble/collapse; e-learning; public
    policy issues (Internet-related); Web
    Services
    adoption rates for, 9–10
    collapse of, 34
    competitive model of, 37
    development of, 4
    e-mail messaging standards of, 9
    era of, 44
    for-free mind-set, 126
    governmental support of, 15
    Internet Corporation for Assigned Names
        and Numbers (ICANN), 187
    Internet-based cooperative entities, 214
    Internet radio, 77, 193
    open-source model in, 172–174
    payment systems of, 136–142
    tax policy on, 194
    World Wide Web, 21–22, 48
    W3C, 102, 116, 194
interoperability, 99, 102, 117
IT industry, 43, 44–45
    consolidation within, 216
    copyright compromises in, 219–220
    cost structure of, 33
    drivers of, 25–26, 55–56
    government value chain influence on,
        184, 185
    growth, 18, 86–88, 95–96, 142–143,
        210–211, 213
    mapping new usage in, 41–42
    market scandals, 199, 204, 222
    Return On Investment (ROI) perspective
        in, 89, 91
    services leadership, 217–218
    statistics for, 86
    structural evolution timeline, 46
    supplier cooperation, 61
    talent migration, 219
    vision of, 40

launching of new industries, 10–15
leadership, 53–55, 81
    challenges for industry, 119
    distributed, 212
    e-learning market leaders, 156
    implications for industry, 117–118
    industry leaders, 27, 226
    services, 217–218
    standards, 54, 118
    testing of, 18

Index

pornography, 199–200
research and development, 189–190
security, 188
spectrum allocation, 186–187
tax policies, 194
telecom regulation, 190–191
universal service, 202–203
voting/registration, 197–198
workforce preparation, 203
public sector IT agenda categories, 185
public trust, 206, 222
publishing industry, 158–159
pure-play companies, 129

racial profiling, 198
radio, 3. *See also* music industry
  on Internet, 193
  Radio Act of 1912, 13
  Radio Frequency Identification (RFID),
    58, 67–68, 211
  radio spectrum management, 13–14
rating scheme for government value-chain
    contribution, 185–186
recording industry, 61, 64, 120–125,
    177–178, 219
reengineered content, 124, 125. *See also* con-
    tent management
research and development (R&D), 189–190
reshaping of IT industry, candidates for, 55–60
resources, 92–95, 179–180, 230–234
royalty tracking systems, 64

scandals, 199, 204, 222
sector consolidation, 216
security, 102, 187, 188, 202
Semantic Applications, 98–103, 109–116,
    121, 210, 211
services, 29, 125
  industry, 31–32
  leadership, 217–218
service utilities, 101
SETI@home, 179–180
Shared Content Object Reference Model
    (SCORM), 155, 187
shared resources, 179–180
Simple Object Access Protocol (SOAP), 109
social welfare, 201–203
software. *See also* Semantic Applications;
    standards; Web Services
  companies, 157–158
  continuous upgrades of, 16, 17
  customer-created content, 174–181
  Independent Software Vendors (ISVs), 62
  industry, 219
  replacing packaged with Web Services,
    100–101
  simple applications, importance of, 25–33

unbundling of, 29
spectrum management, 186–187
standards, 229
  American National Standards Institute
    (ANSI), 78
  bar code, 65–68
  e-mail, 166
  emerging industry, 115–116
  Global Positioning Systems (GPS), 58
  government value-chain contribution,
    187–188
  IBM PC, 30
  industry leadership, 118
  instant messaging, 24
  by international organizations, 116
  leadership, 54
  management of, 232
  minicomputers, 23
  National Television Systems Committee
    (NTSC), 14
  online advertising format, 126
  process for, 102
  Shared Content Object Reference Model
    (SCORM), 155
  stages of IT industry, 98
  strength of industry, 22–24
  Web Services, 102
start-ups, 54–55, 220
Sun Microsystems, 23–24
suppliers, 53, 85, 96
  cooperation of, 61–62
  effects on, 215–223
  e-learning, 154
  growth dependency, 215–216
  repercussions for, 223
  technology frontiers for, 99
  Web Services initiatives by, 97
synchronous communications, 167–169. *See
    also* asynchronous communications
system market launch models, 80

tax issues, 135, 194, 206
taxonomy, 113–114, 163
technology, 3–4, 6, 7–9
  biotechnology, 59
  disruptive, 24, 152–153
  enabling, 198
  frontier, of supplier, 99
  hype of, 81
  nanotechnology, 59
  simple, 212
telephones/telecom industry, 3. *See also*
    wireless communications
  compatibility problems, 8
  competitive model of, 37
  launch of, 8–9
  nationwide telephone system, 14
  regulation of, 190–191

About the Author

David Moschella is an author, consultant, and a regular columnist for *Computerworld*. He is the author of the influential 1997 book, *Waves of Power*, which assessed the evolution of the IT supplier industry.

Mr. Moschella was previously head of worldwide research for International Data Corporation, the leading research and consulting company in the IT industry. He currently serves on the Technology Advisory Board of Merrill Lynch.